Houghton
Mifflin
Harcourt

SCIENCE
FUSiON

fusion [FYOO • zhuhn] a combination of two
or more things that releases energy

This **Interactive Student Edition** belongs to

_____

Teacher/Room

_____

Consulting Authors

Michael A. DiSpezio

Global Educator
North Falmouth, Massachusetts

Michael DiSpezio is a renaissance educator who moved from the research laboratory of a Nobel Prize winner to the K–12 science classroom. He has authored or co-authored numerous textbooks and written more than 25 trade books. For nearly a decade he worked with the JASON Project, under the auspices of the National Geographic Society, where he designed curriculum, wrote lessons, and hosted dozens of studio and location broadcasts. Over the past two decades, he has developed supplementary material for organizations and shows that include PBS *Scientific American Frontiers, Discover* magazine, and the Discovery Channel. He has extended his reach outside the United States and into topics of crucial importance today. To all his projects, he brings his extensive background in science and his expertise in classroom teaching at the elementary, middle, and high school levels.

Marjorie Frank

*Science Writer and
Content-Area Reading Specialist*
Brooklyn, New York

An educator and linguist by training, a writer and poet by nature, Marjorie Frank has authored and designed a generation of instructional materials in all subject areas, including past HMH Science programs. Her other credits include authoring science issues of an award-winning children's magazine; writing game-based digital assessments in math, reading, and language arts; and serving as instructional designer and co-author of pioneering school-to-work software for Classroom Inc., a nonprofit organization dedicated to improving reading and math skills for middle and high school learners. She wrote lyrics and music for *SCIENCE SONGS,* which was an American Library Association nominee for notable recording. In addition, she has served on the adjunct faculty of Hunter, Manhattan, and Brooklyn Colleges, teaching courses in science methods, literacy, and writing.

Acknowledgments for Covers

Front cover: *Volcanic eruption* (bg) ©Photo Researchers, Inc.

Michael R. Heithaus

Dean, College of Arts, Sciences & Education
Florida International University
North Miami, Florida

Mike Heithaus joined the Florida International University Biology Department in 2003. He is a professor in the Department of Biological Sciences and has served as Director of the Marine Sciences Program and Executive Director of the School of Environment and Society. His research focuses on predator-prey interactions and the ecological roles of large marine species including sharks, sea turtles, and marine mammals. His long-term studies include the Shark Bay Ecosystem Project in Western Australia. He also served as a Research Fellow with National Geographic, using remote imaging in his research and hosting a *Crittercam* television series on the National Geographic Channel.

Donna M. Ogle

Professor of Reading and Language
National-Louis University
Chicago, Illinois

Creator of the well-known KWL strategy, Donna Ogle has directed many staff development projects translating theory and research into school practice in middle and secondary schools throughout the United States. She is a past president of the International Reading Association and has served as a consultant on literacy projects worldwide. Her extensive international experience includes coordinating the Reading and Writing for Critical Thinking Project in Eastern Europe, developing an integrated curriculum for a USAID Afghan Education Project, and speaking and consulting on projects in several Latin American countries and in Asia. Her books include *Coming Together as Readers; Reading Comprehension: Strategies for Independent Learners; All Children Read;* and *Literacy for a Democratic Society.*

Program Reviewers

Content Reviewers

Paul D. Asimow, PhD
Professor of Geology and Geochemistry
Division of Geological and Planetary Sciences
California Institute of Technology
Pasadena, CA

Laura K. Baumgartner, PhD
Postdoctoral Researcher
Molecular, Cellular, and Developmental Biology
University of Colorado
Boulder, CO

Eileen Cashman, PhD
Professor
Department of Environmental Resources Engineering
Humboldt State University
Arcata, CA

Hilary Clement Olson, PhD
Research Scientist Associate V
Institute for Geophysics, Jackson School of Geosciences
The University of Texas at Austin
Austin, TX

Joe W. Crim, PhD
Professor Emeritus
Department of Cellular Biology
The University of Georgia
Athens, GA

Elizabeth A. De Stasio, PhD
Raymond H. Herzog Professor of Science
Professor of Biology
Department of Biology
Lawrence University
Appleton, WI

Dan Franck, PhD
Botany Education Consultant
Chatham, NY

Julia R. Greer, PhD
Assistant Professor of Materials Science and Mechanics
Division of Engineering and Applied Science
California Institute of Technology
Pasadena, CA

John E. Hoover, PhD
Professor
Department of Biology
Millersville University
Millersville, PA

William H. Ingham, PhD
Professor (Emeritus)
Department of Physics and Astronomy
James Madison University
Harrisonburg, VA

Charles W. Johnson, PhD
Chairman, Division of Natural Sciences, Mathematics, and Physical Education
Associate Professor of Physics
South Georgia College
Douglas, GA

Program Reviewers *(continued)*

Tatiana A. Krivosheev, PhD
Associate Professor of Physics
Department of Natural Sciences
Clayton State University
Morrow, GA

Joseph A. McClure, PhD
Associate Professor Emeritus
Department of Physics
Georgetown University
Washington, DC

Mark Moldwin, PhD
Professor of Space Sciences
Atmospheric, Oceanic, and
Space Sciences
University of Michigan
Ann Arbor, MI

Russell Patrick, PhD
Professor of Physics
Department of Biology,
Chemistry, and Physics
Southern Polytechnic State
University
Marietta, GA

Patricia M. Pauley, PhD
*Meteorologist, Data Assimilation
Group*
Naval Research Laboratory
Monterey, CA

Stephen F. Pavkovic, PhD
Professor Emeritus
Department of Chemistry
Loyola University of Chicago
Chicago, IL

L. Jeanne Perry, PhD
Director (Retired)
Protein Expression Technology
Center
Institute for Genomics and
Proteomics
University of California, Los
Angeles
Los Angeles, CA

Kenneth H. Rubin, PhD
Professor
Department of Geology and
Geophysics
University of Hawaii
Honolulu, HI

Brandon E. Schwab, PhD
Associate Professor
Department of Geology
Humboldt State University
Arcata, CA

Marllin L. Simon, Ph.D.
Associate Professor
Department of Physics
Auburn University
Auburn, AL

Larry Stookey, PE
Upper Iowa University
Wausau, WI

Kim Withers, PhD
Associate Research Scientist
Center for Coastal Studies
Texas A&M University-Corpus
Christi
Corpus Christi, TX

Matthew A. Wood, PhD
Professor
Department of Physics & Space
Sciences
Florida Institute of Technology
Melbourne, FL

Adam D. Woods, PhD
Associate Professor
Department of Geological
Sciences
California State University,
Fullerton
Fullerton, CA

Natalie Zayas, MS, EdD
Lecturer
Division of Science and
Environmental Policy
California State University,
Monterey Bay
Seaside, CA

Teacher Reviewers

Ann Barrette, MST
Whitman Middle School
Wauwatosa, WI

Barbara Brege
Crestwood Middle School
Kentwood, MI

**Katherine Eaton Campbell,
M Ed**
Chicago Public Schools-Area 2
Office
Chicago, IL

**Karen Cavalluzzi, M Ed,
NBCT**
Sunny Vale Middle School
Blue Springs, MO

Katie Demorest, MA Ed Tech
Marshall Middle School
Marshall, MI

Jennifer Eddy, M Ed
Lindale Middle School
Linthicum, MD

Tully Fenner
George Fox Middle School
Pasadena, MD

Dave Grabski, MS Ed
PJ Jacobs Junior High School
Stevens Point, WI

Amelia C. Holm, M Ed
McKinley Middle School
Kenosha, WI

Ben Hondorp
Creekside Middle School
Zeeland, MI

George E. Hunkele, M Ed
Harborside Middle School
Milford, CT

Jude Kesl
Science Teaching Specialist 6–8
Milwaukee Public Schools
Milwaukee, WI

Joe Kubasta, M Ed
Rockwood Valley Middle School
St. Louis, MO

Mary Larsen
Science Instructional Coach
Helena Public Schools
Helena, MT

Angie Larson
Bernard Campbell Middle School
Lee's Summit, MO

Christy Leier
Horizon Middle School
Moorhead, MN

Helen Mihm, NBCT
Crofton Middle School
Crofton, MD

Jeff Moravec, Sr., MS Ed
Teaching Specialist
Milwaukee Public Schools
Milwaukee, WI

**Nancy Kawecki Nega, MST,
NBCT, PAESMT**
Churchville Middle School
Elmhurst, IL

Mark E. Poggensee, MS Ed
Elkhorn Middle School
Elkhorn, WI

Sherry Rich
Bernard Campbell Middle School
Lee's Summit, MO

Mike Szydlowski, M Ed
Science Coordinator
Columbia Public Schools
Columbia, MO

Nichole Trzasko, M Ed
Clarkston Junior High School
Clarkston, MI

Heather Wares, M Ed
Traverse City West Middle School
Traverse City, MI

Contents in Brief

Program Overview x

Unit 1
Earth's Surface 1

Unit 2
Earth's History 75

Unit 3
Minerals and Rocks 137

Unit 4
The Restless Earth 189

21st Century Skills: Technology and Coding 275

Look It Up! Reference Section R1

Glossary R49

Index R57

This pyramid and Sphinx are a little more than 4,500 years old. Some of the limestone blocks used weigh 2.5 tons each!

Contents

		Assigned	Due
Unit 1 Earth's Surface 1	☐	_____
Lesson 1 Earth's Spheres 4	☐	_____
Lesson 2 Weathering 18	☐	_____
Lesson 3 Erosion and Deposition by Water 28	☐	_____
Think Science 42	☐	_____
Lesson 4 Erosion and Deposition by Wind, Ice, and Gravity 44	☐	_____
Lesson 5 Soil Formation 56	☐	_____
Unit Review 70	☐	_____

Although most of Earth's water is found in the oceans and in ice, a large amount of water is also part of the atmosphere.

What can last for millions of years? Fossils. This is a fossil of a dinosaur that roamed Earth long ago.

The trilobite was a marine organism.

		Assigned	Due
Unit 2 Earth's History 75		☐	_____
Lesson 1 Geologic Change over Time 78		☐	_____
Lesson 2 Relative Dating 92		☐	_____
Think Science 104		☐	_____
Lesson 3 Absolute Dating 106		☐	_____
Lesson 4 The Geologic Time Scale 118		☐	_____
Unit Review 132		☐	_____

Assignments:

_____

_____

_____

_____

_____

_____

_____

Contents (continued)

		Assigned	Due
Unit 3 Minerals and Rocks 137		☐	____
Lesson 1 Minerals 140		☐	____
Lesson 2 The Rock Cycle 154		☐	____
S.T.E.M. Engineering and Technology 166		☐	____
Lesson 3 Three Classes of Rock 170		☐	____
Unit Review 184		☐	____

The huge White Cliffs of Dover were formed from the skeletons of organisms like the microscopic marine algae shown here.

Assignments:

© Houghton Mifflin Harcourt Publishing Company • Image Credits: (l) ©David Dixon/Ardea London Ltd.; (r) ©Andrew Syred/Photo Researchers, Inc.

Imagine how hot it must be for rock to melt and flow like water! That's lava for you.

		Assigned	Due
Unit 4 The Restless Earth	189	☐	_____
Lesson 1 Earth's Layers	192	☐	_____
Lesson 2 Plate Tectonics	200	☐	_____
People in Science	214	☐	_____
Lesson 3 Mountain Building	216	☐	_____
Lesson 4 Volcanoes	226	☐	_____
Lesson 5 Earthquakes	238	☐	_____
S.T.E.M. Engineering and Technology	248	☐	_____
Lesson 6 Measuring Earthquake Waves	252	☐	_____
Unit Review	268	☐	_____

Movement in Earth's crust releases tremendous amounts of energy, which can cause a lot of damage.

© Houghton Mifflin Harcourt Publishing Company • Image Credits: (t) ©Douglas Peebles Photography/Alamy; (b) ©Michael S. Yamashita/Corbis

Power up with *Science Fusion!*

Your program fuses...

e-Learning and Virtual Labs

Labs and Activities

Write-In Student Edition

... to generate energy for today's science learner — you.

S.T.E.M. activities throughout the program!

Write-In Student Edition

Be an active reader and make this book your own!

You can answer questions, ask questions, create graphs, make notes, write your own ideas, and highlight information right in your book.

Learn science concepts and skills by interacting with every page.

Labs and Activities

ScienceFusion includes lots of exciting hands-on inquiry labs and activities, each one designed to bring science skills and concepts to life and get you involved.

By asking questions, testing your ideas, organizing and analyzing data, drawing conclusions, and sharing what you learn...

You are the scientist!

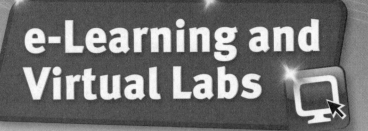

e-Learning and Virtual Labs

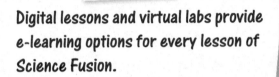

Digital lessons and virtual labs provide e-learning options for every lesson of Science Fusion.

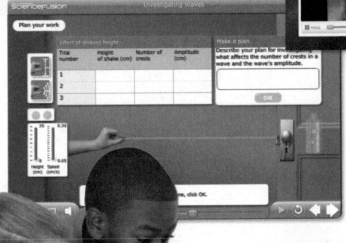

On your own or with a group, explore science concepts in a digital world.

360° of Inquiry

Earth's Surface

Big Idea

Continuous processes on Earth's surface result in the formation and destruction of landforms and the formation of soil.

Most of Florida's underground caves are also under water, which makes them ideal for diving.

What do you think?

Florida has many caves underground. If a cave is close to Earth's surface and its roof is weak, the roof may fall in, forming a sinkhole. How might these caves have formed?

Sinkholes often form suddenly.

Unit 1
Earth's Surface

Lesson 1
Earth's Spheres 4

Lesson 2
Weathering 18

Lesson 3
**Erosion and Deposition
by Water** 28

Think Science 42

Lesson 4
**Erosion and Deposition
by Wind, Ice, and Gravity** 44

Lesson 5
Soil Formation 56

Unit Review 70

CITIZEN SCIENCE

Save a Beach

Like many other features on land, beaches can also change over time. But what could be powerful enough to wash away a beach? Waves and currents.

① Define The Problem

People love to visit the beach. Many businesses along the beach survive because of the tourists that visit the area. But in many places, the beach is being washed away by ocean waves and currents.

Beaches draw lots of tourists.

② Think About It

When waves from the ocean hit the beach at an angle, the waves will often pull some of the sand back into the ocean with them. This sand may then be carried away by the current. In this way, a beach can be washed away. What could you do to prevent a sandy beach from washing away? Looking at the photo below, design a way to prevent the beach from washing away. Then, conduct an experiment to test your design.

Check off the questions below as you use them to design your experiment.

✔ How will you create waves?

✔ At what angle should the waves hit the beach?

✔ Will people still be able to use the beach if your method were used?

Waves carry the sand back into the ocean with them.

③ Make A Plan

A Make a list of the materials you will need for your experiment in the space below.

_____

_____

_____

B Draw a sketch of the setup of your experiment in the space below.

C Conduct your experiment. Briefly state your findings.

_____

_____

_____

Take It Home

Find an area, such as the banks of a pond or a road, which may be eroding in your neighborhood. Study the area. Then, prepare a short presentation for your class on how to prevent erosion in this area. See *ScienceSaurus®* for more information about erosion.

© Houghton Mifflin Harcourt Publishing Company • Image Credits: ©Franz Marc Frei/Photolibrary

Earth's Spheres

ESSENTIAL QUESTION

How do matter and energy move through Earth's spheres?

By the end of this lesson, you should be able to describe Earth's spheres, give examples of their interactions, and explain the flow of energy that makes up Earth's energy budget.

Emperor penguins spend time on land and need to breathe in oxygen from the air.

These penguins also swim and hold their breath for about 18 minutes as they hunt for fish. What do you have in common with these penguins?

Lesson Labs

Quick Labs
- Explaining Earth's Systems
- Model Earth's Spheres

S.T.E.M. Lab
- Change and Balance Between Spheres

Engage Your Brain

1 Predict Check T or F to show whether you think each statement is true or false.

T	F	
☐	☐	Earth is made up completely of solid rocks.
☐	☐	Animals live only on land.
☐	☐	Water in rivers often flows into the ocean.
☐	☐	Air in the atmosphere can move all over the world.

2 Analyze Think about your daily activities, and list some of the ways in which you interact with Earth.

_____
_____
_____
_____
_____
_____

Active Reading

3 Synthesize You can often define an unknown word if you know the meaning of its word parts. Use the word parts and sentence below to make an educated guess about the meaning of the word *geosphere*.

Word part	Meaning
geo-	earth
-sphere	ball

Example sentence:
Water flows across the surface of the geosphere.

geosphere:

_____
_____
_____

Vocabulary Terms

- Earth system
- geosphere
- hydrosphere
- cryosphere
- atmosphere
- biosphere
- energy budget

4 Apply As you learn the definition of each vocabulary term in this lesson, create your own notecards to help you remember the meaning of the term.

What on Earth?

What is the Earth system?

A system is a group of related objects or parts that work together to form a whole. From the center of the planet to the outer edge of the atmosphere, Earth is a system. The **Earth system** is all of the matter, energy, and processes within Earth's boundary. Earth is a complex system made up of many smaller systems. The Earth system is made of nonliving things, such as rocks, air, and water. It also contains living things, such as trees, animals, and people. Matter and energy continuously cycle through the smaller systems that make up the Earth system. The Earth system can be divided into five main parts—the geosphere (JEE•oh•sfir), the hydrosphere (HY•druh•sfir), the cryosphere (KRY•uh•sfir), the atmosphere, and the biosphere.

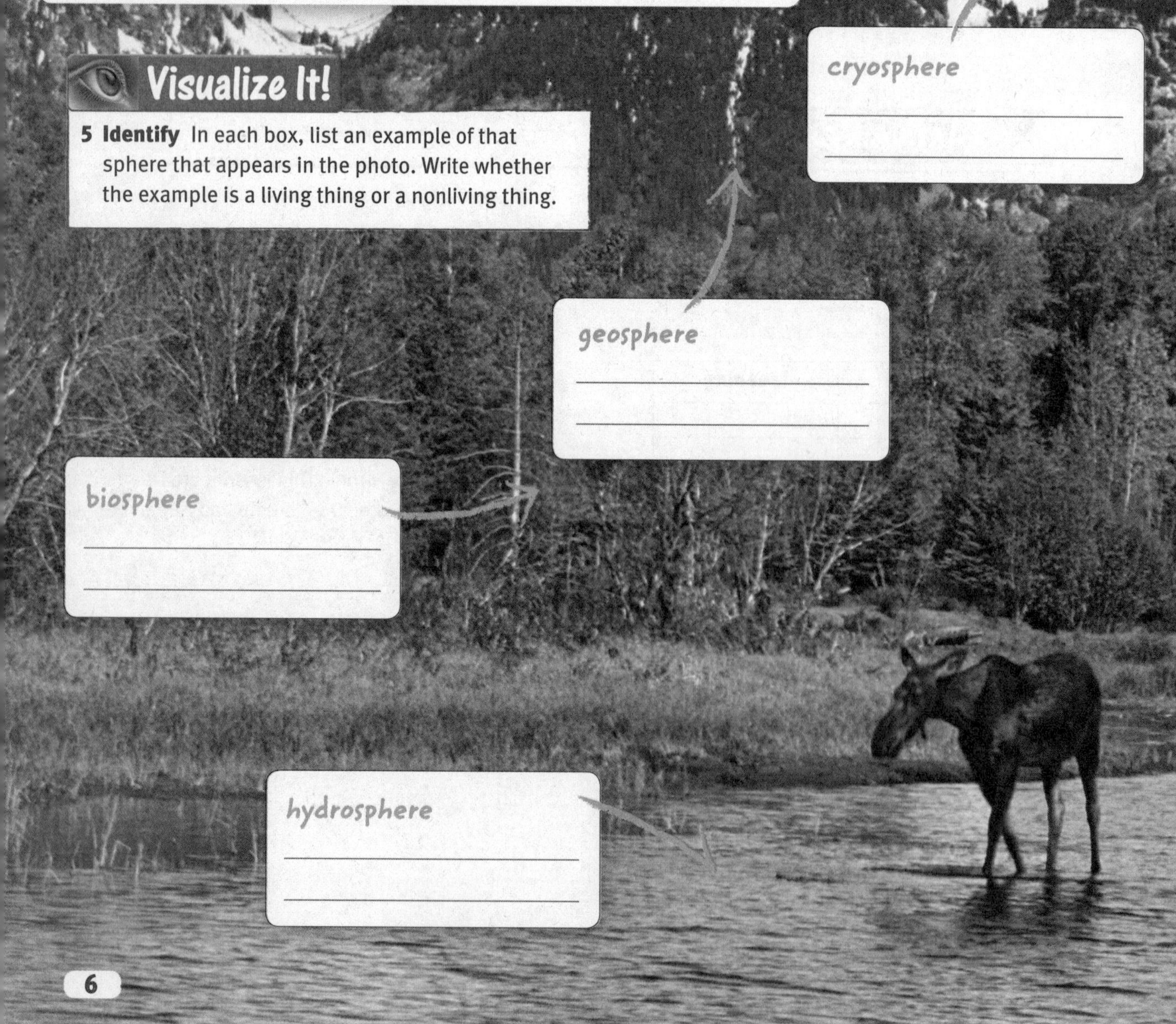

atmosphere
_____
_____

cryosphere
_____
_____

Visualize It!

5 Identify In each box, list an example of that sphere that appears in the photo. Write whether the example is a living thing or a nonliving thing.

geosphere
_____
_____

biosphere
_____
_____

hydrosphere
_____
_____

What is the geosphere?

6 Identify As you read, underline what each of the three different compositional layers of the geosphere is made up of.

The **geosphere** is the mostly solid, rocky part of Earth. It extends from the center of Earth to the surface of Earth. The geosphere is divided into three layers based on chemical composition: the crust, the mantle, and the core.

The thin, outermost layer of the geosphere is called the crust. It is made mostly of silicate minerals. The crust beneath the oceans is called oceanic crust and is only 5 to 10 km thick. The continents are made of continental crust and range in thickness from about 35 to 70 km. Continental crust is thickest beneath mountain ranges.

The mantle lies below the crust. The mantle is made of hot, very slow-flowing, solid rock. The mantle is about 2,900 km thick. It is made of silicate minerals that are denser than the silicates in the crust.

The central part of Earth is the core, which has a radius of about 3,500 km. It is made of iron and nickel and is the densest layer. The core is actually composed of a solid inner core and a liquid outer core.

Crust
The crust is the thin, rigid outermost layer of Earth.

Mantle
The mantle is the hot layer of rock between Earth's crust and core. The mantle is denser than Earth's crust.

Core
The core is Earth's center. The core is about twice as dense as the mantle.

7 Summarize Fill in the table below with the characteristics of each of the geosphere's compositional layers.

Compositional layer	Thickness	Relative density
crust	5–10 km (oceanic) 35–70 km (continental)	least dense

Got Water?

What is the hydrosphere?

The **hydrosphere** is the part of Earth that is liquid water. Ninety-seven percent of all of the water on Earth is the salt water found in the oceans. Oceans cover 71% of Earth's surface. The hydrosphere also includes the freshwater in lakes, rivers, and marshes. Rain and the water droplets in clouds are also parts of the hydrosphere. Even water that is underground is part of the hydrosphere.

The water on Earth is constantly moving. It moves through the ocean in currents because of wind and differences in the density of ocean waters. Water also moves from Earth's surface to the air by evaporation. It falls back to Earth as rain. It flows in rivers and through rocks under the ground. It even moves into and out of living things.

Active Reading

8 Identify What are two things through which water moves?

_____

_____

Visualize It!

9 Identify After you read, write whether the example of water in each photo is part of the hydrosphere or the cryosphere.

Ⓐ

Water droplets form clouds.

Water flows over Earth's surface.

Ⓑ

What is the cryosphere?

Earth's **cryosphere** is made up of all of the frozen water on Earth. Therefore, all of the ice, sea ice, glaciers, ice shelves, and icebergs are a part of the cryosphere. So is permafrost, the frozen ground found at high latitudes. Most of the frozen water on Earth is found in the ice caps in Antarctica and in the Arctic. However, glaciers are found in mountains and at high latitudes all over the world. The amount of frozen water in most of these areas often changes with the seasons. These changes, in turn, play an important role in Earth's climate and in the survival of many species.

10 Compare Fill in the Venn diagram to compare and contrast the hydrosphere and the cryosphere.

Hydrosphere   Both   Cryosphere

Ships can get stuck in sea ice.

C

D

Water moves in ocean currents across huge distances.

What a Gas!

What is the atmosphere?

The **atmosphere** is mostly made of invisible gases that surround Earth. The atmosphere extends outward about 500 to 600 km from the surface of Earth. But most of the gases lie within 8 to 50 km of Earth's surface. The main gases that make up the atmosphere are nitrogen and oxygen. About 78% of the atmosphere is nitrogen. Oxygen makes up 21% of the atmosphere. The remaining 1% is made of many other gases, including argon, carbon dioxide, and water vapor.

The atmosphere contains the air we breathe. The atmosphere also absorbs some of the energy from the sun's rays. This energy helps keep Earth warm enough for living things to survive and multiply. Uneven warming by the sun gives rise to winds and air currents that move air and energy around the world.

Some gases in the atmosphere absorb and reflect harmful ultraviolet (UV) rays from the sun, protecting Earth and its living things. The atmosphere also causes space debris to burn up before reaching Earth's surface and causing harm. Have you ever seen the tail of a meteor across the sky? Then you have seen a meteoroid burning up as it moves through the atmosphere!

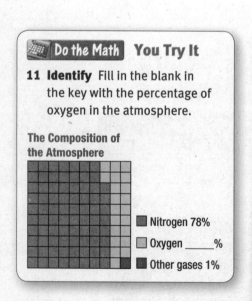

Do the Math **You Try It**

11 Identify Fill in the blank in the key with the percentage of oxygen in the atmosphere.

The Composition of the Atmosphere

■ Nitrogen 78%
□ Oxygen _____%
■ Other gases 1%

The atmosphere is a very thin layer around Earth. It is made up of a mixture of gases.

Think Outside the Book

12 Apply Design a magazine ad for the atmosphere to show what it does for Earth.

What is the biosphere?

The **biosphere** is made up of living things and the areas of Earth where they are found. The rocks, soil, oceans, lakes, rivers, and lower atmosphere all support life. Organisms have even been found deep in Earth's crust and high in clouds. But no matter where they live, all organisms need certain factors to survive.

Many organisms need oxygen or carbon dioxide to carry out life processes. Liquid water is also important for most living things. Many organisms also need moderate temperatures. You will not find a polar bear living in the Sahara, because it is too hot for the bear. However, some organisms do live in extreme environments, such as in ice at the poles and at volcanic vents on the sea floor.

A stable source of energy is also important for life. For example, plants and algae use the energy from sunlight to make their food. Other organisms get their energy by eating these plants or algae.

Active Reading

13 Identify What factors are needed for life?

_____

_____

© Houghton Mifflin Harcourt Publishing Company • Image Credits: (bkgd) ©Blaine Harrington III/Corbis; (cl) ©Gaertner/Alamy; (tubeworms) ©NOAA Okeanos Explorer Program, Galapagos Rift Expedition 2011

Visualize It! (Inquiry)

14 Predict What would happen if the biosphere in this picture stopped interacting with the atmosphere?

_____

_____

_____

_____

_____

_____

These giant tubeworms live on the deep ocean floor where it is pitch dark. The tubeworms depend on nutrients produced by bacteria that grow inside their bodies. The bacteria take in compounds from the water and turn them into forms the worms can use.

The hair on the sloth looks green because it has algae in it. The green color helps the sloth hide from predators. This is very useful because the sloth moves very, very slowly.

What's the Matter?

How do Earth's spheres interact?

Earth's spheres interact as matter and energy change and cycle between the five different spheres. A result of these interactions is that they make life on Earth possible. Remember that the Earth system includes all of the matter, energy, and processes within Earth's boundary.

If matter or energy never changed from one form to another, life on Earth would not be possible. Imagine what would happen if there were no more rain and all of the freshwater drained into the oceans. Most of the life on land would quickly die. But how do these different spheres interact? An example of an interaction is when water cycles between land, ocean, air, and living things. To move between these different spheres, water absorbs, releases, and transports energy all over the world in its different forms.

Visualize It!

15 Analyze Fill in the boxes below each photo with the names of two spheres that are interacting in that photo.

Rain provides water for living things.

A

Decomposing organisms release nutrients into the soil.

B

By Exchanging Matter

Earth's spheres interact as matter moves between spheres. For example, the atmosphere interacts with the hydrosphere or cryosphere when water vapor condenses to form clouds. An interaction also happens as water from the hydrosphere or cryosphere evaporates to enter the atmosphere.

In some processes, matter moves through several spheres. For example, some bacteria in the biosphere remove nitrogen gas from the atmosphere. These bacteria then release a different form of nitrogen into the soil, or geosphere. Plants in the biosphere use this nitrogen to grow. When the plant dies and decays, the nitrogen is released in several forms. One of these forms returns to the atmosphere.

Active Reading **16 Identify** What is the relationship between Earth's spheres and matter?

_____

_____

By Exchanging Energy

Earth's spheres also interact as energy moves between them. For example, plants use solar energy to make their food. Some of this energy is passed on to animals that eat plants. Some of the energy is released into the atmosphere as heat as the animals move. Some energy is released into the geosphere when organisms die and decay. In this case, energy has entered the biosphere and moved into the atmosphere and geosphere.

Energy also moves back and forth between spheres. For example, solar energy re-emitted by Earth's surface warms up the atmosphere, creating winds. Winds create waves and surface ocean currents that travel across Earth's oceans. When warm winds and ocean currents reach colder areas, thermal energy is transferred to the colder air and water, and warms them up. In this case, the energy has cycled between the atmosphere and the hydrosphere.

Icebergs melt in the sun.

Ⓓ

Waves break where the sea floor is shallow.

Ⓒ

Balancing the Budget

What is the source of Earth's energy?

17 Identify As you read, underline the sources of Earth's energy.

Almost all of Earth's energy comes from the sun. Part of this solar energy is reflected into space. The rest is absorbed by Earth's surface. A tiny fraction of Earth's energy comes from ocean tides and geothermal sources such as lava and magma.

Energy on Earth moves through and between the five Earth spheres. These spheres are open systems that constantly exchange energy with each other. Energy is transferred between spheres, but it is not created anew or destroyed. It simply moves between spheres or changes into other forms of energy.

In any system, input must equal output in order to keep the system balanced. The same is true for the flow of energy through Earth's spheres. In Earth's energy system, any addition in energy must be balanced by an equal subtraction of energy. For example, energy taken away from the atmosphere may be added to the oceans or to the geosphere. Earth's **energy budget** is a way to keep track of energy transfers into and out of the Earth system.

The chart on the next page shows the net flow of energy that forms Earth's energy budget. Energy from the sun may be reflected back to space or absorbed by Earth's surface. Earth radiates energy into space in the form of heat.

When Earth's energy flow is balanced, global temperatures stay relatively stable over long periods of time. But sometimes changes in the system cause Earth's energy budget to become unbalanced.

The sun is Earth's main source of energy.

Think Outside the Book Inquiry

18 Apply With your classmates, discuss the idea that energy can never be created or destroyed. Think of an example from your daily life in which energy is changed from one form to another.

Earth's Energy Budget

Incoming solar energy

Reflected by clouds and atmosphere: 26%

Reflected by Earth's surface: 4%

Absorbed by clouds and atmosphere: 19%

Outgoing energy

Radiated from clouds and atmosphere to space: 64%

Radiated from Earth to space: 6%

Lost as heat through rising warm air: 7%

Evaporated from Earth to clouds and atmosphere: 23%

Absorbed by Earth's surface: 51%

What can disturb Earth's energy budget?

An unbalanced energy budget can increase or decrease global temperatures and disrupt the balance of energy in Earth's system. Two things that can disturb Earth's energy budget are an increase in greenhouse gases and a decrease in polar ice caps.

Greenhouse Gases

Greenhouse gases, such as carbon dioxide and water vapor, absorb energy from Earth's surface and keep that energy in the atmosphere. An increase in greenhouse gases decreases the amount of energy radiated out to space. Earth's temperatures then rise over time, which may lead to climate changes.

Melting Polar Ice

Bright white areas such as the snow-covered polar regions and glaciers reflect sunlight. In contrast, bodies of water and bare rock appear dark. They tend to absorb solar radiation. When snow and ice melt, the exposed water and land absorb and then radiate more energy back into the atmosphere than the snow or ice did. Earth's atmosphere becomes warmer, leading to increased global temperatures and climate changes.

Visualize It!

19 Describe Describe what happens to solar energy as it enters Earth's atmosphere.

_____

_____

_____

Visual Summary

To complete this summary, fill in the box below each photo with the name of the sphere being shown in the photo. Then use the key below to check your answers. You can use this page to review the main concepts of the lesson.

20 _____

Earth's Spheres

21 _____

24 _____

23 _____

22 _____

Answers: 20 geosphere; 21 biosphere; 22 cryosphere; 23 hydrosphere; 24 atmosphere

25 Synthesize Diagram an interaction between any two of Earth's spheres.

Lesson Review

Vocabulary

Underline the term that best completes each of the following sentences.

1 The ice caps in the Antarctic and the Arctic are a part of the *geosphere/cryosphere/biosphere*.

2 Most of the water on Earth can be found in the *biosphere/hydrosphere/geosphere*.

3 The *hydrosphere/geosphere/atmosphere* protects organisms that live on Earth by blocking out harmful UV rays from the sun.

Key Concepts

Location	Sphere
4 Identify Forms a thin layer of gases around Earth	
5 Identify Extends from Earth's core to Earth's surface	
6 Identify Extends from inside Earth's crust to the lower atmosphere	

7 Describe What does the Earth system include?

_____

_____

_____

8 Analyze Which spheres are interacting when a volcano erupts and releases gases into the air?

_____

_____

9 Identify What are the two most abundant gases in the atmosphere?

_____

10 Describe How do Earth's spheres interact?

_____

_____

_____

Critical Thinking

Use this graph to answer the following question.

Earth's Solar Energy Balance

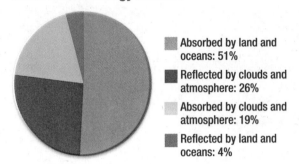

- Absorbed by land and oceans: 51%
- Reflected by clouds and atmosphere: 26%
- Absorbed by clouds and atmosphere: 19%
- Reflected by land and oceans: 4%

11 Infer Which parts of the graph would increase if all of Earth's polar ice melts? Which parts would decrease?

_____

_____

_____

12 Identify Name two ways in which the Earth system relies on energy from the sun.

_____

_____

_____

13 Analyze How does the biosphere rely on the other spheres for survival?

_____

_____

_____

14 Infer Where is most of Earth's liquid water? What must be done so humans can drink it?

_____

_____

_____

_____

My Notes

Weathering

ESSENTIAL QUESTION

How does weathering change Earth's surface?

By the end of this lesson, you should be able to analyze the effects of physical and chemical weathering on Earth's surface, including examples of each kind of weathering.

Wave Rock in Australia may look like an ocean wave, but it was actually formed when the rock in the middle of this formation weathered faster than the rock at the top.

✋ **Lesson Labs**

Quick Labs
- Mechanical Weathering
- Weathering Chalk
- How Can Materials on Earth's Surface Change?

Engage Your Brain

1 Predict Check T or F to show whether you think each statement is true or false.

T   F
☐   ☐   Rocks can change shape and composition over time.

☐   ☐   Rocks cannot be weathered by wind and chemicals in the air.

☐   ☐   A rusty car is an example of weathering.

☐   ☐   Plants and animals can cause weathering of rocks.

2 Describe Your class has taken a field trip to a local stream. You notice that the rocks in the water are rounded and smooth. Write a brief description of how you think the rocks changed over time.

_____

_____

_____

_____

_____

_____

_____

Active Reading

3 Synthesize You can often find clues to the meaning of a word by examining the use of that word in a sentence. Read the following sentences and write your own definition for the word *abrasion*.

Example sentences
Bobby fell on the sidewalk and scraped his knee. The abrasion on his knee was painful because of the loss of several layers of skin.

Vocabulary Terms

- weathering
- physical weathering
- abrasion
- chemical weathering
- oxidation
- acid precipitation

4 Apply As you learn the definition of each vocabulary term in this lesson, create your own definition or sketch to help you remember the meaning of the term.

abrasion:

_____

_____

_____

BreakItDown

What is weathering?

Did you know that sand on a beach may have once been a part of a large boulder? Over millions of years, a boulder can break down into many smaller pieces. The breakdown of rock material by physical and chemical processes is called **weathering**. Two kinds of weathering are *physical weathering* and *chemical weathering*.

What causes physical weathering?

Rocks can get smaller and smaller without a change in the composition of the rock. This is an example of a physical change. The process by which rock is broken down into smaller pieces by physical changes is **physical weathering**. Temperature changes, pressure changes, plant and animal actions, water, wind, and gravity are all agents of physical weathering.

As materials break apart, they can become even more exposed to physical changes. For instance, a large boulder can be broken apart by ice and water over time. Eventually, the boulder can split in two. Now there are two rocks exposed to the agents of physical weathering. In other words, the amount of surface area exposed to the agents of physical weathering increases. The large boulder can become thousands of tiny rocks over time as each new rock increases the amount of surface area able to be weathered.

5 **Identify** As you read, place the names of some common agents of physical weathering in the graphic organizer below.

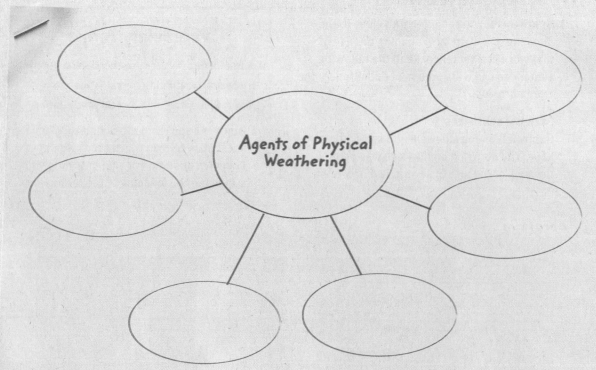

Agents of Physical Weathering

6 Describe Write a caption for each of the images to describe the process of ice wedging

Ice Wedging

Water

_____

Ice

_____

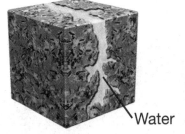

Water

_____

Ice

_____

Temperature Change

Changes in temperatures can cause a rock to break apart. A rise in temperature will cause a rock to expand. A decrease in temperature will cause a rock to contract. Repeated temperature changes can weaken the structure of a rock, causing the rock to crumble. Even changes in temperature between day and night can cause rocks to expand and contract. In desert regions differences in day and night temperatures can be significant. Rocks can weaken and crumble from the stress caused by these temperature changes.

Ice wedging, sometimes known as _frost wedging_, can also cause rocks to physically break apart, as shown in the image below. Ice wedging causes cracks in rocks to expand as water seeps in and freezes. When water collects in cracks in rock and the temperature drops, the water may freeze. Water expands as it freezes to become ice. As the ice expands, the crack will widen. As more water enters the crack, it can expand to an even larger size. Eventually, a small crack in a rock can cause even the largest of rocks to split apart.

7 Hypothesize Where on Earth would physical weathering from temperature changes be most common? Least common? Explain.

_____

_____

_____

These cracks, which were caused by ice wedging, will continue to expand over time.

Enchanted Rock was once buried deep inside Earth.

Pressure Change

Physical weathering can be caused by pressure changes. Rocks formed under pressure deep within Earth can become exposed at the surface. As overlying materials are removed above the rock, the pressure decreases. As a result, the rock expands, causing the outermost layers of rock to separate from the underlying layers, as shown to the left. *Exfoliation* (ex•foh•lee•AY•shun) is the process by which the outer layers of rock slowly peel away due to pressure changes. Enchanted Rock in Texas is a 130 m–high dome of granite that is slowly losing the outermost layers of rock due to exfoliation and other processes.

Animal Action

Animals can cause physical weathering. Many animals dig burrows into the ground, allowing more rock to be exposed. Common burrowing animals include ground squirrels, prairie dogs, ants, and earthworms. These animals move soils and allow new rocks, soils, and other materials to be exposed at the surface, as shown below. Materials can undergo weathering below the surface, but are more likely to be weathered once exposed at the surface.

Visualize It!

8 Describe Write a caption for each animal describing how it might cause physical weathering.

Prairie dog

A _____

Earthworm

B _____

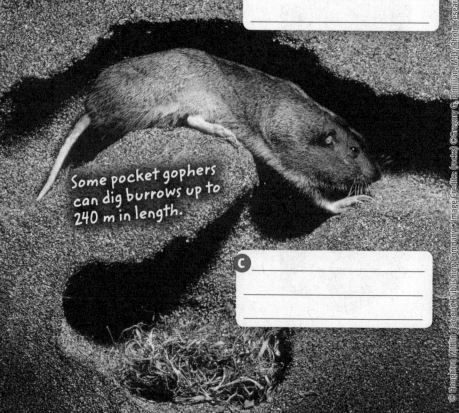
Some pocket gophers can dig burrows up to 240 m in length.

C _____

© Houghton Mifflin Harcourt Publishing Company • Image Credits: (rocks) ©Gregory G. Dimijian, M.D./Photo Researchers, Inc.; (worm) ©Dr. Jeremy Burgess/Photo Researchers, Inc.; (gopher) ©Tom McHugh/Photo Researchers, Inc.; (prairie dog) ©L. Zacharie/Alamy

Wind, Water, and Gravity

Rock can be broken down by the action of other rocks over time. **Abrasion** (uh•BRAY•zhuhn) is the breaking down and wearing away of rock material by the mechanical action of other rock. Three agents of physical weathering that can cause abrasion are moving water, wind, and gravity. Also, rocks suspended in the ice of a glacier can cause abrasion of other rocks on Earth's surface.

In moving water, rock can become rounded and smooth. Abrasion occurs as rocks are tumbled in water, hitting other rocks. Wind abrasion occurs when wind lifts and carries small particles in the air. The small particles can blast away at surfaces and slowly wear them away. During a landslide, large rocks can fall from higher up a slope and break more rocks below, causing abrasion.

Active Reading

9 Identify As you read, underline the agents of weathering that cause abrasion.

Rocks are tumbled in water, causing abrasion.

Wind-blown sand can blast small particles away.

Rocks can be broken down in a landslide.

Plant Growth

You have probably noticed that just one crack in a sidewalk can be the opening for a tiny bit of grass to grow. Over time, a neglected sidewalk can become crumbly from a combination of several agents of physical weathering, including plant growth. Why?

Roots of plants do not start out large. Roots start as tiny strands of plant matter that can grow inside small cracks in rocks. As the plant gets bigger, so do the roots. The larger a root grows, the more pressure it puts on rock. More pressure causes the rock to expand, as seen to the right. Eventually, the rock can break apart.

Think Outside the Book Inquiry

10 Summarize Imagine you are a rock. Write a short biography of your life as a rock, describing the changes you have gone through over time.

This tree started as a tiny seedling and eventually grew to split the rock in half.

Reaction

What causes chemical weathering?

Chemical weathering changes both the composition and appearance of rocks. **Chemical weathering** is the breakdown of rocks by chemical reactions. Agents of chemical weathering include oxygen in the air and acids.

Reactions with Oxygen

Oxygen in the air or in water can cause chemical weathering. Oxygen reacts with the compounds that make up rock, causing chemical reactions. The process by which other chemicals combine with oxygen is called **oxidation** (ahk•si•DAY•shun).

Rock surfaces sometimes change color. A color change can mean that a chemical reaction has taken place. Rocks containing iron can easily undergo chemical weathering. Iron in rocks and soils combines quickly with oxygen that is dissolved in water. The result is a rock that turns reddish orange. This is rust! The red color of much of the soil in the southeastern United States and of rock formations in the southwestern United States is due to the presence of rust, as seen in the image below.

Reactions with Acid Precipitation

Acids break down most minerals faster than water alone. Increased amounts of acid from various sources can cause chemical weathering of rock. Acids in the atmosphere are created when chemicals combine with water in the air. Rain is normally slightly acidic. When fossil fuels are burned, other chemicals combine with water in the atmosphere to produce even stronger acids. When these stronger acids fall to Earth, they are called **acid precipitation** (AS•id prih•sip•ih•TAY•shun). Acid precipitation is recognized as a problem all around the world and causes rocks to break down and change composition.

**Active Reading** 12 **Describe** How does acid precipitation cause rocks to weather faster?

_____

_____

**Active Reading**

11 **Identify** As you read, underline examples of chemical weathering.

These rocks in Arizona are red because of oxidation.

Reactions with Acids in Groundwater

Water in the ground, or groundwater, can cause chemical weathering. As groundwater moves through spaces or cracks in rock, acids in the water can cause rocks to dissolve. A small crack in a rock can result in the formation of extensive cave systems that are carved out over time under Earth's surface, as shown to the right. The dissolved rock material is carried in water until it is later deposited. Stalactites (stuh•LAHK•tyt) and stalagmites (stuh•LAHG•myt) are common features in cave systems as dissolved chemicals are deposited by dripping water underground.

Reactions with Acids in Living Things

Acids are produced naturally by certain living organisms. For instance, lichens (LY•kuhns) and mosses often grow on rocks and trees. As they grow on rocks, they produce weak acids that can weather the rock's surface. As the acids move through tiny spaces in the rocks, chemical reactions can occur. The acids will eventually break down the rocks. As the acids seep deeper into the rocks, cracks can form. The rock can eventually break apart when the cracks get too large.

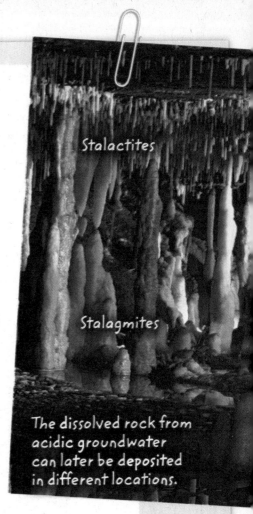

Stalactites

Stalagmites

The dissolved rock from acidic groundwater can later be deposited in different locations.

This gear is rusted, which indicates that a chemical reaction has taken place.

Think Outside the Book

13 Apply Think of an item made by humans that could be broken down by the agents of physical and chemical weathering. Describe to your classmates all of the ways the item could change over time.

Visual Summary

To complete this summary, fill in the blanks with the correct word or phrase. Then use the answer key to check your answers. You can use this page to review the main concepts of the lesson.

Weathering

Physical weathering breaks rock into smaller pieces by physical means.

Chemical weathering breaks down rock by chemical reactions.

14 Label the images with the type of physical weathering shown.

A _____

B _____

C _____

15 Label the images with the type of chemical weathering shown.

A _____

B _____

Answers: 14 A, plant growth; B, animal action; C, ice wedging; 15 A, oxidation; B, reactions with acids

16 **Relate** Why are some rocks more easily weathered than other rocks?

Lesson Review

Vocabulary

Fill in the blank with the term that best completes the following sentences.

1 Acid precipitation is an agent of _____ weathering.

2 The gradual wearing away or breaking down of rocks by abrasion is a type of _____ weathering.

3 The process of _____ causes rocks to change composition when reacting with oxygen.

4 The mechanical breakdown of rocks by the action of other rocks and sand particles is called _____.

Key Concepts

5 Compare What are some similarities and differences between physical and chemical weathering?

_____

_____

_____

_____

6 List Provide examples of physical weathering and chemical weathering in the chart below.

Physical Weathering	Chemical Weathering

7 Compare What are some similarities between ice wedging and plant root growth in a rock?

_____

_____

_____

_____

Critical Thinking

Use the graph to answer the following questions.

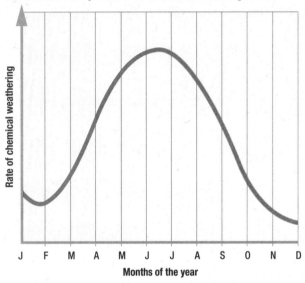

The Effect of Temperature on Rates of Weathering

(y-axis: Rate of chemical weathering; x-axis: Months of the year — J F M A M J J A S O N D)

8 Analyze Which two months had the highest rates of chemical weathering?

_____

_____

9 Apply Why do you think those two months had the highest rates of chemical weathering?

_____

_____

_____

_____

_____

_____

10 Infer Coastal regions are often affected by abrasion. What processes would cause increased abrasion along a coastal region? Explain.

_____

_____

_____

_____

My Notes

Erosion and Deposition by Water

ESSENTIAL QUESTION

How does water change Earth's surface?

By the end of this lesson, you should be able to relate the processes of erosion and deposition by water to the landforms that result from these processes.

Rivers aren't only found on Earth's surface. They also flow underground! Underground rivers can carve out caves full of channels, waterfalls, and even lakes.

Lesson Labs

Quick Labs
• Wave Action on the Shoreline
• Moving Sediment
• Modeling Stalactites and Stalagmites

Exploration Lab
• Exploring Stream Erosion and Deposition

Engage Your Brain

1 Predict Check T or F to show whether you think each statement is true or false.

T	F	
☐	☐	Water is able to move rocks as big as boulders.
☐	☐	Rivers can help to break down mountains.
☐	☐	Water cannot change rock underneath Earth's surface.
☐	☐	Waves and currents help to form beaches.

2 Explain Write a caption that explains how you think this canyon formed.

_____

_____

_____

Active Reading

3 Synthesize Several of the vocabulary terms in this lesson are compound words, or two separate words combined to form a new word that has a new meaning. Use the meanings of the two separate words to make an educated guess about the meaning of the compound terms shown below.

flood + plain = floodplain

_____

_____

ground + water = groundwater

_____

_____

shore + line = shoreline

_____

_____

sand + bar = sandbar

_____

_____

Vocabulary Terms

• erosion
• deposition
• floodplain
• delta
• alluvial fan

• groundwater
• shoreline
• beach
• sandbar
• barrier island

4 Apply As you learn the definition of each vocabulary term in this lesson, create your own definition or sketch to help you remember the meaning of the term.

Go with the Flow

How does flowing water change Earth's surface?

If your job was to carry millions of tons of rock and soil across the United States, how would you do it? You might use a bulldozer or a dump truck, but your job would still take a long time. Did you know that rivers and other bodies of flowing water do this job every day? Flowing water, as well as wind and ice, can move large amounts of material, such as soil and rock. Gravity also has a role to play. Gravity causes water to flow and rocks to fall downhill.

By Erosion

Acting as liquid conveyor belts, rivers and streams erode soil, rock, and sediment. *Sediment* is tiny grains of broken-down rock. **Erosion** is the process by which sediment and other materials are moved from one place to another. Eroded materials in streams may come from the stream's own bed and banks or from materials carried to the stream by rainwater runoff. Over time, erosion causes streams to widen and deepen.

By Deposition

After streams erode rock and soil, they eventually drop, or deposit, their load downstream. **Deposition** is the process by which eroded material is dropped. Deposition occurs when gravity's downward pull on sediment is greater than the push of flowing water or wind. This usually happens when the water or wind slows down. A stream deposits materials along its bed, banks, and mouth, which can form different landforms.

---

5 Compare Fill in the Venn diagram to compare and contrast erosion and deposition.

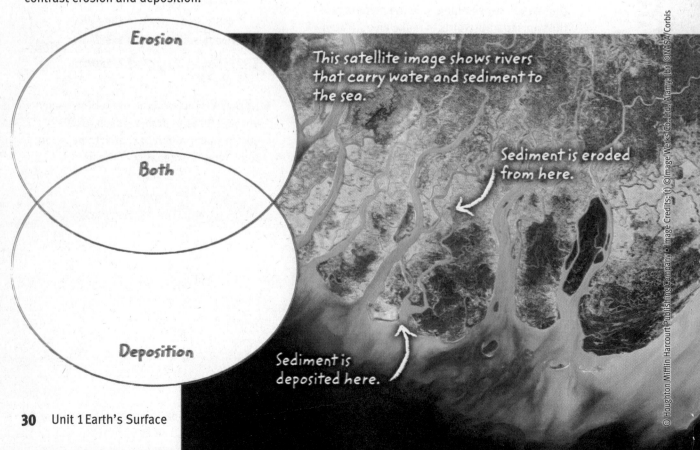

Erosion

Both

Deposition

This satellite image shows rivers that carry water and sediment to the sea.

Sediment is eroded from here.

Sediment is deposited here.

What factors relate to a stream's ability to erode material?

Some streams are able to erode large rocks, while others can erode only very fine sediment. Some streams move many tons of material each day, while others move very little sediment. So what determines how much material a stream can erode? A stream's gradient, discharge, and load are the three main factors that control what sediment a stream can carry.

Gradient

Gradient is the measure of the change in elevation over a certain distance. You can think of gradient as the steepness of a slope. The water in a stream that has a high gradient—or steep slope—moves very rapidly because of the downward pull of gravity. This rapid water flow gives the stream a lot of energy to erode rock and soil. A river or stream that has a low gradient has less energy for erosion, or erosive energy.

Load

Materials carried by a stream are called the stream's *load*. The size of the particles in a stream's load is affected by the stream's speed. Fast-moving streams can carry large particles. The large particles bounce and scrape along the bottom and sides of the streambed. Thus, a stream that has a load of large particles has a high erosion rate. Slow-moving streams carry smaller particles and have less erosive energy.

Discharge

The amount of water that a stream carries in a given amount of time is called *discharge*. The discharge of a stream increases when a major storm occurs or when warm weather rapidly melts snow. As the stream's discharge increases, its erosive energy, speed, and load increase.

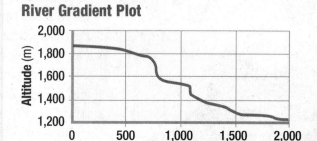

A river gradient plot shows how quickly the elevation of a river falls along its course. The slope of the line is the river's gradient. The line has a steep slope at points along the river where the gradient is steep. The line has a nearly level slope where the river gradient is shallow.

Identify

7 Along this river, at which two approximate altitude ranges are the gradients the steepest?

_____

_____

_____

8 At which altitude ranges would you expect the highest streambed erosion rate?

_____

_____

_____

9 At which altitude ranges would you expect the slowest streambed erosion rate?

_____

_____

_____

▶ Active Reading

6 Explain Why do some streams and rivers cause more erosion and deposition than others?

_____

_____

_____

Run of a River

What landforms can streams create?

A stream forms as water erodes soil and rock to make a channel. A *channel* is the path that a stream follows. As the stream continues to erode rock and soil, the channel gets wider and deeper. Over time, canyons and valleys can form.

Canyons and Valleys by Erosion

The processes that changed Earth's surface in the past continue to be at work today. For example, erosion and deposition have taken place throughout Earth's history. Six million years ago, Earth's surface in the area now known as the Grand Canyon was flat. The Colorado River cut down into the rock and formed the Grand Canyon over millions of years. Landforms, such as canyons and valleys, are created by the flow of water through streams and rivers. As the water moves, it erodes rock and sediment from the streambed. The flowing water can cut through rock, forming steep canyons and valleys.

10 Apply Discuss with your classmates some landforms near your town that were likely made by flowing water.

Visualize It!

11 Apply On the lines below, label where erosion and deposition are occurring.

Canyon

A _____

B _____

Meander

Floodplains by Deposition

When a stream floods, a layer of sediment is deposited over the flooded land. Many layers of deposited sediment can form a flat area called a **floodplain**. Sediment often contains nutrients needed for plant growth. Because of this, floodplains are often very fertile.

As a stream flows through an area, its channel may run straight in some parts and curve in other parts. Curves and bends that form a twisting, looping pattern in a stream channel are called *meanders*. The moving water erodes the outside banks and deposits sediment along the inside banks. Over many years, meanders shift position. During a flood, a stream may cut a new channel that bypasses a meander. The cut-off meander forms a crescent-shaped lake, which is called an *oxbow lake*.

Deltas and Alluvial Fans by Deposition

When a stream empties into a body of water, such as a lake or an ocean, its current slows and it deposits its load. Streams often deposit their loads in a fan-shaped pattern called a **delta**. Over time, sediment builds up in a delta, forming new land. Sometimes the new land can extend far into the lake or ocean. A similar process occurs when a stream flows onto a flat land surface from mountains or hills. On land, the sediment forms an alluvial fan. An **alluvial fan** is a fan-shaped deposit that forms on dry land.

Active Reading

12 Identify As you read, underline the definitions of *delta* and *alluvial fan*.

13 Compare Compare and contrast alluvial fans and deltas.

_____
_____
_____
_____
_____

Alluvial fan

Floodplain

C _____

Oxbow lake

Delta

What landforms are made by groundwater erosion?

As you have learned, rivers cause erosion when water picks up and moves rock and soil. The movement of water underground can also cause erosion. **Groundwater** is the water located within the rocks below Earth's surface. Slightly acidic groundwater can cause erosion by dissolving rock. When underground erosion happens, caves can form. Most of the world's caves formed over thousands of years as groundwater dissolved limestone underground. Although caves are formed by erosion, they also show signs of deposition. Water that drips from cracks in a cave's ceiling leaves behind icicle-shaped deposits known as *stalactites* and *stalagmites*. When the groundwater level is lower than the level of a cave, the cave roof may no longer be supported by the water underneath. If the roof of a cave collapses, it may leave a circular depression called a *sinkhole*.

Active Reading 14 **Explain** How does groundwater cause caves to form?

_____

_____

Stalactites are caused by deposition.

Groundwater can erode rock, causing caves to form.

Visualize It!

15 **Apply** Describe what may have happened underground to cause this sinkhole to form.

_____

_____

_____

_____

What forces shape a shoreline?

A **shoreline** is the place where land and a body of water meet. Ocean water along a shoreline moves differently than river water moves. Ocean waves crashing against the shoreline have a great deal of energy. Strong waves may erode material. Gentle waves may deposit materials. In addition to waves, ocean water has *currents,* or streamlike movements of water. Like waves, currents can also erode and deposit materials.

Waves

Waves play a major part in building up and breaking down a shoreline. Waves slow down as they approach a shoreline. The first parts of the shoreline that waves meet are the *headlands,* or pieces of land that project into the water. The slowing waves bend toward the headlands, which concentrates the waves' energy. A huge amount of energy is released when waves crash into headlands, causing the land to erode. The waves striking the areas between headlands have less energy. Therefore, these waves are more likely to deposit materials rather than erode materials.

Currents

When water travels almost parallel to the shoreline very near shore, the current is called a *longshore current.* Longshore currents are caused by waves hitting the shore at an angle. Waves that break at angles move sediment along the coast. The waves push the sand in the same angled direction in which they break. But the return water flow moves sand directly away from the beach. The end result is a zigzag movement of the sand. As sand moves down a beach, the upcurrent end of the beach is eroded away while the downcurrent end of the beach is built up.

As waves approach a shoreline, they bend toward the headlands and crash against them. The energy in the waves between the headlands is spread out, so they have less erosive power.

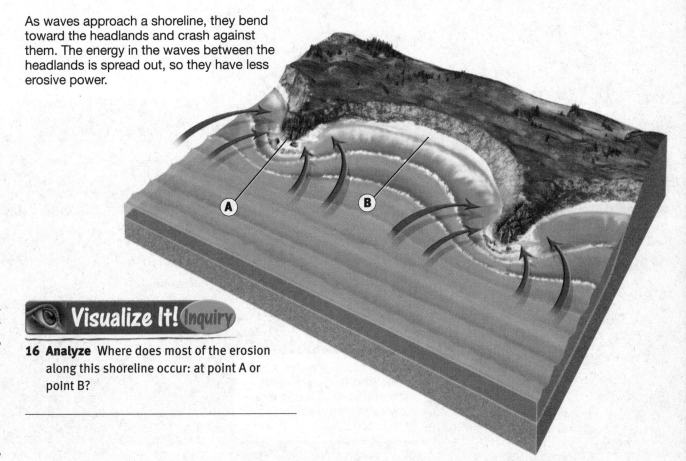

![Visualize It! Inquiry]

16 Analyze Where does most of the erosion along this shoreline occur: at point A or point B?

_____

Surf Versus Turf

What coastal landforms are made by erosion?

Wave erosion produces a variety of features along a shoreline. The rate at which rock erodes depends on the hardness of the rock and the energy of the waves. Gentle waves cause very little erosion. Strong waves from heavy storms can increase the rate of erosion. During storms, huge blocks of rock can be broken off and eroded away. In fact, a severe storm can noticeably change the appearance of a shoreline in a single day.

In addition to wave energy, the hardness of the rock making up the coastline affects how quickly the coastline is eroded. Very hard rock can slow the rate of erosion because it takes a great deal of wave energy to break up hard rock. Soft rock erodes more rapidly. Many shoreline features are caused by differences in rock hardness. Over time, a large area of softer rock can be eroded by strong waves. As a result, part of the shoreline is carved out and forms a bay.

Active Reading

17 Identify As you read, underline the sentence that summarizes the factors that determine how fast a shoreline erodes.

Sea caves form when waves cut large holes into fractured or weak rock along the base of sea cliffs.

Wave-cut platforms form when a sea cliff is worn back from shore, producing a nearly level platform beneath the water at the base of the cliff.

Headlands are finger-shaped projections that form when cliffs of hard rock erode more slowly than the surrounding softer rock does.

Sea Cliffs and Wave-cut Platforms

A *sea cliff* forms when waves erode and undercut rock to make steep slopes. Waves strike the cliff's base, wearing away the rock. This process makes the cliff steeper. As a sea cliff erodes above the waterline, a bench of rock usually remains beneath the water at the cliff's base. This bench is called a *wave-cut platform*. Wave-cut platforms are almost flat because the rocks eroded from the cliff often scrape away at the platform.

Sea Caves, Arches, and Stacks

Sea cliffs seldom erode evenly. Often, headlands form as some parts of a cliff are cut back faster than other parts. As the rock making up sea cliffs and headlands erodes, it breaks and cracks. Waves can cut deeply into the cracks and form large holes. As the holes continue to erode, they become *sea caves*. A sea cave may erode even further and eventually become a *sea arch*. When the top of a sea arch collapses, its sides become *sea stacks*.

18 Summarize Complete the chart by filling in descriptions of each coastal landform.

Coastal Landform	Description
Headland	
Sea cave	
Sea arch	
Sea stack	
Wave-cut platform	

Sea arches form when wave action erodes sea caves until a hole cuts through a headland.

Sea stacks form when the tops of sea arches collapse and leave behind isolated columns of rock.

19 Analyze Which of these features do you think took longer to form: the sea stack, sea arch, or sea cave? Explain.

_____

_____

_____

© Houghton Mifflin Harcourt Publishing Company

Shifting Sands

What coastal landforms are made by deposition?

Waves and currents carry a variety of materials, including sand, rock, dead coral, and shells. Often, these materials are deposited on a shoreline, where they form a beach. A **beach** is an area of shoreline that is made up of material deposited by waves and currents. A great deal of beach material is also deposited by rivers and then is moved down the shoreline by currents.

Beaches

You may think of beaches as sandy places. However, not all beaches are made of sand. The size and shape of beach material depend on how far the material has traveled from its source. Size and shape also depend on the type of material and how it is eroded. For example, in areas with stormy seas, beaches may be made of pebbles and boulders deposited by powerful waves. These waves erode smaller particles such as sand.

👁 Visualize It!

20 Infer Would it take more wave energy to deposit sand or the rocks shown on this beach? Explain.

_____

_____

Barrier islands lie nearly parallel to the shore.

Barrier islands are ridges of sand.

Sandbars and Barrier Islands

When waves erode material from the shoreline, longshore currents can transport and deposit this material offshore. This process creates landforms in open water.

A **sandbar** is an underwater or exposed ridge of sand, gravel, or shell material. A **barrier island** is a long, narrow island, usually made of sand, that forms parallel to the shoreline a short distance offshore.

Living on the Edge

Barrier islands are dynamic landforms that are constantly changing shape. What's here today may be gone tomorrow!

Barrier islands

Landform in Limbo

Barrier islands are found all over the world, including the United States. They can be eroded away by tides and large storms. The barrier island at the left was eroded by a hurricane. Because of erosion, the shape of a barrier island is always changing.

Building on Barriers

Barrier islands are popular spots to build vacation homes and hotels. Residents of barrier islands often use anti-erosion strategies to protect their property from erosion by tides and storms. Short-term solutions include using sand bags, like those shown on the right, to slow down erosion.

Extend

Inquiry

21 Explain Give a step-by-step description of how a barrier island could form.

22 Identify Research different technologies and strategies people can use to slow the erosion of a barrier island.

23 Model Choose one of the anti-erosion methods identified in your research and design an experiment to test how well the technology or strategy slows down the process of erosion.

Visual Summary

To complete this summary, fill in the blanks. Then use the key below to check your answers. You can use this page to review the main concepts of the lesson.

Erosion and Deposition by Water

Streams alter the shape of Earth's surface.

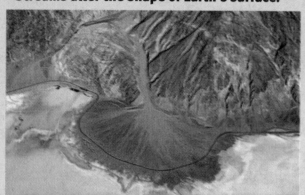

24 Caused by erosion: canyons, valleys

Caused by deposition: floodplains, deltas, _____

Groundwater erodes and deposits materials.

25 Caused by erosion: caves, _____

Caused by deposition: stalactites, stalagmites

Waves and currents change the shape of the shoreline.

26 Caused by erosion: bays, inlets, headlands, wave-cut platforms, sea cliffs, sea caves, sea stacks, _____

Caused by deposition: beaches, sandbars, barrier islands

Answers: 24 alluvial fans; 25 sinkholes; 26 sea arches

27 Explain How do erosion and deposition work together to form a delta?

Lesson Review

Vocabulary

Circle the term that best completes the following sentences.

1 *Erosion/Deposition* occurs when materials drop out of wind or water.

2 When a river flows into an ocean, it slows down and deposits materials in its *alluvial fan/delta*.

3 When a river periodically floods and deposits its sediments, a flat area known as a *floodplain/shoreline* forms over time.

Key Concepts

Complete the table below.

Landform	How It Forms
Canyon	**4 Explain**
Sinkhole	**5 Explain**
Sea cave	**6 Explain**

7 Synthesize How does gravity relate to a stream's ability to erode and deposit materials?

_____

_____

_____

8 Identify What are the two main factors that affect how quickly a coastline erodes?

_____

9 Describe How does a longshore current change a beach?

_____

_____

_____

Critical Thinking

Use this graph, which shows erosion and deposition on a beach, to answer questions 10–11.

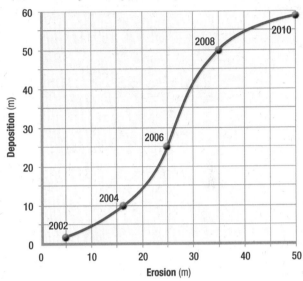

Erosion and Deposition (2002-2010)

10 Analyze In 2004, was there more erosion or deposition taking place?

_____

11 Evaluate Explain how waves and currents are affecting this beach over time.

_____

_____

_____

_____

_____

12 Hypothesize Many communities pump groundwater to irrigate crops and supply homes with water. How do you think overpumping groundwater is related to the formation of sinkholes?

_____

_____

_____

_____

_____

My Notes

Searching the Internet

The Internet can be a great tool for finding scientific information and reference material. But, because the Internet contains so much information, finding useful information on it may be difficult. Or, you may find information that is unreliable or not suitable.

Tutorial

The procedure below can help you retrieve useful, reliable information from the Internet.

Choose a search engine There are many search engines available for finding information. Evaluate different search engines using the following criteria:

- number of relevant sites listed in search results;
- how easy the search engine is to use;
- how fast the search is; and
- how easy the documents on the site are to access, and what type of documents they are.

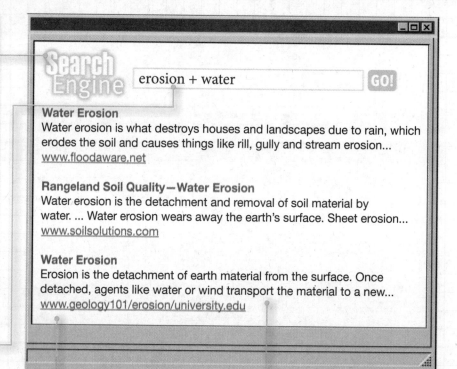

Search Engine

erosion + water   **GO!**

Water Erosion
Water erosion is what destroys houses and landscapes due to rain, which erodes the soil and causes things like rill, gully and stream erosion...
www.floodaware.net

Rangeland Soil Quality—Water Erosion
Water erosion is the detachment and removal of soil material by water. ... Water erosion wears away the earth's surface. Sheet erosion...
www.soilsolutions.com

Water Erosion
Erosion is the detachment of earth material from the surface. Once detached, agents like water or wind transport the material to a new...
www.geology101/erosion/university.edu

Choose and enter keywords Identify specific keywords for the topic of interest. You can make lists or draw concept maps to help you think of keywords or key phrases. Enter your keyword(s) into the search engine. You can enter one keyword at a time, or you can enter multiple keywords. You can put the word *and* or + between two keywords to find both words on the site. Use the word *or* between two keywords to find at least one of the keywords on the site. Use quotations ("like this") around keywords to find exact matches.

Look at the URL Examine the address in the search results list. Ask yourself if a reliable organization is behind the webpage such as government agencies (.gov or .mil), educational institutions (.edu), and non-profit organizations (.org). Avoid personal sites and biased sources, which may tell only one side of a story. These types of sources may lead to inaccurate information or a false impression.

Look at the content of the webpage Decide whether the webpage contains useful information. Read the page's title and headings. Read the first sentences of several paragraphs. Look at tables and diagrams. Ask yourself: How current is the webpage?; Are the sources documented?; and Are there links to more information? Decide whether the webpage contains the kind of information that you need.

You Try It!

Weathering is the physical and chemical alteration of rock.

Weathering processes have led to the formations you see here in Bryce Canyon. Study the photo and then do some research on the Internet to find out more about weathering processes.

Morning light on Thor's Hammer in Bryce Canyon National Park in Utah

1 Choosing Keywords Think about what you want to learn about mechanical weathering. You may want to focus on one topic, such as frost wedging, exfoliation, or thermal expansion. Choose relevant keyword(s) or phrases for the topic that you are researching.

_____

_____

_____

_____

_____

_____

2 Searching the Internet Enter the keywords in a search engine. Which keywords or phrases prompted the most relevant and reliable sites?

_____

_____

_____

_____

_____

3 Evaluating Websites Use the table below to evaluate websites on how useful they are and on the quality of the information. As you visit different websites for your research, make notes about each site's relevance and suitability.

Webpage	Comments

© Houghton Mifflin Harcourt Publishing Company • Image Credits: © William Manning/Alamy

Lesson 4

Erosion and Deposition by Wind, Ice, and Gravity

ESSENTIAL QUESTION

How do wind, ice, and gravity change Earth's surface?

By the end of this lesson, you should be able to describe erosion and deposition by wind, ice, and gravity as well as identify the landforms that result from these processes.

In this desert, wind has sculpted hills of sand, spreading them out like fingers.

© Houghton Mifflin Harcourt Publishing Company • Image Credits: ©George Steinmetz/Corbis

Engage Your Brain

1 Predict How do you think wind can erode materials?

_____

_____

_____

_____

_____

2 Infer The dark bands you see in the photo on the right are dirt and rocks frozen in the ice. What do you think will happen to the dirt and rocks when the ice melts?

_____

_____

_____

_____

_____

Active Reading

3 Define In this lesson, you will be learning about how different agents of erosion can abrade rock. Use a dictionary to look up the meaning of the word *abrade*. Record the definition:

_____

_____

Now use the word *abrade* in your own sentence:

_____

_____

_____

As you read this lesson, circle the word *abrade* whenever you come across it. Compare the sentences that include this word with the sentence you wrote above.

Vocabulary Terms

• dune   • creep
• loess   • rockfall
• glacier   • landslide
• glacial drift   • mudflow

4 Apply As you learn the definition of each vocabulary term in this lesson, create your own definition or sketch to help you remember the meaning of the term.

Gone with the

How can wind shape Earth?

Have you ever been outside and had a gust of wind blow a stack of papers all over the place? If so, you have seen how wind erosion works. In the same way that wind moved your papers, wind moves soil, sand, and rock particles. When wind moves soil, sand, and rock particles, it acts as an agent of erosion.

Abraded Rock

When wind blows sand and other particles against a surface, it can wear down the surface over time. The grinding and wearing down of rock surfaces by other rock or by sand particles is called *abrasion*. Abrasion happens in areas where there are strong winds, loose sand, and soft rocks. The blowing of millions of grains of sand causes a sandblasting effect. The sandblasting effect slowly erodes the rock by stripping away its surface. Over time, the rock can become smooth and polished.

Desert Pavement

The removal of fine sediment by wind is called *deflation*. This process is shown in the diagram below. During deflation, wind removes the top layer of fine sediment or soil. Deflation leaves behind rock fragments that are too heavy to be lifted by the wind. After a while, these rocks may be the only materials left on the surface. The resulting landscape is known as desert pavement. As you can see in the photo below, desert pavement is a surface made up mostly of pebbles and small, broken rocks.

Wind Direction

Desert Pavement

Visualize It!

5 Describe How did the desert pavement in this photo most likely form?

_____

_____

_____

Wind

Dunes

Wind carries sediment in much the same way that rivers do. Just as rivers deposit their loads, winds eventually drop the materials that they are carrying. For example, when wind hits an obstacle, it slows and drops materials on top of the obstacle. As the material builds up, the obstacle gets larger. This obstacle causes the wind to slow more and deposit more material, which forms a mound. Eventually, the original obstacle is buried. Mounds of wind-deposited sand are called **dunes**. Dunes are common in deserts and along the shores of lakes and oceans.

Generally, dunes move in the same direction the wind is blowing. Usually, a dune's gently sloped side faces the wind. Wind constantly moves material up this side of the dune. As sand moves over the crest of the dune, the sand slides down the slip face and makes a steep slope.

Loess

Wind can carry extremely fine material long distances. Thick deposits of this windblown, fine-grained sediment are known as **loess** (LOH•uhs). Loess can feel like the talcum powder a person may use after a shower. Because wind carries fine-grained material much higher and farther than it carries sand, loess deposits are sometimes found far away from their source. Loess deposits can build up over thousands and even millions of years. Loess is a valuable resource because it forms good soil for growing crops.

Visualize It!

Wind direction →

Windward slope

Slip face

Direction of dune movement →

Inquiry

6 Infer Why do you think loess can be carried further than sand?

_____

_____

_____

7 Determine Look at the photo above the illustration. Which direction does the wind blow across the photographed dune: from left to right or right to left?

_____

8 Identify Which side of the dune in the photograph is the slip face: A or B?

_____

Groovy Glaciers

What kinds of ice shape Earth?

Have you ever made a snowball from a scoop of fluffy snow? If so, you know that when the snow is pressed against itself, it becomes harder and more compact. The same idea explains how a glacier forms. A **glacier** is a large mass of moving ice that forms by the compacting of snow by natural forces.

Flowing Ice

Glaciers can be found anywhere on land where it is cold enough for ice to stay frozen year round. Gravity causes glaciers to move. When enough ice builds up on a slope, the ice begins to move downhill. The steeper the slope is, the faster the glacier moves.

As glaciers move, they pick up materials. These materials become embedded in the ice. As the glacier moves forward, the materials scratch and abrade the rock and soil underneath the glacier. This abrasion causes more erosion. Glaciers are also agents of deposition. As a glacier melts, it drops the materials that it carried. **Glacial drift** is the general term for all of the materials carried and deposited by a glacier.

Active Reading **10 Infer** Where in North America would you expect to find glaciers?

_____

_____

_____

Think Outside the Book

9 Apply Find out whether glaciers have ever covered your state. If so, what landforms did they leave behind?

As a glacier flowed over this rock, it scratched out these grooves.

This glacier is moving down the valley like a river of ice.

© Houghton Mifflin Harcourt Publishing Company • Image Credits: (l) © Bernhard Edmaier/Photo Researchers, Inc.; (r) ©Mark Burnett/Photo Researchers, Inc.

Alpine Glaciers

An alpine glacier is a glacier that forms in a mountainous area. Alpine glaciers flow down the sides of mountains and create rugged landscapes. Glaciers may form in valleys originally created by stream erosion. The flow of water in a stream forms a V-shaped valley. As a glacier slowly flows through a V-shaped valley, it scrapes away the valley floor and walls. The glacier widens and straightens the valley into a broad U-shape. An alpine glacier can also carve out bowl-shaped depressions, called *cirques* (surks), at the head of a valley. A sharp ridge called an *arête* (uh•RAYT) forms between two cirques that are next to each other. When three or more arêtes join, they form a sharp peak called a *horn*.

Visualize It!

11 Summarize Use the illustration below to write a description for each of the following landforms.

Landforms made by alpine glaciers	Description
Arête	
Cirque	
Horn	
U-shaped valley	

Horns are sharp, pyramid-shaped peaks that form when several arêtes join at the top of a mountain.

Arêtes are jagged ridges that form between two or more cirques that cut into the same mountain.

Hanging valleys are small glacial valleys that join the deeper, main valley. Many hanging valleys form waterfalls after the ice is gone.

Cirques are bowl-shaped depressions where glacial ice cuts back into the mountain walls.

U-shaped valleys form when a glacier erodes a river valley. The valley changes from its original V-shape to a U-shape.

Continental Glaciers

Continental glaciers are thick sheets of ice that may spread over large areas, including across entire continents. These glaciers are huge, continuous masses of ice. Continental glaciers create very different landforms than alpine glaciers do. Alpine glaciers form sharp and rugged features, whereas continental glaciers flatten and smooth the landscape. Continental glaciers erode and remove features that existed before the ice appeared. These glaciers smooth and round exposed rock surfaces in a way similar to the way that bulldozers can flatten landscapes.

Erosion and deposition by continental glaciers result in specific, recognizable landforms. Some of the landforms are shown below. Similar landforms can be found in the northern United States, which was once covered by continental glaciers.

Visualize It!

12 Compare What does the formation of erratics and kettle lakes have in common?

_____

_____

_____

_____

_____

_____

Erratics are large boulders that were transported and deposited by glaciers.

Kettle lakes form when chunks of ice are deposited by a glacier and glacial drift builds up around the ice blocks. When the ice melts, a lake forms.

Melting the Ice

A CHANGING WORLD

What would you do if an Ice Age glacial dam broke and let loose millions of gallons of water? Get out of the way and get ready for some erosion!

A Crack in the Ice

During the last Ice Age, a huge ice dam held back Glacial Lake Missoula, a 320-km-long body of water. Then one day, the dam burst. Water roared out, emptying the lake in less than 48 hours!

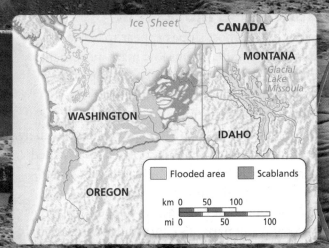

Giant ripple marks from the Missoula floods

Large-Scale Landforms

The erosion caused by the roaring water carved out a landscape of huge waterfalls, deep canyons, and three-story-high ripple marks. Many of these features are in an area called the Scablands.

History Repeats Itself

Lake Missoula eventually reformed behind another ice dam. The breaking of the dam and the floods repeated about 40 more times, ripping away topsoil and exposing and cracking the bedrock.

Extend

Inquiry

13 **Relate** Where have you seen ripple marks before and how do they compare to the ripple marks shown in the photo on this page?

14 **Explain** How do you think the three-story-high ripple marks shown here were formed?

15 **Model** Use sand, pebbles, and other materials to model how a severe flood can alter the landscape. Photograph or illustrate the results of your investigation. Present your results in the form of an animation, slide show, or illustrated report.

Slippery Slopes

How can gravity shape Earth?

Although you can't see it, the force of gravity, like water, wind, and ice, is an agent of erosion and deposition. Gravity not only influences the movement of water and ice, but it also causes rocks and soil to move downslope. This shifting of materials is called *mass movement*. Mass movement plays a major role in shaping Earth's surface.

Slow Mass Movement

Even though most slopes appear to be stable, they are actually undergoing slow mass movement. In fact, all the rocks and soil on a slope travel slowly downhill. The ground beneath the tree shown on the left is moving so slowly that the tree trunk curved as the tree grew. The extremely slow movement of material downslope is called **creep**. Many factors contribute to creep. Water loosens soil and allows the soil to move freely. In addition, plant roots act as wedges that force rocks and soil particles apart. Burrowing animals, such as gophers and groundhogs, also loosen rock and soil particles, making it easier for the particles to be pulled downward.

 **Visualize It!**

16 Analyze As the soil on this hill shifts, how is the tree changing so that it continues to grow upright?

_____

_____

_____

The shape of this tree trunk indicates that creep has occurred along the slope.

© Houghton Mifflin Harcourt Publishing Company • Image Credits: ©ThinkStock/age fotostock

Rapid Mass Movement

The most destructive mass movements happen suddenly and rapidly. Rapid mass movement can be very dangerous and can destroy everything in its path. Rapid mass movement tends to happen on steep slopes because materials are more likely to fall down a steep slope than a shallow slope.

While traveling along a mountain road, you may have noticed signs along the road that warn of falling rocks. A **rockfall** happens when loose rocks fall down a steep slope. Steep slopes are common in mountainous areas. Gravity causes loosened and exposed rocks to fall down steep slopes. The rocks in a rockfall can range in size from small fragments to large boulders.

Another kind of rapid mass movement is a landslide. A **landslide** is the sudden and rapid movement of a large amount of material downslope. As you can see in the photo on the right, landslides can carry away plants. They can also carry away animals, vehicles, and buildings. Heavy rains, deforestation, construction on unstable slopes, and earthquakes increase the chances of a landslide.

A rapid movement of a large mass of mud is a **mudflow**. Mudflows happen when a large amount of water mixes with soil and rock. The water causes the slippery mud to flow rapidly downslope. Mudflows happen in mountainous regions after deforestation has occurred or when a long dry season is followed by heavy rains. Volcanic eruptions or heavy rains on volcanic ash can produce some of the most dangerous mudflows. Mudflows of volcanic origin are called lahars. Lahars can travel at speeds greater than 80 km/h and can be as thick as wet cement.

This landslide in California was caused by heavy rains.

17 Identify List five events that can trigger a mass movement.

_____

_____

_____

_____

_____

Visualize It!

18 Infer On which slope, A or B, would a landslide be more likely to occur? Explain.

_____

_____

© Houghton Mifflin Harcourt Publishing Company • Image Credits: (t) ©Randy Jibson, USGS

Visual Summary

To complete this summary, fill in the blanks with the correct word or phrase. Then, use the key below to check your answers. You can use this page to review the main concepts of the lesson.

Erosion and Deposition by Wind, Ice, and Gravity

Wind forms dunes and desert pavement.

19 Wind forms dunes through:

_____

20 Wind forms desert pavement through:

_____

Ice erodes and deposits rock.

21 Alpine glaciers make landforms such as:

_____
_____
_____
_____

22 Continental glaciers make landforms such as:

_____
_____
_____

Gravity pulls materials downward.

23 Type of slow mass movement: _____

24 Three major types of rapid mass movement:

_____ _____ _____

25 Summarize Describe the role that gravity plays in almost all examples of erosion and deposition.

_____

Lesson Review

Vocabulary

Use a term from the section to complete each sentence below.

1 When an obstacle causes wind to slow down and deposit materials, the materials pile up and eventually form a _____

2 Large masses of flowing ice called _____ are typically found near Earth's poles and in other cold regions.

3 Very fine sediments called _____ can be carried by wind over long distances.

4 As glaciers retreat, they leave behind deposits of _____

Key Concepts

5 Explain How can glaciers cause deposition?

_____

_____

_____

_____

6 Compare Compare and contrast how wind and glaciers abrade rock.

_____

_____

_____

_____

_____

_____

_____

_____

7 Distinguish What is the difference between creep and a landslide?

_____

_____

_____

_____

_____

Critical Thinking

Use the diagram to answer the question below.

8 Synthesize Which of the four locations would be the best and worst places to build a house? Rank the four locations and explain your reasoning.

_____

_____

_____

_____

_____

_____

9 Integrate Wind erosion occurs at a faster rate in deserts than in places with a thick layer of vegetation covering the ground. Why do you think this is the case?

_____

_____

_____

_____

_____

_____

_____

_____

My Notes

Lesson 5

Soil Formation

ESSENTIAL QUESTION

How does soil form?

By the end of this lesson, you should be able to describe the physical and chemical characteristics of soil layers and identify the factors that affect soil formation, including the action of living things.

Living things, such as this shelf fungus (*Laetiporus sulphureus*), help to break down organic matter. The organic matter mixes with minerals, weathered sediment, water, and air to form soil.

© Houghton Mifflin Harcourt Publishing Company • Image Credits: (bkgd) ©Frank Paul/Alamy

Lesson Labs

Quick Labs
- Observing Life in Soil
- Modeling a Soil Profile
- Observing the Impact of Earthworms on Soil

Field Lab
- Comparing Soil Characteristics

Engage Your Brain

1 Predict Check T or F to show whether you think each statement is true or false.

T	F	
☐	☐	Soil contains air and water.
☐	☐	Soil does not contain living things.
☐	☐	Soils are the same from place to place.
☐	☐	Climate can affect how fertile soils are.

2 Explain How might the burrows formed by ants affect the soil?

_____

_____

_____

Active Reading

3 Apply Many scientific words, such as *weather*, have more than one meaning. Use context clues to write your own definition for each meaning of the word *weather*.

Example sentence
The <u>weather</u> outside is nice.

weather:

_____

_____

Example sentence
Wind, water, and plant roots <u>weather</u> rock into sediment.

weather:

_____

_____

Vocabulary Terms

- soil
- humus
- soil profile
- soil horizon

4 Apply As you learn the definition of each vocabulary term in this lesson, write your own definition or sketch to help you remember the meaning of the term.

The Dirt on Soil

What causes soil to form?

Soil is important to your life. You walk on grass that is rooted in soil. You eat foods that need soil in order to grow. But what exactly is soil? Where does it come from? How does it form?

A scientist might define **soil** as a loose mixture of small rock fragments, organic matter, water, and air that can support the growth of vegetation. The very first step in soil formation is the weathering of *parent rock*. Parent rock is the source of inorganic soil particles. Soil forms directly above the parent rock. Soil either develops here, or it is eroded and transported to another location.

Weathering of Parent Rock

Weathering breaks down parent rock into smaller and smaller pieces. These pieces of rock eventually become very small particles that are mixed in with organic matter to form soil. The process of soil formation can take a very long time. The amount of time it takes depends on many factors that you will learn about later in this lesson.

Active Reading

5 Identify As you read, underline the different substances that make up soil.

Soil formation begins when parent rock weathers into small fragments.

Plant roots grow and can break down sediment even further.

Burrowing animals increase the rate of weathering. They mix the soil, allowing more air to enter. They bring sediment to the surface where it is weathered more quickly by water, wind, and organisms.

Decomposition and Mixing by Living Things

Some microorganisms, such as bacteria and fungi, are decomposers that live in soil. These tiny decomposers perform the important task of breaking down the remains of plants and animals. These remains are decayed organic matter called **humus**. Humus is found in the top layer of soils. It is important because it contains nutrients that plants need to grow. Plants take up these nutrients through their roots. When plants or animals die, they are broken down by decomposers, and the nutrients are returned to the soil.

Larger animals, such as earthworms and moles, also live in soil. They loosen and mix the soil as they burrow through it. The mixing increases the amount of air in soil and improves the ability of soil to drain water.

6 Apply How might a fallen leaf eventually become part of soil?

_____

_____

7 Summarize How do decomposers and plants cycle nutrients in soil?

_____

_____

At least a million microorganisms can fit into one spoonful of soil! These tiny organisms have the big job of decomposing plant and animal remains.

Thick Tops, Rocky Bottoms

What factors determine how long it takes for soils to form?

Soil formation and development are processes that take place over a very long period of time. There are four main factors in determining exactly how long these processes take. They include the parent rock type, climate, topography, and plants and animals.

Image Credits: (tl) ©Premaphotos/Alamy; (bl) ©Peter Hulme; Ecoscene/Corbis; (br) ©Premaphotos/Alamy

- Rock type: Certain rock types weather at different rates and in different ways. The rate of weathering depends on the structure of the rock and minerals that make up the rock.
- Climate: Soil usually develops more quickly in warm, wet areas than in cold, dry areas.
- Topography: Sediments on steep slopes are often eroded. Soils usually develop faster in flatter areas where sediments are not easily eroded.
- Plants and animals: Plant roots hold sediments in place, allowing soil to develop quickly. Areas teeming with life have higher rates of decomposition and mixing. Soils tend to develop more quickly in these areas. Without a lot of plants and animals, soil tends to develop slowly.

Active Reading

8 Identify As you read, underline the factors that affect how long it takes for soils to form and develop.

9 Compare List some possible characteristics of an area where soils would develop quickly. Then do the same for an area where soils would develop slowly.

Area where Soils Develop Quickly	*Area where Soils Develop Slowly*

© Houghton Mifflin Harcourt Publishing Company

What are the main soil horizons?

Picture the rich, dark soil in a garden. Now imagine what the soil looks like as you dig deeper beneath the surface. Does the soil look and feel the same as you dig deeper? A vertical section of soil that shows all of the different layers is a **soil profile**. Each layer in the soil profile that has different physical properties is called a **soil horizon**. The main horizons include the A horizon, B horizon, and C horizon. There are many other horizons as well.

A Horizon

The A horizon is at the top of the soil profile. It is often referred to as *topsoil*. Decomposers live in this horizon, so it has the most decayed organic matter. This humus gives it a dark color. Plant roots break up fragments and animals burrow and mix the the soil. These processes increase the rate of weathering, so the A horizon is usually the most developed. As you'll learn later in this lesson, rich soils generally have high amounts of humus. Dead leaves, branches, and other organic matter may cover the surface of the A horizon.

B Horizon

The B horizon lies below the A horizon. It is not as developed as the A horizon and has less humus. Following precipitation events, water seeps down through the A horizon. Water carries material, such as iron minerals and clay, from the A horizon down to the B horizon. This is known as *leaching*. The leached materials commonly give the B horizon a reddish or brownish color.

C Horizon

The C horizon lies below the B horizon. It is the least-developed soil horizon. It contains the largest rock fragments and usually has no organic matter. The C horizon lies directly above the parent rock. Recall that this is the weathered rock from which the soil was formed.

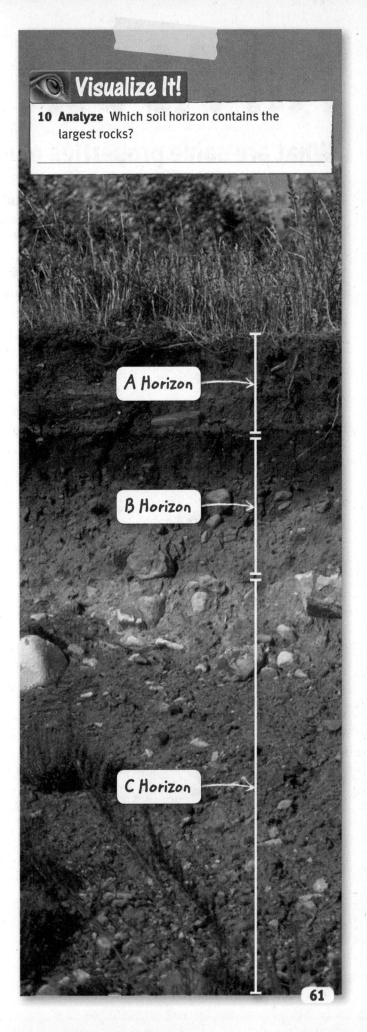

Visualize It!

10 Analyze Which soil horizon contains the largest rocks?

_____

A Horizon

B Horizon

C Horizon

All About Soil

What are some properties of soil?

Plants grow well in some soils and poorly in others. Soils look and feel different. They also contain different minerals and particles. Soil properties are used to classify different soils. These properties include soil texture, color, chemistry, pore space, and fertility.

11 Identify As you read, underline the three kinds of soil particles.

Soil Texture

The term *soil texture* is a property that describes the relative amounts of differently sized soil particles. Soil particles are classified as sand, silt, or clay. Most soils are a mixture of all three. Sand is the largest particle, ranging from 0.05 mm to 2 mm. Soils containing a lot of sand feel coarse. Silt particles are smaller than sand particles. They range from 0.002 mm to 0.05 mm. Silty soils have a smooth, silky feel. At less than 0.002 mm, clay particles are the smallest soil particles. Clayey soils feel very smooth and are usually sticky when they are wet.

Visualize It!

12 Distinguish The last space in each row contains three circles. Fill in the circle that shows the correct relative size of the particle shown in that row.

Particle	Size Range	Relative Size
sand	0.05 mm–2 mm	
silt	0.002 mm–0.05 mm	
clay	less than 0.002 mm	

Soil Color

Soils can be black, brown, red, orange, yellow, gray, and even white. Soil color is a clue to the types and amounts of minerals and organic matter in the soil. Iron minerals make soil orange or reddish. Soils that contain a lot of humus are black or brown. Color can also be a clue about the environmental conditions. Gray soil can indicate that an area is often wet and has poor drainage.

Soils are usually a mixture of colors, such as reddish brown. Scientists use the Munsell System of Color Notation to describe soil colors. The system uses a book of color chips, much like the paint chips found in a paint store. Scientists compare a soil to the color chips in the book to classify soils.

Soil and Climate

Climate can affect how soil forms in different regions on Earth. Warm, rainy regions produce tropical soils and temperate soils. Dry regions produce desert soils and arctic soils.

Tropical Soils form in warm, wet regions. Heavy rains wash away and leach soils, leaving only a thin layer of humus. Soil development is fast in these regions. They are not suitable for growing most crops.

Desert Soils form in dry regions. These soils are shallow and contain little organic matter. Because of the low rainfall, chemical weathering and soil development is slow in desert regions.

Temperate Soils form in regions with moderate rainfall and temperatures. Some temperate soils are dark-colored, rich in organic matter and minerals, and good for growing crops.

Arctic Soils form in cold, dry regions where chemical weathering is slow. They typically do not have well-developed horizons. Arctic soils may contain many rock fragments.

Soil Chemistry

Soil pH is determined by the combination of minerals, sediment, and organic matter found in soil. The pH of soil is a measure of how acidic or basic a soil is. The pH is based on a scale of 0 to 14. If pH is less than 7, the soil is acidic. If pH is above 7, the soil is basic. In the middle of the pH scale is 7, which means the soil is neither acidic nor basic; it is neutral. Scientists measure soil pH to determine whether the soil can support different plants. For example, soybeans grow best in a soil with a pH between 6.0 and 7.0. Peanuts thrive when the pH of soil is between 5.3 and 6.6.

Farmers can adjust the pH of soil to meet the needs of their plants. They can add lime to make acidic soils more basic. They can add acids to make basic soils more acidic.

Pore Space

Pore space describes the spaces between soil particles. Water and air are found in the pore spaces of soils. Water and air move easily through soils with many well-connected pore spaces. Soils with this property are well-drained and typically good for plant growth.

Plants need both water and air to grow. About 25 to 60 percent of the volume of most soils is pore space. The best soil for growing most plants has about 50 percent of its volume as pore space, with that volume equally divided between water and air.

The pH of a soil can be tested to make sure it will support the plants being grown.

Visualize It!

14 Describe Write a caption that describes the pore space for each diagram below.

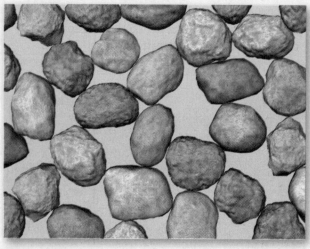

A _____
_____
_____
_____

B _____
_____
_____
_____

Soil Fertility

Soil fertility describes how well a soil can support plant growth. This quality is affected by factors that include the climate of the area; the amount of humus, minerals, and nutrients in the soil; and the topography of the area.

Fertile soils are often found in areas with moderate rainfall and temperatures. Soils with a lot of humus and the proper proportions of minerals and nutrients have high soil fertility. Soils found in dry areas or on steep hillsides often have low fertility. Farmers can add chemical fertilizers or organic material to soils to improve soil fertility. They also can grow crops, such as legumes, to restore certain nutrients to soil or leave cropland unplanted for a season to replenish its fertility.

Active Reading **15 Apply** What could you do to improve the fertility of the soil in your garden?

_____

_____

This meadow's bluebonnets thrive in well-drained soil. Bluebonnets also grow best in slightly basic soils.

Inquiry

16 Infer Use what you have learned to infer why Soils A and B have the following soils properties.

Soil Properties	Possible Reasons for Soil Properties
Soil A is black, well-drained, and good for growing plants.	
Soil B feels smooth and sticky and is gray in color.	

Visual Summary

To complete this summary, fill in the blanks with the correct word. Then use the key below to check your answers. You can use this page to review the main concepts of the lesson.

Soil Formation

Soil formation involves weathering of rock, addition of organic material, and actions by plants and animals that live in the soil.

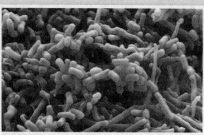

17 In general, soils in cold, dry areas will take _____ to develop than soils in warm, wet areas.

Characteristics of soil include texture, color, chemistry, pore space, and soil fertility.

19 _____ describes the spaces between soil particles.

A soil profile commonly has the A horizon, B horizon, and C horizon. They each have distinct physical characteristics.

18 The _____ contains the most organic matter; leaching carries minerals and humus down to the _____.

Answers: 17 longer; 18 A horizon, B horizon; 19 Pore space

20 Summarize Describe how living things can affect the different characteristics and development of soil.

_____

Lesson Review

Vocabulary

Draw a line to connect the following terms to their definitions.

1 soil

2 humus

3 soil profile

4 soil horizon

A decomposed organic matter

B layer of soil with distinct physical properties in a soil profile

C vertical section showing the soil horizons

D mixture of weathered sediment, organic material, water, and air

Key Concepts

5 Identify What is the first step of soil formation?

_____

_____

6 Explain What are the main factors that determine how long it takes for a soil to form and develop?

_____

_____

_____

7 Describe How would a soil that developed in a warm, wet place be different than one that developed in a hot, dry place?

_____

_____

_____

_____

8 Compare How might a dark colored, coarse soil differ from a reddish, smooth soil?

_____

_____

_____

_____

Critical Thinking

Use this table to answer the following question.

Climate Data for Locations A and B		
	Average Yearly Temperature (°C)	Average Yearly Precipitation (cm)
Location A	27	190
Location B	3	26

9 Analyze In which location would soils develop faster? Explain.

_____

_____

_____

_____

10 Infer Which soil would you expect to be better developed: the soil on a hillside or the soil on a valley floor? Why?

_____

_____

_____

_____

11 Synthesize Describe the cycle that involves soil, decomposers, and other living things.

_____

_____

_____

_____

My Notes

Unit 1

Big Idea > Continuous processes on Earth's surface result in the formation and destruction of landforms and the formation of soil.

Lesson 1

ESSENTIAL QUESTION
How do matter and energy move through Earth's spheres?

Describe Earth's spheres, give examples of their interactions, and explain the flow of energy that makes up Earth's energy budget.

Lesson 2

ESSENTIAL QUESTION
How does weathering change Earth's surface?

Analyze the effects of physical and chemical weathering on Earth's surface, including examples of each kind of weathering.

Lesson 3

ESSENTIAL QUESTION
How does water change Earth's surface?

Relate the processes of erosion and deposition by water to the landforms that result from these processes.

Lesson 4

ESSENTIAL QUESTION
How do wind, ice, and gravity change Earth's surface?

Describe erosion and deposition by wind, ice, and gravity as well as identify the landforms that result from these processes.

Lesson 5

ESSENTIAL QUESTION
How does soil form?

Describe the physical and chemical characteristics of soil layers and identify the factors that affect soil formation, including the action of living things.

Connect ESSENTIAL QUESTIONS
Lessons 2 and 4

1 Synthesize Explain how gravity causes erosion.

_____
_____
_____

Think Outside the Book

2 Synthesize Choose one of these activities to help synthesize what you have learned in this unit.

☐ Using what you learned in lessons 2, 4, and 5, explain the role that physical weathering plays in soil formation by making a flipbook.

☐ Using what you learned in lessons 1 and 2, write a short essay explaining how different spheres of Earth interact with each other during the process of chemical weathering.

Unit 1 Review

Name _____

Vocabulary

Fill in each blank with the term that best completes the following sentences.

1 _____ is the dark, organic-rich material formed as a top layer in soil from the decayed remains of plants and animals.

2 The process by which rocks break down as a result of chemical reactions is called _____.

3 The fan-shaped mass of sediment deposited by a stream into an ocean or a lake is called a _____.

4 The rock material deposited by glaciers as they melt and retreat is called _____.

5 The _____ is the part of Earth where life exists and extends from the deep ocean floors up into the lower atmosphere.

Key Concepts

Read each question below, and circle the best answer.

6 Which term describes the ability a soil has to support plant growth?

  A chemistry

  B fertility

  C texture

  D pore space

7 What are two processes that result in rocks being broken down into smaller pieces?

  A sunlight and glacial melting

  B chemical weathering and physical weathering

  C chemical weathering and deposition

  D physical weathering and humus

8 This diagram shows a landform called an alluvial fan.

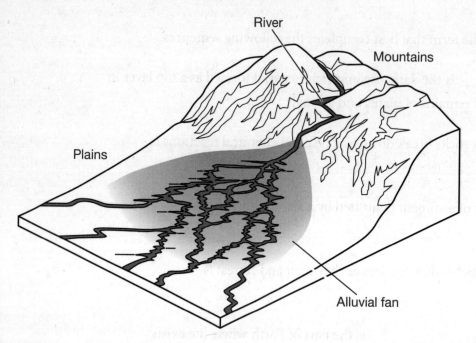

How does an alluvial fan form?

A It forms where a stream enters an ocean or lake, slows down, and deposits sediments there over time.

B It forms from a stream overflowing and depositing sediments.

C It forms where part of a meandering stream is cut off.

D It forms where a stream reaches a flat area of land, slows down, and deposits sediments there over time.

9 While walking along a seashore, Antonio determined that the shore has been affected by stormy seas and rough waves. What did Antonio observe?

A The beach was sandy.   **C** The beach was rocky.

B There were sandbars.   **D** There was a sea stack.

10 Landslides, rockfalls, and creep are examples of erosion and deposition by which erosion agent?

A gravity   **C** oxidation

B solar energy   **D** wind

11 The diagram below shows a landform called a sinkhole.

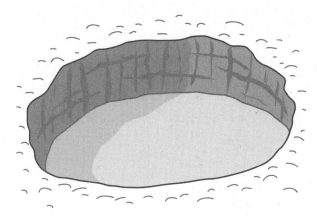

How does a sinkhole form?

A Stalactites erode the ceiling of a cavern.

B A flowing stream in the mountains erodes sediment and the ground caves in.

C Underground water erodes rock forming a cavern, and over time the cavern's roof collapses.

D A flowing stream erodes soil and rock making the stream deeper and wider.

12 A glacier is a large mass of moving ice. What conditions are necessary for a glacier to form?

A The weather must be below freezing and very dry.

B The weather must be below freezing, and more snow must fall than melt.

C The weather must be mild, and there must be a lot of precipitation.

D The weather must be below freezing, and more snow must melt than fall.

Critical Thinking

Answer the following questions in the space provided.

13 Explain whether water is a cause of either chemical weathering, physical weathering, or both.

_____

_____

_____

_____

_____

14 Below is a diagram of the soil profile of three layers of soil.

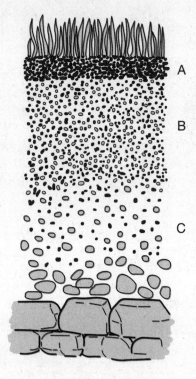

Describe the characteristics and properties of the three layers of soil.

_____

_____

_____

_____

_____

Connect ESSENTIAL QUESTIONS
Lessons 3 and 4

Answer the following question in the space provided.

15 How can water and gravity work together to erode soil, sediment, and rock?
Give two examples. _____

_____

_____

_____

Explain how water deposits soil, sediment, and rock. Give two examples. _____

_____

_____

_____

Earth's History

Big Idea

Rock, fossils, and other types of natural evidence are used to study Earth's history and measure geologic time.

The rocks and sand on some beaches contain clues about an area's past.

What do you think?

Earth's landscape is constantly changing. But Earth's history has not been erased. Look closely at the fossils that make up this coquina. What might the environment have been like when these organisms were living?

Coquina is fossilized shell and coral.

Unit 2
Earth's History

Lesson 1
Geologic Change Over Time 78

Lesson 2
Relative Dating 92

Think Science.................... 104

Lesson 3
Absolute Dating 106

Lesson 4
The Geologic Time Scale 118

Unit Review.................... 132

CITIZEN SCIENCE

Preserving the Past

Fossils are found throughout the United States. Fossils contain information about the organisms that lived both on land and in the ocean. How would you research the fossil history of an area?

① Think About It

Do some research to find out where fossils have been found. List some of these areas below.

_____

_____

What are the most common types of fossils found in these areas?

_____

_____

Do some further research about an interesting fossil discovery in one of these areas. Take notes on your findings on a separate sheet of paper.

Scientists use grids to record where things are found.

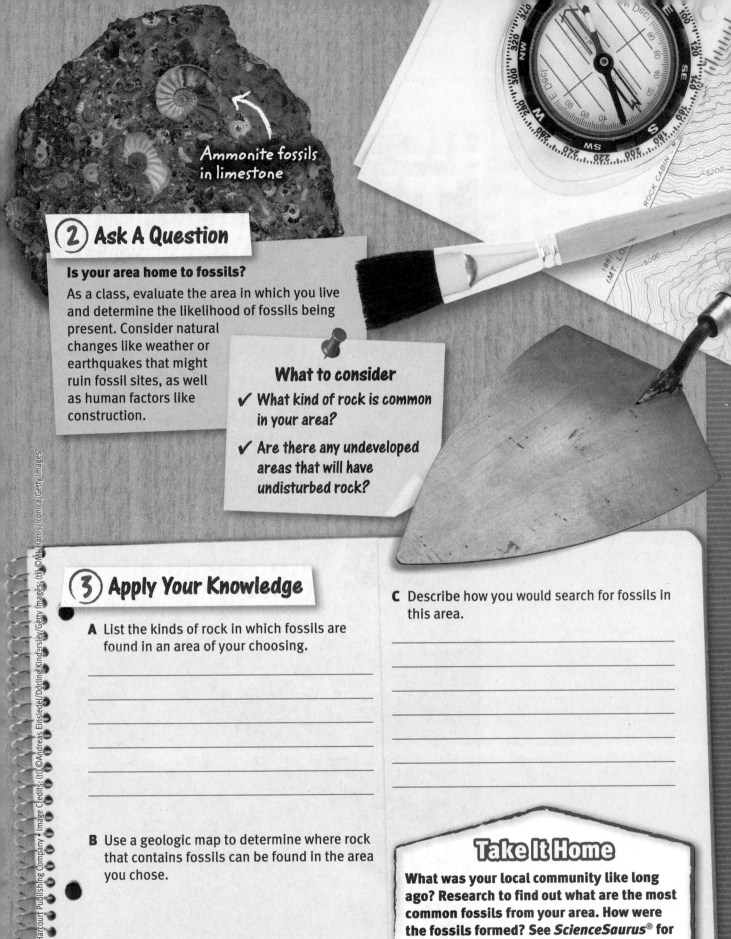

Ammonite fossils
in limestone

② Ask A Question

Is your area home to fossils?

As a class, evaluate the area in which you live and determine the likelihood of fossils being present. Consider natural changes like weather or earthquakes that might ruin fossil sites, as well as human factors like construction.

What to consider

✔ What kind of rock is common in your area?

✔ Are there any undeveloped areas that will have undisturbed rock?

③ Apply Your Knowledge

A List the kinds of rock in which fossils are found in an area of your choosing.

_____

_____

_____

_____

_____

_____

B Use a geologic map to determine where rock that contains fossils can be found in the area you chose.

C Describe how you would search for fossils in this area.

_____

_____

_____

_____

_____

Take It Home

What was your local community like long ago? Research to find out what are the most common fossils from your area. How were the fossils formed? See *ScienceSaurus®* for more information about fossils.

Geologic Change over Time

ESSENTIAL QUESTION

How do we learn about Earth's history?

By the end of this lesson, you should be able to explain how Earth materials, such as rock, fossils, and ice, show that Earth has changed over time.

Scientists learn about Earth's history by studying materials such as these rhinoceros fossils in Nebraska.

Lesson Labs

Quick Labs
• Modeling the Fossil Record
• Fossil Flipbooks

S.T.E.M. Lab
• Exploring Landforms

Engage Your Brain

1 Predict Check T or F to show whether you think each statement is true or false.

T	F	
☐	☐	Once rock forms, it never changes.
☐	☐	Fossils can tell us which animals lived at a certain time.
☐	☐	The climate is exactly the same all over the world.
☐	☐	A volcano erupting is an example of a geologic process.

2 Explain What can you infer about the environment in which this fossil probably formed?

_____

_____

_____

Active Reading

3 Synthesize You can often define an unknown word if you know the meaning of its word parts. Use the word parts and sentence below to make an educated guess about the meaning of the word *uniformitarianism*.

Word part	Meaning
uniform-	the same in all cases and at all times
-ism	a system of beliefs or actions

Vocabulary Terms

• uniformitarianism • climate
• fossil • ice core
• trace fossil

4 Identify This list contains vocabulary terms you'll learn in this lesson. As you read, circle the definition of each term.

Example sentence
The idea that erosion has occurred the same way throughout Earth's history is an example of underlineuniformitarianism.

uniformitarianism:

_____

_____

© Houghton Mifflin Harcourt Publishing Company • Image Credits: (bkgd) ©Annie Griffiths Belt/National Geographic/Getty Images; (inset) ©eltramo nature/Getty Images

Been There,

This inactive volcano last erupted over 4,000 years ago.

This is an active volcano.

What is the principle of uniformitarianism?

The principle of **uniformitarianism** (yoo•n uh•fohr•mi•TAIR•ee•uh•niz•uhm) states that geologic processes that happened in the past can be explained by current geologic processes. Processes such as volcanism and erosion that go on today happened in a similar way in the past. Because geologic processes tend to happen at a slow rate, this means that Earth must be very old. In fact, scientists have shown that Earth is about 4.6 billion years old.

Most geologic change is slow and gradual, but sudden changes have also affected Earth's history. An asteroid hitting Earth may have led to the extinction of the dinosaurs. However, scientists see these as a normal part of geologic change.

Active Reading **5 Describe** In your own words, describe the principle of uniformitarianism.

_____
_____
_____
_____

Visualize It!

6 Identify How do these photos show the principle of uniformitarianism?

_____
_____
_____

© Houghton Mifflin Harcourt Publishing Company • Image Credits: (t) ©USGS; (b) ©Tom Pfeiffer/VolcanoDiscovery/Getty Images

Done That

How do organisms become preserved as fossils?

Fossils are the trace or remains of an organism that lived long ago, most commonly preserved in sedimentary rock. Fossils may be skeletons or body parts, shells, burrows, or ancient coral reefs. Fossils form in many different ways.

 **Visualize It!**

Trapped in Amber

Imagine that an insect is caught in soft, sticky tree sap. Suppose that the insect is covered by more sap, which hardens with the body of the insect inside. Amber is formed when hardened tree sap is buried and preserved in sediment. Some of the best insect fossils, such as the one shown below, are found in amber. Fossil spiders, frogs, and lizards have also been found in amber.

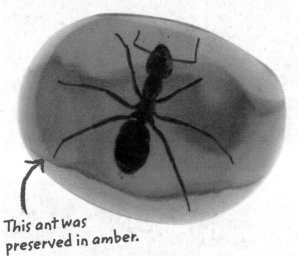

This ant was preserved in amber.

7 Analyze What features of the ant can you still see in this fossil?

_____

_____

_____

Trapped in Asphalt

There are places where asphalt wells up at Earth's surface in thick, sticky pools. One such place is La Brea Tar Pits in California. These asphalt pools have trapped and preserved many fossils over the past 40,000 years, such as the one shown below. Fossils such as these show a lot about what life was like in Southern California in the past.

This water beetle was preserved in asphalt.

8 Describe How did this organism become a fossil?

_____

_____

_____

_____

Buried in Rock

When an organism dies, it often starts to decay or is eaten by other organisms. Sometimes, however, organisms are quickly buried by sediment when they die. The sediment slows down decay and can protect parts of the body from damage. Hard parts of organisms, such as shells and bones, do not break down as easily as soft parts do. So, when sediments become rock, the hard parts of animals are preserved and become part of the rock as the sediments harden.

Visualize It! **9 Analyze** What part of the organism was preserved as a fossil in this rock?

_____

_____

Ammonites once lived in shells in ancient seas.

Become Frozen

In very cold places on Earth, the soil can be frozen all the time. An animal that dies there may also be frozen. It is frozen with skin and flesh, as well as bones. Because cold temperatures slow down decay, many types of frozen fossils are preserved from the last ice age.

Visualize It! **10 Compare** What information can this fossil give that fossils preserved in rock cannot?

_____

_____

This frozen mammoth was discovered in Siberia.

Become Petrified

Petrification (pet•ruh•fi•KAY•shuhn) happens when an organism's tissues are replaced by minerals. In some petrified wood, minerals have replaced all of the wood. A sample of petrified wood is shown at the right. This wood is in the Petrified Forest National Park in Arizona.

A similar thing happens when the pore space in an organism's hard tissue, such as bone, is filled up with minerals.

This petrified wood is in Arizona.

What are trace fossils?

Active Reading 11 **Identify** As you read, underline examples of trace fossils.

Fossils of organisms can tell us a lot about the bodies of life forms. Another type of fossil may also give evidence about how some animals behaved. A **trace fossil** is a fossilized structure that formed in sedimentary rock by animal activity on or in soft sediment.

Tracks, like the ones across this page, are one type of trace fossil. They are footprints made by animals in soft sediment that later became hard rock. Tracks show a lot about the animal that made them, such as how it lived, how big it was, and how fast it moved. For example, scientists have found paths of tracks showing that a group of dinosaurs moved in the same direction. This has led scientists to hypothesize that some dinosaurs moved in herds.

Burrows are another kind of trace fossil. Burrows are pathways or shelters made by animals, such as clams on the sea floor or rodents on land, that dig in sediment. Some scientists also classify animal dung, called coprolite (KAHP•ruh•lyt), as a trace fossil. Some coprolites are shown at the right.

These tracks were made by dinosaurs that once lived in Utah.

Visualize It! Inquiry

12 **Illustrate** Draw two sets of tracks that represent what you might leave for future scientists to study. Draw one set of you walking and another set of you running.

Walking

Running

Time Is on Our Side

Visualize It!

13 Infer What do these fossils of tropical plants from Antarctica tell you about what the climate was once like?

_____

_____

_____

A piece of Antarctica's past

Antarctica today

Active Reading

14 Identify As you read, underline two types of changes on Earth that fossils can give information about.

What can fossils tell us?

All of the fossils that have been discovered on Earth are called the *fossil record*. The fossil record shows part of the history of life on Earth. It is only part of the history because some things are still unknown. Not all the organisms that ever lived have left behind fossils. Also, there are many fossils that have not been discovered yet. Even so, fossils that are available do provide important information about Earth's history.

Fossils can tell scientists about environmental changes over time. The types of fossils preserved in sedimentary rock show what the environment was like when the organisms were alive. For example, fish fossils indicate that an aquatic environment was present. Palm fronds mean a tropical environment was present. Scientists have found fossils of trees and dinosaurs in Antarctica, so the climate there must have been warm in the past.

Fossils can also tell scientists how life forms have changed over time. Major changes in Earth's environmental conditions and surface can influence an organism's survival and the types of adaptations that a species must have to survive. To learn about how life on Earth has changed, scientists study relationships between different fossils and between fossils and living organisms.

How does sedimentary rock show Earth's history?

Rock and mineral fragments move from one place to another during erosion. Eventually, this sediment is deposited in layers. As new layers of sediment are deposited, they cover older layers. Older layers become compacted. Dissolved minerals, such as calcite and quartz, separate from water that passes through the sediment. This forms a natural cement that holds the rock and mineral fragments together in sedimentary rock.

Scientists use different characteristics to classify sedimentary rock. These provide evidence of the environment that the sedimentary rock formed in.

Composition

The composition of sedimentary rock shows the source of the sediment that makes up the rock. Some sedimentary rock forms when rock or mineral fragments are cemented together. Sandstone, shown below, forms when sand grains are deposited and buried, then cemented together. Other sedimentary rock forms from the remains of once-living plants and animals. Most limestone forms from the remains of animals that lived in the ocean. Another sedimentary rock, called coal, forms underground from partially decomposed plant material that is buried beneath sediment.

Active Reading 15 **Describe** What processes can cause rock to break apart into sediment?

_____

_____

_____

Sandstone

Texture and Features

The texture of sedimentary rock shows the environment in which the sediment was carried and deposited. Sedimentary rock is arranged in layers. Layers can differ from one another, depending on the kind, size, and color of their sediment. Features on sedimentary rock called *ripple marks* record the motion of wind or water waves over sediment. An example of sedimentary rock with ripple marks is shown below. Other features, called *mud cracks,* form when fine-grained sediments at the bottom of a shallow body of water are exposed to the air and dry out. Mud cracks show that an ancient lake, stream, or ocean shoreline was once a part of an area.

Visualize It!

16 Identify Which arrow shows the direction that water was moving to make these ripple marks?

_____

A   B   C

These are ripple marks in sandstone.

What do Earth's surface features tell us?

Earth's surface is always changing. Continents change position continuously as tectonic plates move across Earth's surface.

Continents Move

The continents have been moving throughout Earth's history. For example, at one time the continents formed a single landmass called *Pangaea* (pan•JEE•uh). Pangaea broke apart about 200 million years ago. Since then, the continents have been slowly moving to their present locations, and continue to move today.

Evidence of Pangaea can be seen by the way rock types, mountains, and fossils are now distributed on Earth's surface. For example, mountain-building events from tectonic plate movements produced different mountain belts on Earth. As the map below shows, rock from one of these mountain belts is now on opposite sides of the Atlantic Ocean. Scientists think this mountain belt separated as continents have moved to their current locations.

Today's continents were once part of a landmass called Pangaea.

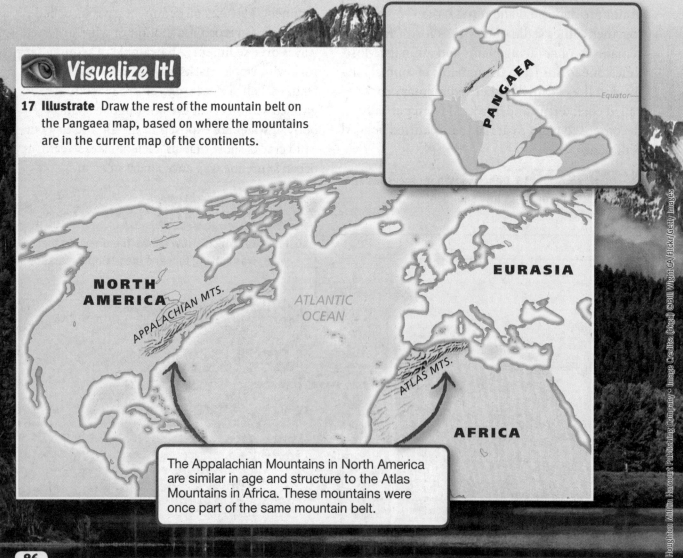

Visualize It!

17 Illustrate Draw the rest of the mountain belt on the Pangaea map, based on where the mountains are in the current map of the continents.

The Appalachian Mountains in North America are similar in age and structure to the Atlas Mountains in Africa. These mountains were once part of the same mountain belt.

© Houghton Mifflin Harcourt Publishing Company • Image Credits: (bkgd) ©Bill Wight CA/Flickr/Getty Images

Landforms Change over Time

The movement of tectonic plates across Earth has resulted in extraordinary events. When continental plates collide, mountain ranges such as the ones shown below can form. As they pull apart, magma can be released in volcanic eruptions. When they grind past one another, breaks in Earth's surface form, where earthquakes can occur. Collisions between oceanic and continental plates can also cause volcanoes and the formation of mountains.

In addition to forces that build up Earth's surface features, there are forces that break them down as well. Weathering and erosion always act on Earth's surface, changing it with time. For example, high, jagged mountains can become lower and more rounded over time. So, the height and shape of mountains can tell scientists about the geologic history of mountains.

Think Outside the Book

19 **Support** Find out about how the continents continue to move today. Draw a map that shows the relative motion along some of the tectonic plate boundaries.

Visualize It!

18 **Analyze** Label the older and younger mountains below. Explain how you decided which was older and which was younger.

_____

_____

_____

Rocky Mountains

Appalachian Mountains

Back to the Future

What other materials tell us about Earth's climate history?

The **climate** of an area describes the weather conditions in the area over a long period of time. Climate is mostly determined by temperature and precipitation. In addition to using fossils, scientists also analyze other materials to study how Earth's climate and environmental conditions have changed over time.

 **Active Reading**

20 Identify As you read the next two pages, underline the evidence that scientists use to learn about Earth's climate history.

Trees

When most trees grow, a new layer of wood is added to the trunk every year. This forms rings around the circumference (suhr•KUHM•fuhr•uhns) of the tree, as shown at the right. These rings tell the age of the tree. Some trees are over 2,000 years old. Scientists can use tree rings to find out about the climate during the life of the tree. If a tree ring is thick, it means the tree grew well—there was plenty of rain and favorable temperatures existed at that time. Thin tree rings mean the growing conditions were poor.

Visualize It! **21 Analyze** What is the time frame for which this tree can give information about Earth's climate?

Tree rings tell the age of a tree and what the climate was like.

Sea-Floor Sediments

Evidence about past climates can also be found deep beneath the ocean floor. Scientists remove and study long cylinders of sediment from the ocean floor, such as the one shown at the right. Preserved in these sediments are fossil remains of microscopic organisms that have died and settled on the ocean floor. These remains build up in layers, over time. If certain organisms are present, it can mean that the climate was particularly cold or warm at a certain time. The chemical composition of sediments, especially of the shells of certain microorganisms, can also be important. It shows what the composition was of the ocean water and atmosphere when the organisms were alive.

These scientists are studying sediment from the Ross Sea in Antarctica.

Ice

Icecaps are found in places such as Iceland and islands in the Arctic. The icecaps formed as older snow was squeezed into ice by new snow falling on top of it. Scientists can drill down into icecaps to collect a long cylinder of ice, called an **ice core**.

Ice cores, such as the ones shown in these photographs, give a history of Earth's climate over time. Some ice cores have regular layers, called bands, which form each year. Band size shows how much precipitation fell during a given time. The composition of water and concentration of gases in the ice core show the conditions of the atmosphere at the time that the ice formed.

Scientists study ice cores to find out about amounts of precipitation in the past.

22 Evaluate Fill in the table by reading the evidence and suggesting what it could mean.

Evidence	What it could mean
A. A scientist finds a fossil of a shark tooth in a layer of rock that is high in the mountains.	
B. Rocks from mountains on two different continents were found to have formed at the same time and to have the same composition.	
C. Upon studying an ice core, scientists find that a particular band is very wide.	

Visual Summary

To complete this summary, check the box that indicates true or false. Then use the key below to check your answers. You can use this page to review the main concepts of the lesson.

Fossils give information about changes in Earth's environments and life forms.

23 Trace fossils give information about animal activity and movement.

☐ True
☐ False

Sedimentary rocks provide information about Earth's geologic history.

24 These are ripple marks in sedimentary rock.

☐ True
☐ False

Studying Earth's History

Earth's surface features reflect its geologic history.

25 Tall, jagged mountains are older than rounded, smaller mountains.

☐ True
☐ False

Besides fossils, other materials give information about Earth's climate history.

26 Scientists study the width of tree rings to learn about past climate conditions.

☐ True
☐ False

Answers: 23 T; 24 T; 25 F; 26 T

---

27 **Explain** Describe three different materials that can be used to study Earth's history. What type of evidence does each give?

Lesson Review

Vocabulary

In your own words, define the following terms.

1 uniformitarianism _____

_____

_____

2 trace fossil _____

_____

_____

Key Concepts

3 Identify How old is Earth?

_____

4 Explain How can sedimentary rock show Earth's history?

_____

_____

_____

_____

5 List Name three examples of trace fossils.

_____

_____

6 Explain Name five ways that organisms can be preserved as fossils, and explain what fossils can show about Earth's history.

_____

_____

_____

_____

_____

7 Describe How do Earth's surface features indicate changes over time?

_____

_____

_____

_____

8 Describe What are two ways that scientists can study Earth's climate history?

_____

_____

_____

_____

Critical Thinking

9 Justify Is a piece of pottery an example of a fossil? Why or why not?

_____

_____

_____

Use this photo to answer the following questions.

10 Synthesize How does the erosion of these mountains support the principle of uniformitarianism?

_____

_____

_____

11 Infer The type and age of rocks found in this mountain range are also found on another continent. What might this mean?

_____

_____

_____

_____

My Notes

Relative Dating

ESSENTIAL QUESTION

How are the relative ages of rock measured?

By the end of this lesson, you should be able to summarize how scientists measure the relative ages of rock layers and identify gaps in the rock record.

Studying these rock layers can tell scientists a great deal about the order in which the different layers formed.

✋ Lesson Labs

Quick Labs
• Layers of Sedimentary Rock
• Ordering Rock Layers

Exploration Lab
• Earth's History

Engage Your Brain

1 Describe Fill in each blank with the word or phrase that you think completes the following sentences.

An example of something young is

_____

An example of something old is

_____

An example of something that is horizontal is

_____

An example of something older than you is

_____

The Liberty Bell

2 Explain Which came first, the bell or the crack in the bell? How do you know?

_____

_____

_____

_____

Active Reading

3 Synthesize You can often define an unknown word if you know the meaning of its word parts. Use the word parts below to make an educated guess about the meaning of the word *superposition*, when used to describe layers of rock.

Word part	Meaning
super-	above
-position	specific place

Vocabulary Terms

• relative dating
• superposition
• unconformity
• fossil
• geologic column

4 Apply As you learn the definition of each vocabulary term in this lesson, make your own definition or sketch to help you remember the meaning of the term.

superposition:

_____

_____

Who's First?

What is relative dating?

Imagine that you are a detective at a crime scene. You must figure out the order of events that took place before you arrived. Scientists have the same goal when studying Earth. They try to find out the order in which events happened during Earth's history. Instead of using fingerprints and witnesses, scientists use rocks and fossils. Determining whether an object or event is older or younger than other objects or events is called **relative dating**.

The telephones shown below show how technologies have changed over time. Layers of rock also show how certain things took place in the past. Using different pieces of information, scientists can find the order in which rock layers formed. Once they know the order, a relative age can be determined for each rock layer. Keep in mind, however, that this does not give scientists a rock's age in years. It only allows scientists to find out what rock layer is older or younger than another rock layer.

Visualize It!

6 **Explain** Use the numbers 1, 2, and 3 to rate these telephones from oldest (1) to youngest (3). Explain your choices. Does this tell you the years that the telephones were made?

_____

_____

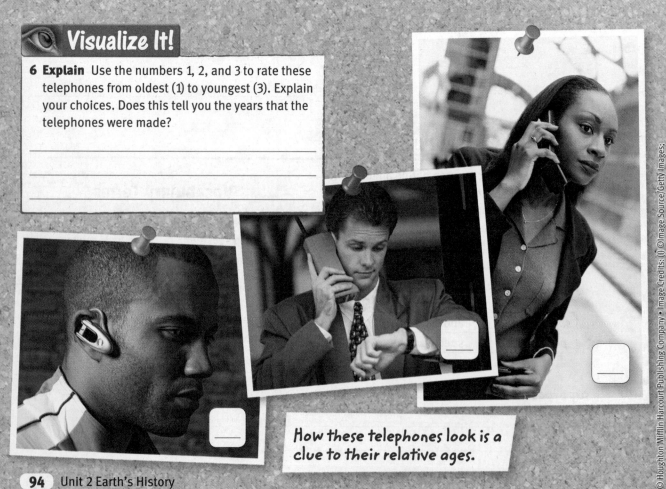

How these telephones look is a clue to their relative ages.

© Houghton Mifflin Harcourt Publishing Company • Image Credits: (l) ©Image Source/Getty Images; (m) ©C.Borland/PhotoLink/Photodisc/Getty Images; (r) ©Corbis

How are undisturbed rock layers dated?

To find the relative ages of rocks, scientists study the layers in sedimentary rocks. Sedimentary rocks form when new sediments are deposited on top of older rock. As more sediment is added, it is compressed and hardens into rock layers.

Scientists know that gravity causes sediment to be deposited in layers that are horizontal (hohr•ih•ZAHN•tuhl). Over time, different layers of sediment pile up on Earth's surface. Younger layers pile on top of older ones. If left undisturbed, the sediment will remain in horizontal layers. Scientists use the order of these layers to date the rock of each layer.

Active Reading **7 Explain** Why does gravity cause layers of sediment to be horizontal?

_____

_____

_____

Using Superposition

Suppose that you have a brother who takes pictures of your family and piles them in a box. Over time, he adds new pictures to the top of the pile. Where are the oldest pictures—the ones taken when you were a baby? Where are the most recent pictures—the ones taken last week? The oldest pictures will be at the bottom of the pile. The youngest pictures will be at the top of the pile. Layers of rock are like the photographs shown below. As you go from top to bottom, the layers get older.

This approach is used to determine the relative age of sedimentary rock layers. The law of **superposition** (soo•per•puh•ZISH•uhn) is the principle that states that younger rocks lie above older rocks if the layers have not been disturbed.

Rock layers are like photographs that have been put in a pile over time.

Visualize It!

8 Apply Use the law of superposition to describe the relative ages of these rock layers.

_____

_____

_____

How Disturbing!

How are sedimentary rock layers disturbed?

If rock layers are not horizontal, then something disturbed them after they formed. Forces in Earth can disturb rock layers so much that older layers end up on top of younger layers. Some of the ways that rock layers can be disturbed are shown below and on the next page.

By Tilting and Folding

Tilting happens when Earth's forces move rock layers up or down unevenly. The layers become slanted. *Folding* is the bending of rocks that can happen when rock layers are squeezed together. The bending is from stress on the rock. Folding can cause rock layers to be turned over by so much that older layers end up on top of younger layers.

By Faults and Intrusions

Scientists often find features that cut across existing layers of rock. A *fault* is a break or crack in Earth's crust where rocks can move. An *intrusion* (in•TROO•zhuhn) is igneous rock that forms when magma is injected into rock and then cools and becomes hard.

Folding, tilting, faults, and intrusions can make finding out the relative ages of rock layers difficult. This can be even more complicated when a layer of rock is missing. Scientists call this missing layer of rock an *unconformity*.

 **Visualize It!**

9 Describe Write a caption for this group of images.

_____

_____

_____

Tilting

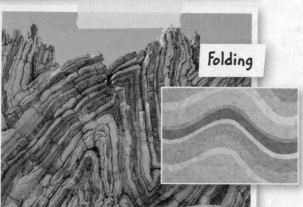
Folding

Faults

Intrusions

By Unconformities

A missing layer of rock forms a gap in Earth's geologic history, also called the geologic record. An **unconformity** (uhn•kuhn•FAWR•mih•tee) is a break in the geologic record that is made when rock layers are eroded or when sediment is not deposited for a long period of time. When scientists find an unconformity, they must question if the "missing layer" was simply never present or if it was removed. Two examples of unconformities are shown below.

Active Reading 10 **Describe** What are two ways that a rock layer can cause a gap in the geologic record?

_____

_____

_____

_____

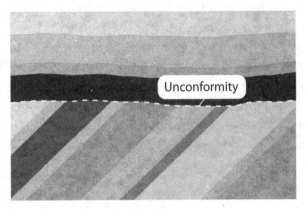

Unconformity

An unconformity can happen between horizontal layers and layers that are tilted or folded. The older layers were tilted or folded and then eroded before horizontal layers formed above them.

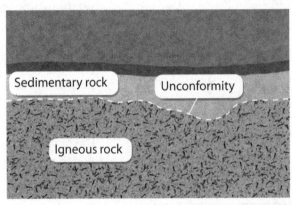

Sedimentary rock

Unconformity

Igneous rock

An unconformity can also happen when igneous or metamorphic rocks are exposed at Earth's surface and become eroded. Later, deposited sediment causes the eroded surface to become buried under sedimentary rock.

11 **Illustrate** Choose two of the following: tilting, folding, fault, intrusion, and an unconformity. Draw and label each one.

I'm Cutting In!

How are rock layers ordered?

Active Reading

12 Identify As you read, underline the law of crosscutting relationships.

Often, the order of rock layers is affected by more than one thing. Finding out what happened to form a group of rock layers is like piecing together a jigsaw puzzle. The law of superposition helps scientists to do this.

The idea that layers of rock have to be in place before anything can disturb them is also used. The law of crosscutting relationships states that a fault or a body of rock, such as an intrusion, must be younger than any feature or layer of rock that the fault or rock body cuts through. For example, if a fault has broken a rock layer, the fault is younger than the rock layer. If a fault has broken through igneous rock, the igneous rock must have been in place, and cool, before it could have been broken. The same is true for an unconformity. Look at the image below and use the laws of superposition and crosscutting relationships to figure out the relative ages of the rock layers and features.

Visualize It!

13 Analyze What is the order in which layers and features A through J formed?
Fill in the lines according to the relative ages of the layers or features.

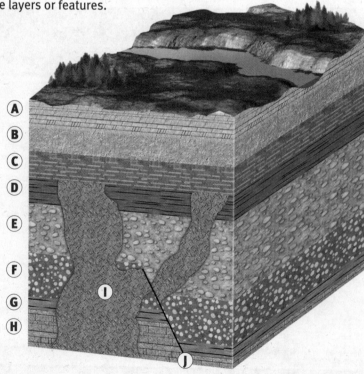

Youngest
_____
_____
_____
_____
_____
_____
_____
_____
Oldest

Dating Mars

NASA's *Mars Odyssey* orbiter and the *Hubble Space Telescope* have produced a large collection of images of the surface of Mars. These are studied to find the relative ages of features on Mars, using the laws of superposition and crosscutting relationships. Here are two examples of crosscutting relationships.

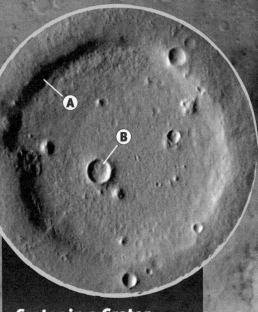

The Crater Came First
A crater can be cut by another feature, such as a fracture.

Crater in a Crater
A crater (A) can be cut by another crater (B) that formed from a later impact.

Hellas Crater
The many craters on Mars are studied to determine relative ages of features. This is Hellas Impact Basin, which is almost 2100 km wide.

Extend

Inquiry

14 Analyze What are the relative ages of crater A and crater B? Explain your answer.

15 Apply How can scientists use erosion as a way to determine the relative ages of craters on Mars? Describe how erosion could change the appearance of a crater over time.

16 Research Find out how scientists have used relative dating to study the geologic history of other planets, such as Venus. Present what you found out by drawing a graphic novel or making a poster.

So Far Away

How are fossils used to determine relative ages of rocks?

Fossils are the traces or remains of an organism that lived long ago, most commonly preserved in sedimentary rock. Fossil forms of plants and animals show change over time, as they evolve. Scientists can classify fossilized (FAHS•uh•lyzd) organisms based on these changes. Then they can use that classification of fossils to find the relative ages of the rocks in which the fossils are found. Rock that contains fossils of organisms similar to those that live today is most likely younger than rock that contains fossils of ancient organisms. For example, fossilized remains of a 47 million-year-old primate are shown below. Rock that contains these fossils is younger than rock that contains the fossils of a dinosaur that lived over 200 million years ago.

Inquiry

17 Explain In general, would fossils of species that did not change noticeably over time be useful in determining the relative ages of rocks? Explain.

_____

_____

_____

_____

_____

This is a fossil of a dinosaur that lived over 200 million years ago.

This is a fossil of a primate that lived about 47 million years ago.

How are geologic columns used to compare relative ages of rocks?

Relative dating can also be done by comparing the relative ages of rock layers in different areas. The comparison is done using a geologic column. A **geologic column** is an ordered arrangement of rock layers that is based on the relative ages of the rocks, with the oldest rocks at the bottom of the column. It is made by piecing together different rock sequences from different areas. A geologic column represents an ideal image of a rock layer sequence that doesn't actually exist in any one place on Earth.

The rock sequences shown below represent rock layers from different outcrops at different locations. Each has certain rock layers that are common to layers in the geologic column, shown in the middle. Scientists can compare a rock layer with a similar layer in a geologic column that has the same fossils or that has the same relative position. If the two layers match, then they probably formed around the same time.

Active Reading

18 Identify As you read, underline the description of how rock layers are ordered in a geologic column.

Visualize It!

19 Identify Draw lines from the top and bottom of each outcrop to their matching positions in the geologic column.

Outcrop 1

Geologic Column

Outcrop 2

Rock layers from different outcrops can be compared to a geologic column.

Visual Summary

To complete this summary, circle the correct words. Then use the key below to check your answers. You can use this page to review the main concepts of the lesson.

If undisturbed, sedimentary rock exists as horizontal layers.

20 For undisturbed rock layers, younger rocks are above/below older rocks.

Forces in Earth can cause horizontal layers of rock to be disturbed.

21 This photo shows folding/tilting.

Relative Dating

Fossils can be used to determine the relative ages of rock layers.

22 In undisturbed rock layers, fossils of a more recent organism will be in rock that is above/below rock containing fossils of older organisms.

Rock layers from different areas can be compared to a geologic column.

23 In geologic columns, the oldest rock layers are at the bottom/top.

Answers: 20 above; 21 folding; 22 above; 23 bottom

24 Apply How might the law of superposition relate to a stack of magazines that you have been saving over the past few years?

Lesson Review

Vocabulary

In your own words, define the following terms.

1 relative dating

_____

_____

2 unconformity

_____

_____

Key Concepts

3 Describe How are sedimentary rock layers deposited?

_____

_____

4 List Name five ways that the order of rock layers can be disturbed.

_____

_____

_____

5 Explain How are the laws of superposition and crosscutting relationships used to determine the relative ages of rocks?

_____

_____

_____

_____

_____

_____

6 Explain How can fossils be used to determine the relative ages of rock layers?

_____

_____

_____

_____

7 Describe How is the geologic column used in relative dating?

_____

_____

_____

_____

Critical Thinking

8 Justify Does the law of crosscutting relationships involve sedimentary rock only? Why or why not?

_____

_____

_____

Use this image to answer the following questions.

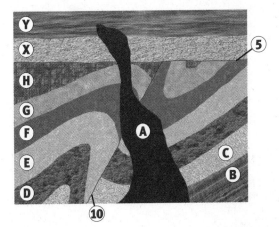

9 Analyze Is intrusion A younger or older than layer X? Explain.

_____

_____

10 Analyze What feature is marked by 5?

_____

11 Analyze Other than intrusion and faulting, what happened in layers B, C, D, E, F, G, and H?

My Notes

Forming a Hypothesis

When conducting an investigation to test a hypothesis, a scientist must not let personal bias affect the results of the investigation. A scientist must be open to the fact that the results of an investigation may not completely support the hypothesis. They may even contradict it! Revising or forming a new hypothesis may lead a scientist to make a breakthrough that could be the basis of a new discovery.

Tutorial

The following procedure explains the steps that you will use to develop and evaluate a hypothesis.

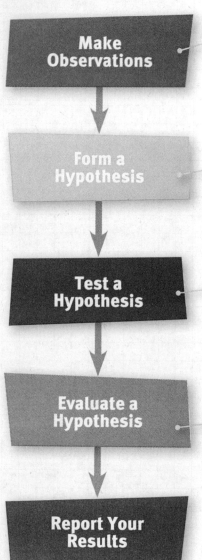

1 Making Observations Scientific investigations commonly begin with observations. Your observations may lead to a question. For example, you may wonder how, why, or when something happens.

2 Forming a Hypothesis To answer your question, you can start by forming a hypothesis. A hypothesis is a clear statement of what you expect will be the answer to your question. Start to form a hypothesis by stating the probable answer to your question based on your observations.

3 Testing a Hypothesis A useful hypothesis must be testable. To determine whether your hypothesis is testable, identify experiments that you can perform or observations that you can make to find out whether the hypothesis is supported or not.

4 Evaluating a Hypothesis After analyzing your data, you can determine if your results support your hypothesis. If your data support your hypothesis, you may want to repeat your observations or experiments to verify your results. If your data do not support your hypothesis, you may have to check your procedure for errors. You may even have to reject your hypothesis and form a new one.

You Try It!

The table provides observations about the latest eruptions of several volcanoes in Hawai'i.

Latest Eruption of Volcanoes in Hawai'i	
Volcano	**Year**
East Maui (Haleakala)	1460
Hualalai	1801
Mauna Loa	1984
Kilauea	still active

Map of the Hawaiian Islands showing: Kauai, Niihau, Oahu, Molokai, Maui (West Maui Volcano, East Maui Volcano (Haleakala)), Hawaii (Hualalai, Mauna Loa, Kilauea, Loihi). Legend: ▲ Volcano. PACIFIC OCEAN. Scale: km 0 50 100, mi 0 50 100. 160°W, 155°W.

1 Making Observations On the map, label the volcanoes with the years shown. What do you observe about the dates and the locations of the volcanoes?

_____

_____

_____

_____

_____

_____

_____

2 Forming a Hypothesis Use the observations above to form a hypothesis about the history of the area. Focus on the relationship between the activity of the volcanoes and the location of the volcanoes. Your hypothesis should be supported by all of your data. Summarize your completed hypothesis in a single paragraph.

_____

_____

_____

_____

_____

_____

3 Testing a Hypothesis Loihi is currently active, but West Maui has not erupted in recent history. Describe whether these new observations support your hypothesis or disprove it.

_____

_____

_____

_____

4 Revising a Hypothesis Share your hypothesis with your classmates. Rewrite your hypothesis so that it includes the changes suggested by your classmates.

_____

_____

_____

Take It Home

While you already know the word *hypothesis*, you might not know the word *hypothetical*. Use the dictionary to look up the meaning of the suffix *-ical*. Combine the meanings of these two word parts, and write an original definition of *hypothetical* in your notebook.

Absolute Dating

ESSENTIAL QUESTION

How is the absolute age of rock measured?

By the end of this lesson, you should be able to summarize how scientists measure the absolute age of rock layers, including by radiometric dating.

A clock is one way of measuring absolute time.

Engage Your Brain

1 Predict Check T or F to show whether you think each statement is true or false.

T	F	
☐	☐	All rocks are made of matter and all matter is made of atoms.
☐	☐	We use calendars to measure the absolute age of people.
☐	☐	Someone tells you that he is older than you are. This tells you his absolute age.
☐	☐	If you cut a clay ball in two and then cut one of the halves in two, you will end up with four pieces of clay.

2 Explain What is the age of this person? How do you know?

_____

_____

_____

_____

Active Reading

3 Synthesize You can often define an unknown word if you know the meaning of its word parts. Use the word parts and sentence below to make an educated guess about the meaning of the phrase *radiometric dating*.

Word part	Meaning
radio-	relating to radiation
-metric	relating to measurement

Example sentence
By using radiometric dating, the scientist found that the rock was 25 million years old.

radiometric dating:

_____

_____

Vocabulary Terms

• absolute dating
• radioactive decay
• half-life
• radiometric dating

4 Apply As you learn the definition of each vocabulary term in this lesson, create your own definition or sketch to help you remember the meaning of the term.

It's About

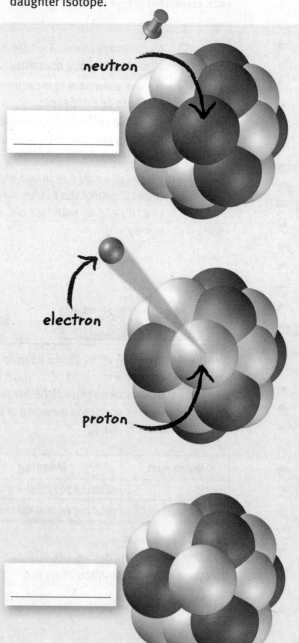

How can the absolute age of rock be determined?

Determining the actual age of an event or object in years is called **absolute dating**. Scientists use many different ways to find the absolute age of rock and other materials. One way is by using radioactive isotopes (ray•dee•oh•AK•tiv EYE•suh•tohpz).

Using Radioactive Isotopes

Atoms of the same element that have a different number of neutrons are called isotopes. Many isotopes are stable, meaning that they stay in their original form. But some isotopes are unstable, and break down to form different isotopes. The unstable isotopes are called *radioactive*. The breakdown of a radioactive isotope into a stable isotope of the same element or of another element is called **radioactive decay**. As shown on the right, radioactive decay for many isotopes happens when a neutron is converted to a proton, with the release of an electron. A radioactive isotope is called a *parent isotope*. The stable isotope formed by its breakdown is called the *daughter isotope*.

Each radioactive isotope decays at a specific, constant rate. **Half-life** is the time needed for half of a sample of a radioactive substance to undergo radioactive decay to form daughter isotopes. Half-life is always given in units of time.

Active Reading **5 Describe** How much of a radioactive parent isotope remains after one half-life has passed? Explain your answer.

_____

_____

_____

Visualize It!

6 Identify Label the parent isotope and the daughter isotope.

neutron

_____

electron

proton

_____

Time!

By Radiometric Dating

Some radioactive isotopes in mineral crystals can act as clocks. These mineral crystals record the ages of the rocks in which the minerals formed. Scientists study the amounts of parent and daughter isotopes to date samples. If you know how fast a radioactive isotope decays, you can figure out the sample's absolute age. Finding the absolute age of a sample by determining the relative percentages of a radioactive parent isotope and a stable daughter isotope is called **radiometric dating** (ray•dee•oh•MET•rik DAYT•ing). The figure on the right shows how the relative percentages of a parent isotope and a daughter isotope change with the passing of each half-life. The following is an example of how radiometric dating can be used:

- You want to determine the age of a sample that contains a radioactive isotope that has a half-life of 10 million years.
- You analyze the sample and find equal amounts of parent and daughter isotopes.
- Because 50%, or ½, of the parent isotope has decayed, you know that 1 half-life has passed.
- So, the sample is 10 million years old.

What is the best rock for radiometric dating?

Igneous rock is often the best type of rock sample to use for radiometric dating. When igneous rock forms, elements are separated into different minerals in the rock. When they form, minerals in igneous rocks often contain only a parent isotope and none of the daughter isotope. This makes the isotope percentages easier to interpret and helps dating to be more accurate.

Visualize It!

7 Calculate Fill in the number of parent isotopes and daughter isotopes in the spaces beside the images below.

0 years
Parent isotope = 16
Daughter isotope = 0
100% of the sample is parent isotope.

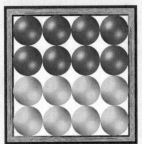

After 1 half-life
Parent isotope = 8
Daughter isotope = 8
50%, or $\frac{1}{2}$, of the sample is parent isotope.

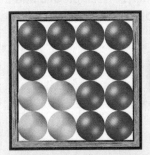

After 2 half-lives
Parent isotope = 4
Daughter isotope = ___
25%, or $\frac{1}{4}$, of the sample is parent isotope.

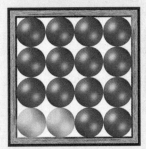

After 3 half-lives
Parent isotope = ___
Daughter isotope = ___
12.5%, or $\frac{1}{8}$, of the sample is parent isotope.

Do the Math Sample Problem

A crystal contains a radioactive isotope that has a half-life of 10,000 years. One-fourth (25%) of the parent isotope remains in a sample. How old is the sample?

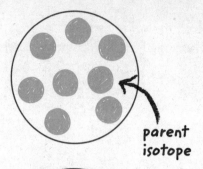

parent isotope

Identify

A. What do you know? Half-life = 10,000 years, parent isotope = 25%

B. What do you want to find out? How old the sample is. So, you need to know how many half-lives have gone by since the crystal formed.

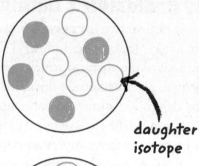

daughter isotope

Plan

C. Draw the parent-to-daughter isotope ratios for each half-life.

Solve

D. The third drawing on the right shows a sample that contains 25% parent isotope. This amount is present after 2 half-lives have passed.

E. Find the age of the sample. Because the half-life of the radioactive isotope is 10,000 years and 2 half-lives have passed, the age of the sample is:

$$2 \times 10,000 \text{ years} = 20,000 \text{ years}$$

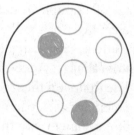

 Do the Math You Try It

8 Calculate A crystal contains a radioactive isotope that has a half-life of 20,000 years. You analyze a sample and find that one-eighth (12.5%) of the parent isotope remains. How old is the sample?

Identify

A. What do you know? _____

B. What do you want to find out? _____

Plan

C. Draw the parent-to-daughter isotope ratios on the right.

Solve

D. Figure out how many half-lives have passed: _____

E. Find the age of the sample:

_____

Answer: _____

Time for a Change

What are some radiometric dating methods?

Scientists use many different isotopes for radiometric dating. The half-life of an isotope is very important in determining the time range that it is useful for dating. If the half-life is too short compared with the age of the sample, there will be too little parent isotope left to measure. If the half-life is too long, there will not be enough daughter isotope to measure. Also, different methods may only be useful for certain types of materials.

Active Reading

9 Identify As you read, underline the time frame for which radiocarbon dating is useful.

Radiocarbon Dating

The ages of wood, bones, shells, and other organic remains can be found by radiocarbon dating. The radioactive isotope carbon-14 combines with oxygen to form radioactive carbon dioxide, CO_2. Most CO_2 in the atmosphere contains nonradioactive carbon-12, but radioactive carbon-14 is also present.

Plants absorb CO_2 from the atmosphere, which they use to build their bodies through photosynthesis. As long as a plant is alive, the plant takes in carbon dioxide with the same carbon-14 to carbon-12 ratio. Similarly, animals convert the carbon from the food they eat into bone and other tissues. So, animals inherit the carbon isotope ratio of their food sources.

Once a plant or animal dies, carbon is no longer taken in. The ratio of carbon-14 to carbon-12 decreases in the dead organism because carbon-14 undergoes radioactive decay to nitrogen-14. The half-life of carbon-14 is only 5,730 years. Also, radiocarbon dating can only be used to date organic matter. So this method is used to date things that lived in the last 45,000 years.

Active Reading **10 Explain** You have found a bone in a layer of rock that you think is about 500,000 years old. Would you use radiocarbon dating to find the age of this bone? Why or why not?

Materials such as these woolly mammoth teeth can be radiocarbon dated.

_____

_____

Radiometric dating has been done on Mammoth Mountain's volcanic rock.

Active Reading **11 Identify** As you read this page, underline the time frame for which each method is most useful.

Potassium-Argon Dating

The element potassium (puh•TAS•ee•uhm) occurs in two stable isotopes, potassium-41 and potassium-39, and one radioactive isotope that occurs naturally, potassium-40. Potassium-40 decays to argon and calcium. It has a half-life of 1.25 billion years. Scientists measure argon as the daughter isotope. Potassium-argon dating is often used to date igneous volcanic rocks. This method is used to date rocks that are between about 100,000 years and a few billion years old.

Scientist and astronaut Harrison Schmitt collected samples of rock on the moon during the *Apollo 17* mission in 1972.

Uranium-Lead Dating

An isotope of uranium (yoo•RAY•nee•uhm), called uranium-238, is a radioactive isotope that decays to lead-206. Uranium-lead dating is based on measuring the amount of the lead-206 daughter isotope in a sample. Uranium-238 has a half-life of 4.5 billion years.

Uranium-lead dating can be used to determine the age of igneous rocks that are between 100 million years and billions of years old. Younger rocks do not have enough daughter isotope to be accurately measured by this method. Uranium-lead dating was used to find the earliest accurate age of Earth.

Time Will Tell

How is radiometric dating used to determine the age of Earth?

Radiometric dating can be used to find the age of Earth, though not by dating Earth rocks. The first rocks that formed on Earth have long ago been eroded or melted, or buried under younger rocks. So, there are no Earth rocks which can be directly studied that are as old as our planet. But other bodies in space do have rock that is as old as our solar system.

Meteorites (MEE•tee•uh•rytz) are small, rocky bodies that have traveled through space and fallen to Earth's surface. Scientists have found meteorites on Earth, such as the one shown below. Rocks from the moon have also been collected. Radiometric dating has been done on these rocks from other parts of our solar system. The absolute ages of these samples show that our solar system, including Earth, is about 4.6 billion years old.

Active Reading

12 Identify As you read, underline the reason why scientists cannot use rocks from Earth to measure the age of Earth.

Think Outside the Book **Inquiry**

13 Model Develop a way to help people understand how large the number 4.6 billion is.

This 4.5 billion-year-old rock is part of a meteorite that landed in Antarctica. It is thought to be from Mars.

Showing Your Age

How can fossils help to determine the age of sedimentary rock?

Sedimentary rock layers and the fossils within these layers cannot be dated directly. But igneous rock layers on either side of a fossil layer can be dated radiometrically. Once the older and younger rock layers are dated, scientists can assign an absolute age range to the sedimentary rock layer that the fossils are found in.

Using Index Fossils

Scientists have found that particular types of fossils appear only in certain layers of rock. By dating igneous rock layers above and below these fossil layers, scientists can determine the time span in which the organisms lived. *Index fossils,* such as the ones shown below, are fossils that are used to estimate the absolute age of the rock layers in which they are found. Once the absolute age of an index fossil is known, it can be used to determine the age of rock layers that contain the same index fossil anywhere on Earth.

To be an index fossil, the organism from which the fossil formed must have lived during a relatively short geologic time span. The fossils of the organism must be relatively common and must be found over a large area. Index fossils must also have features that make them different from other fossils.

Phacops rana fossils are used as index fossils. This trilobite lived between 405 million and 360 million years ago.

How are index fossils used?

Index fossils act as markers for the time that the organisms lived on Earth. Organisms that formed index fossils lived during short periods of geologic time. So, the rock layer that an index fossil is found in can be dated accurately. For example, ammonites were marine mollusks, similar to a modern squid. They lived in coiled shells in ancient seas. The ammonite *Tropites* (troh•PY•teez) lived between 230 million and 208 million years ago. So, whenever scientists find a fossil of *Tropites*, they know that the rock layer the fossil was found in formed between 230 million and 208 million years ago. As shown below, this can also tell scientists something about the ages of surrounding rock layers.

Trilobite (TRY•luh•byt) fossils are another example of a good index fossil. The closest living relatives of trilobites are the horseshoe crab, spiders, and scorpions. *Phacops rana* is a trilobite that lived between 405 million and 360 million years ago. The *Phacops rana* fossil, shown on the previous page, is the state fossil of Pennsylvania.

Index fossils can also be used to date rock layers in separate areas. The appearance of the same index fossil in rock of different areas shows that the rock layers formed at about the same time.

Active Reading

15 Identify As you read, underline examples of organisms whose fossils are index fossils. Include the time frame for which they are used to date rock.

Visualize It!

16 Infer *Tropites* fossils are found in the middle rock layer shown below. Place each of the following ages beside the correct rock layer: 215 million/500 million/100 million.

*Fossils of a genus of ammonites called **Tropites** are good index fossils.*

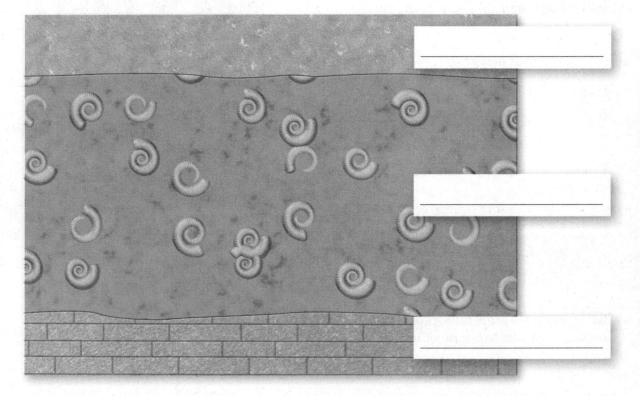

Visual Summary

To complete this summary, fill in the blanks with the correct word or phrase. Then, use the key below to check your answers. You can use this page to review the main concepts of the lesson.

Radiometric dating can be used to find the absolute ages of materials such as igneous rocks. This method uses the radioactive decay of an isotope.

17 During radioactive decay, the amount of _____ isotope decreases by one-half after every _____

Absolute Dating

Index fossils can be used to estimate the absolute ages of some sedimentary rocks.

18 Four things that index fossils should be:

A _____

B _____

C _____

D _____

19 Relate How is the use of radioactive decay in absolute dating similar to how you use a clock?

Lesson Review

Vocabulary

Fill in each blank with the term that best completes the following sentences.

1 The breakdown of a radioactive isotope into a stable isotope is called _____

_____

2 The _____ is the time needed for half of a sample of a radioactive isotope to break down to form daughter isotopes.

3 _____ is a method used to determine the absolute age of a sample by measuring the relative amounts of parent isotope and daughter isotope.

Key Concepts

4 Summarize How are radioactive isotopes used to determine the absolute age of igneous rock? Name two radiometric methods that are used.

_____

_____

_____

_____

5 Describe What happens to an isotope during radioactive decay?

_____

_____

6 Explain Why are igneous rocks the best type of rock sample for radiometric dating?

_____

_____

7 Describe How old is Earth and how did scientists find this out?

_____

_____

8 Explain What are index fossils and how are they used to determine the absolute age of sedimentary rock?

_____

_____

_____

_____

Critical Thinking

9 Justify An igneous rock sample is about 250,000 years old. Would you use uranium-lead radiometric dating to find its age? Explain.

_____

_____

_____

10 Calculate A sample of wood contains 12.5% of its original carbon-14. What is the estimated age of this sample? Show your work.

_____

_____

_____

Use this graph to answer the following questions.

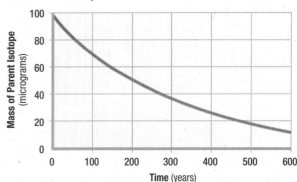

Radioactive Decay

11 Analyze What is the half-life of the radioactive isotope?

12 Analyze What mass of radioactive isotope will be left after three half-lives?

My Notes

The Geologic Time Scale

ESSENTIAL QUESTION

What is the geologic time scale?

By the end of this lesson, you should understand how geologists use the geologic time scale to divide Earth's history.

In Earth's ancient past, molten material cooled and hardened to form new land. This process continues today when lava cools and hardens on Earth's surface. It is just one of many geologic processes that have shaped Earth for billions of years.

Lesson Labs

Quick Labs
• Investigating Events in Earth's History
• Timeline of Earth's History

Engage Your Brain

1 Predict Check T or F to show whether you think each statement is true or false.

T	F	
☐	☐	In Earth's past, mass extinctions wiped out nearly all life in the oceans.
☐	☐	Most changes to Earth's surface happen suddenly.
☐	☐	Early humans and dinosaurs lived side by side during Earth's distant past.
☐	☐	We live in the Cenozoic Era.

2 Compare Describe the mountains that you see in the photo. What do you think they looked like when they were much younger, more than 400 million years ago?

_____

_____

_____

Active Reading

3 Synthesize You can often define an unknown word if you know the meaning of its word parts. Use the word parts and sentence below to make an educated guess about the meaning of the word *geology*.

Word part	Meaning
geo-	Earth
-logy	study of

Example sentence:
Joseph was interested in rocks and minerals, so he decided to study geology.

geology:

_____

_____

Vocabulary Terms
• geology
• geologic time scale

4 Identify As you read, place a question mark next to any words that you don't understand. When you finish reading the lesson, go back and review the text that you marked. If the information is still confusing, consult a classmate or a teacher.

Once Upon a Time

Volcanic eruptions can cause sudden, drastic changes to Earth's surface.

How have geologists described the rate of geologic change?

How old is Earth? How does new rock form? How do mountains form? These are the types of questions asked by scientists who study geology. **Geology** is the scientific study of the origin, history, and structure of Earth and the processes that shape it. Early geologists proposed different ideas to explain how Earth changes over time.

Changes Occur Suddenly: Catastrophism

Some early scientists used catastrophism to explain geologic changes on Earth. *Catastrophism* (kuh•TAS•truh•fiz•uhm) is the principle that states that all geologic change occurs suddenly. Supporters of catastrophism thought that Earth's features, such as mountains and seas, formed during sudden events called *catastrophes* (kuh•TAS•truh•feez). These unpredictable events caused rapid change over large areas, sometimes even globally.

A volcanic eruption is just one example of a catastrophic event. In November 2010, the Merapi volcano in Indonesia erupted with violent explosions that could be heard 20 km away. Millions of cubic meters of ash, dust, and gases were released. Material reportedly fell in areas hundreds of kilometers from the volcano.

Active Reading **5 Identify** What is one example of a geologic catastrophe?

_____

_____

_____

1.75 million years ago

250 million years ago

515 million years ago

Gradual and sudden changes have shaped the Grand Canyon.

Visualize It!

6 Identify How much geologic time is represented by these rock layers in the Grand Canyon?

_____

Changes Occur Gradually: Uniformitarianism

About 250 years ago, a Scottish farmer and scientist named James Hutton studied rock formations in Scotland. His years of observations challenged the principle of catastrophism and led to the foundation of modern geology.

Hutton believed that the key to understanding Earth's history is all around us. The processes that we observe today, such as erosion and deposition, do not change over time. They remain constant, or uniform. This principle is now called uniformitarianism (*yoo•nuh•fohr •mih•TAIR•ee•uh•niz•uhm*). *Uniformitarianism* is the idea that the same geologic processes that shape Earth today have been at work throughout Earth's history. The principle also states that the average rate of geologic change is slow and has remained relatively constant over time.

Changes Occur Both Catastrophically and Gradually

Today, geologists realize that neither uniformitarianism nor catastrophism accounts for all geologic change. While most geologic change is gradual and uniform, modern geologists recognize that catastrophes do cause some geologic change. For example, earthquakes, floods, volcanic eruptions, and asteroid impacts can cause sudden changes to Earth's surface.

Scientists have found huge craters caused by ancient asteroid impacts. About 65 million years ago, an asteroid hit Earth. Scientists think this led to the extinction of the dinosaurs. The impact would have thrown large amounts of debris into the atmosphere, which would have blocked the sun's rays. This likely limited photosynthesis, killing plants and causing the dinosaur food chain to collapse.

7 Contrast Compare catastrophism and uniformitarianism.

Catastrophism	Uniformitarianism

It's About Time

How do geologists use the geologic time scale?

By using radiometric dating techniques on meteorites and moon rocks, geologists estimate that the solar system, and therefore Earth, is about 4.6 billion years old. To help make sense of this vast amount of time, geologists use the geologic time scale to organize Earth's history. The **geologic time scale** divides Earth's history into intervals of time defined by major events or changes on Earth.

To Divide Earth's Long Geologic History

The geologic time scale divides Earth's geologic history into eons, eras, periods, and epochs. The largest unit of geologic time is an *eon*. Earth's 4.6-billion-year history is divided into four eons: the Hadean, Archean, Proterozoic, and Phanerozoic. The Hadean, Archean, and Proterozoic eons together are called *Precambrian time*. Precambrian time makes up almost 90 percent of Earth's history. Eons may be divided into smaller units of time called *eras*. The Phanerozoic Eon is the present eon. This eon is divided into three eras: the Paleozoic, Mesozoic, and Cenozoic. Each era is subdivided into a number of *periods*. The periods of the Cenozoic, the present era, are further divided into *epochs*.

 **Visualize It!**

8 List Use the diagram of the geologic time scale to list the different divisions of time, beginning with the largest division, the eon.

Precambrian time (4600 Ma to 542 Ma)		
EONS Hadean Eon	Archean Eon	

4600 Ma 3850 Ma 2500 Ma

Ma = million years

ERAS Paleozoic Era

PERIODS | Cambrian | Ordovician | Silurian | Devonian | Carboniferous | Permian
542 Ma | 488 Ma | 444 Ma | 416 Ma | 359 Ma | 299 Ma | 251 Ma

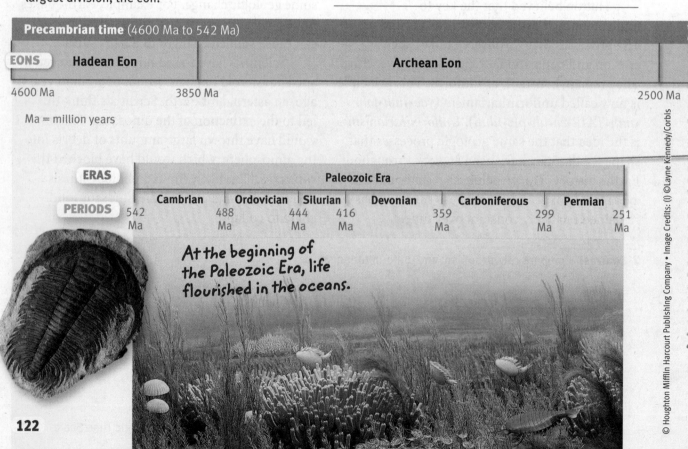

At the beginning of the Paleozoic Era, life flourished in the oceans.

122

To Mark Major Changes in the Fossil Record

Active Reading **9 Identify** As you read, underline the factors used to determine the divisions of geologic time.

Unlike divisions of time such as days or minutes, the divisions of the geologic time scale have no fixed lengths. Many divisions are based on events in Earth's geologic history. Some divisions are based entirely on the fossil record.

At least five divisions of geologic time have ended in large mass extinction events. In mass extinction events, a larger than expected number of organisms "disappear" from the fossil record in rock layers worldwide. For example, the Paleozoic Era ended about 250 million years ago with the largest extinction event known. More than 90% of marine species and 70% of land species are thought to have become extinct. The Mesozoic Era ended with the extinction of dinosaurs and many other organisms about 65 million years ago. Causes of mass extinctions are varied. Movement of the continents, lowering of global sea level, rapid climate change, and asteroid impacts are all thought to be causes.

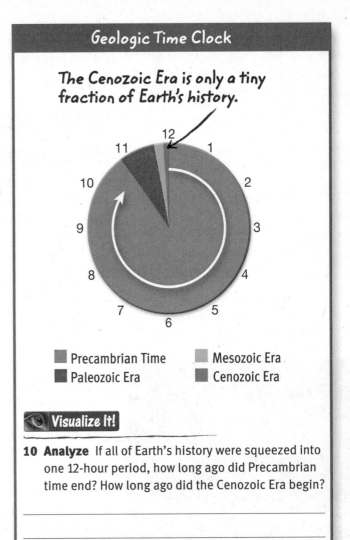

Geologic Time Clock

The Cenozoic Era is only a tiny fraction of Earth's history.

- Precambrian Time
- Paleozoic Era
- Mesozoic Era
- Cenozoic Era

Visualize It!

10 Analyze If all of Earth's history were squeezed into one 12-hour period, how long ago did Precambrian time end? How long ago did the Cenozoic Era begin?

_____

_____

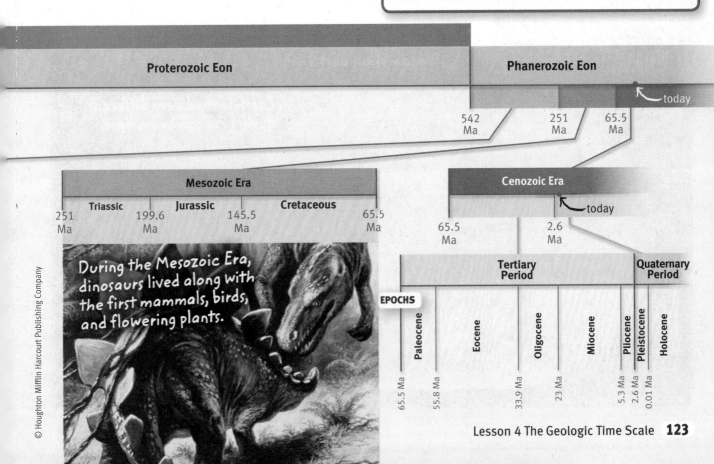

Proterozoic Eon

Phanerozoic Eon

today

542 Ma

251 Ma

65.5 Ma

Mesozoic Era

| Triassic | Jurassic | Cretaceous |

251 Ma

199.6 Ma

145.5 Ma

65.5 Ma

Cenozoic Era

today

65.5 Ma

2.6 Ma

Tertiary Period

Quaternary Period

EPOCHS

Paleocene · Eocene · Oligocene · Miocene · Pliocene · Pleistocene · Holocene

65.5 Ma · 55.8 Ma · 33.9 Ma · 23 Ma · 5.3 Ma · 2.6 Ma · 0.01 Ma

During the Mesozoic Era, dinosaurs lived along with the first mammals, birds, and flowering plants.

Time After Time...

What were some defining events of Precambrian time?

Precambrian time began with the formation of Earth about 4.6 billion years ago. Many changes occurred during this time. From about 4.5 to 3.8 billion years ago, early Earth formed into a spherical planet, and its molten rocks cooled. Continents began to form, and tectonic activity occurred along continental margins. The oldest fossils, life forms in the oceans, date from this time.

Massive supercontinents formed and broke up at least twice during Precambrian time. Earth's early atmosphere was made mainly of gases released by volcanic eruptions. During the Archean Eon, water vapor was added to the atmosphere by almost constant volcanic activity. This water fell as rain and collected in basins to form the first oceans. The atmosphere had no free oxygen until the Proterozoic Eon, when cyanobacteria released oxygen into the air during the process of photosynthesis.

Toward the end of Precambrian time, much of Earth's land surfaces were located near the poles and covered in ice. Land on Earth was largely frozen and lifeless.

Active Reading **11 Identify** What was the first source of oxygen for Earth's atmosphere?

The first continents, oceans, and atmosphere formed during Precambrian time.

Precambrian Earth

Earth looked very different during Precambrian time.

Engage Your Brain

1 Describe Fill in the blank with the word or phrase that you think correctly completes the following sentences.

Most of Earth is made of _____

Rock is _____ changing.

The three main classes of rock are igneous, metamorphic, and _____

2 Describe Write your own caption for this photo.

_____

_____

_____

Active Reading

3 Synthesize Many English words have their roots in other languages. Use the Latin words below to make an educated guess about the meaning of the words *erosion* and *deposition*.

Latin Word	Meaning
erosus	eaten away
depositus	laid down

Vocabulary Terms

- weathering
- erosion
- deposition
- igneous rock
- sedimentary rock
- metamorphic rock
- rock cycle
- uplift
- subsidence
- rift zone

4 Apply As you learn the definition of each vocabulary term in this lesson, create your own definition or sketch to help you remember the meaning of the term.

Erosion:

_____

_____

Deposition:

_____

_____

Let's Rock!

What is rock?

The solid parts of Earth are made almost entirely of rock. Scientists define rock as a naturally occurring solid mixture of one or more minerals that may also include organic matter. Most rock is made of minerals, but some rock is made of nonmineral material that is not organic, such as glass. Rock has been an important natural resource as long as humans have existed. Early humans used rocks as hammers to make other tools. For centuries, people have used different types of rock, including granite, marble, sandstone, and slate, to make buildings, such as the pyramids shown below.

It may be hard to believe, but rocks are always changing. People study rocks to learn how areas have changed through time.

5 List How is rock used today?

_____

_____

_____

The ancient Egyptians used a rock called limestone to construct the Great Sphinx and the pyramids at Giza.

These rock formations in Goreme, Turkey, are known as fairy chimneys. They were shaped by erosion.

Think Outside the Book

6 Design Create a travel brochure for Goreme, Turkey.

What processes change rock?

Natural processes make and destroy rock. They change each type of rock into other types of rock and shape the features of our planet. These processes also influence the type of rock that is found in each area of Earth's surface.

Active Reading **7 Identify** As you read, underline the processes and factors that can change rock.

Weathering, Erosion, and Deposition

The process by which water, wind, ice, and changes in temperature break down rock is called **weathering**. Weathering breaks down rock into fragments called *sediment*. The process by which sediment is moved from one place to another is called **erosion.** Water, wind, ice, and gravity can erode sediments. These sediments are eventually deposited, or laid down, in bodies of water and other low-lying areas. The process by which sediment comes to rest is called **deposition.**

Temperature and Pressure

Rock that is buried can be squeezed by the weight of the rock or the layers of sediment on top of it. As pressure increases with depth beneath Earth's surface, so does temperature. If the temperature and pressure are high enough, the buried rock can change into metamorphic rock. In some cases, the rock gets hot enough to melt and forms *magma*, or molten rock. If magma reaches Earth's surface, it is called *lava*. The magma or lava eventually cool and solidify to form new rock.

Classified Information!

What are the classes of rocks?

Rocks fall into three major classes based on how they form. **Igneous rock** forms when magma or lava cools and hardens to become solid. It forms beneath or on Earth's surface. **Sedimentary rock** forms when minerals that form from solutions or sediment from older rocks get pressed and cemented together. **Metamorphic rock** forms when pressure, temperature, or chemical processes change existing rock. Each class can be divided further, based on differences in the way rocks form. For example, some igneous rocks form when lava cools on Earth's surface, and others form when magma cools deep beneath the surface. Therefore, igneous rock can be classified based on how and where it forms.

Active Reading

8 Identify As you read the paragraph, underline the three main classes of rocks.

Think Outside the Book Inquiry

9 Apply With a classmate, discuss the processes that might have shaped the rock formations in the Valley of Fire State Park.

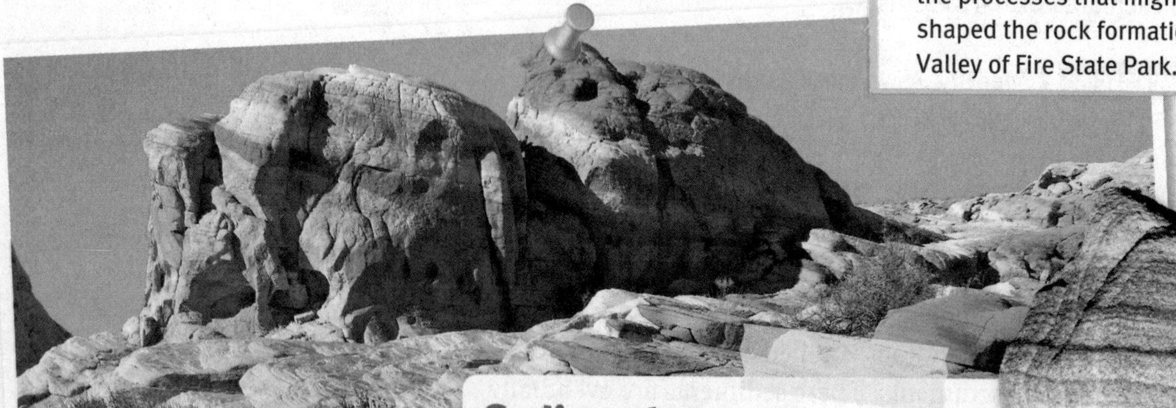

These formations in Valley of Fire State Park in Nevada are made of sandstone, a sedimentary rock.

Sedimentary

Sedimentary rock is composed of minerals formed from solutions or sediments from older rock. Sedimentary rock forms when the weight from above presses down on the layers of minerals or sediment, or when minerals dissolved in water solidify between sediment pieces and cement them together.

Sedimentary rocks are named according to the size and type of the fragments they contain. For example, the rock shown here is made of sand and is called sandstone. Rock made primarily of the mineral calcite (calcium carbonate) is called limestone.

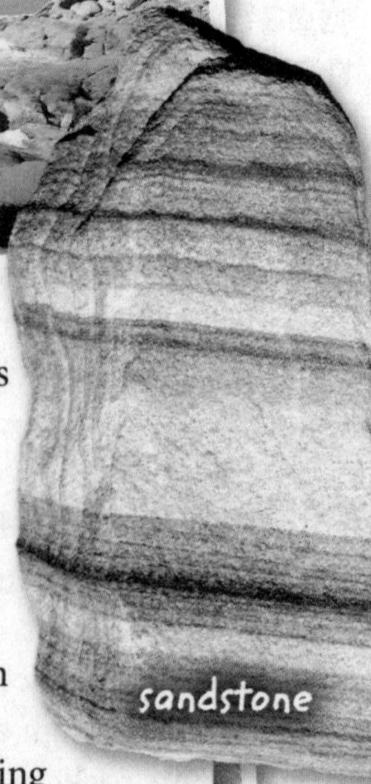

sandstone

Enchanted Rock in Texas is a large dome made of granite, an intrusive igneous rock.

Igneous Rock

Igneous rock forms from cooling lava and magma. As molten rock cools and becomes solid, the minerals crystallize and grow. The longer the cooling takes, the more time the crystals have to grow. The granite shown here cooled slowly and is made of large crystals. Rock that forms when magna cools beneath Earth's surface is called intrusive igneous rock. Rock that forms when lava cools on Earth's surface is called extrusive igneous rock.

granite

Metamorphic Rock

Metamorphic rock forms when high temperature and pressure change the texture and mineral content of rock. For example, a rock can be buried in Earth's crust, where the temperature and pressure are high. Over millions of years, the solid rock changes, and new crystals are formed. Metamorphic rocks may be changed in four ways: by temperature, by pressure, by temperature and pressure combined, or by fluids or other chemicals. Gneiss, shown here, is a metamorphic rock. It forms at high temperatures deep within Earth's crust.

gneiss

Gneiss is a metamorphic rock that is made up of bands of light and dark minerals.

10 Compare Fill in the chart to compare and contrast sedimentary, igneous, and metamorphic rock.

Classes of Rocks

Sedimentary rock	Igneous rock	Metamorphic rock

What is the rock cycle?

Active Reading 11 **Apply** As you read, underline the rock types that metamorphic rock can change into.

Rocks may seem very permanent, solid, and unchanging. But over millions of years, any of the three rock types can be changed into another of the three types. For example, igneous rock can change into sedimentary or metamorphic rock, or back into another kind of igneous rock. This series of processes in which rock changes from one type to another is called the **rock cycle**. Rocks may follow different pathways in the cycle. Examples of these pathways are shown here. Factors, including temperature, pressure, weathering, and erosion, may change a rock's identity. Where rock is located on a tectonic plate and whether the rock is at Earth's surface also influence how it forms and changes.

When igneous rock is exposed at Earth's surface, it may break down into sediment. Igneous rock may also change directly into metamorphic rock while still beneath Earth's surface. It may also melt to form magma that becomes another type of igneous rock.

When sediment is pressed together and cemented, the sediment becomes sedimentary rock. With temperature and pressure changes, sedimentary rocks may become metamorphic rocks, or they may melt and become igneous rock. Sedimentary rock may also be broken down at Earth's surface and become sediment that forms another sedimentary rock.

Under certain temperature and pressure conditions, metamorphic rock will melt and form magma. Metamorphic rock can also be altered by heat and pressure to form a different type of metamorphic rock. Metamorphic rock can also be broken down by weathering and erosion to form sediment that forms sedimentary rock.

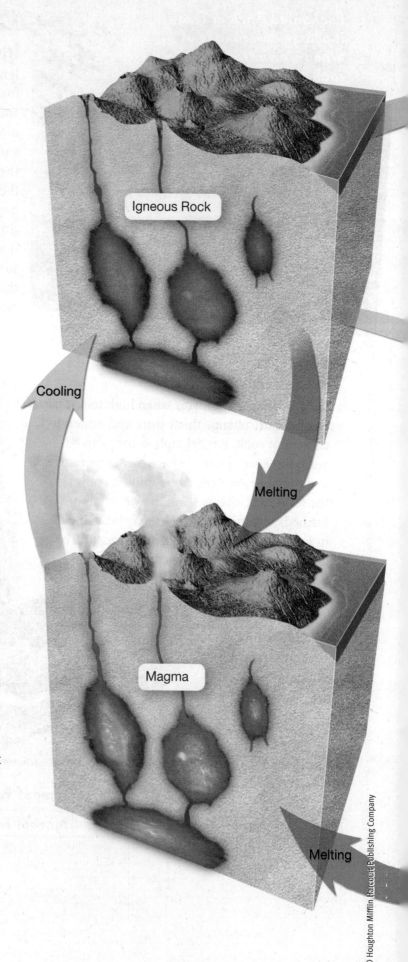

Igneous Rock

Cooling

Melting

Magma

Melting

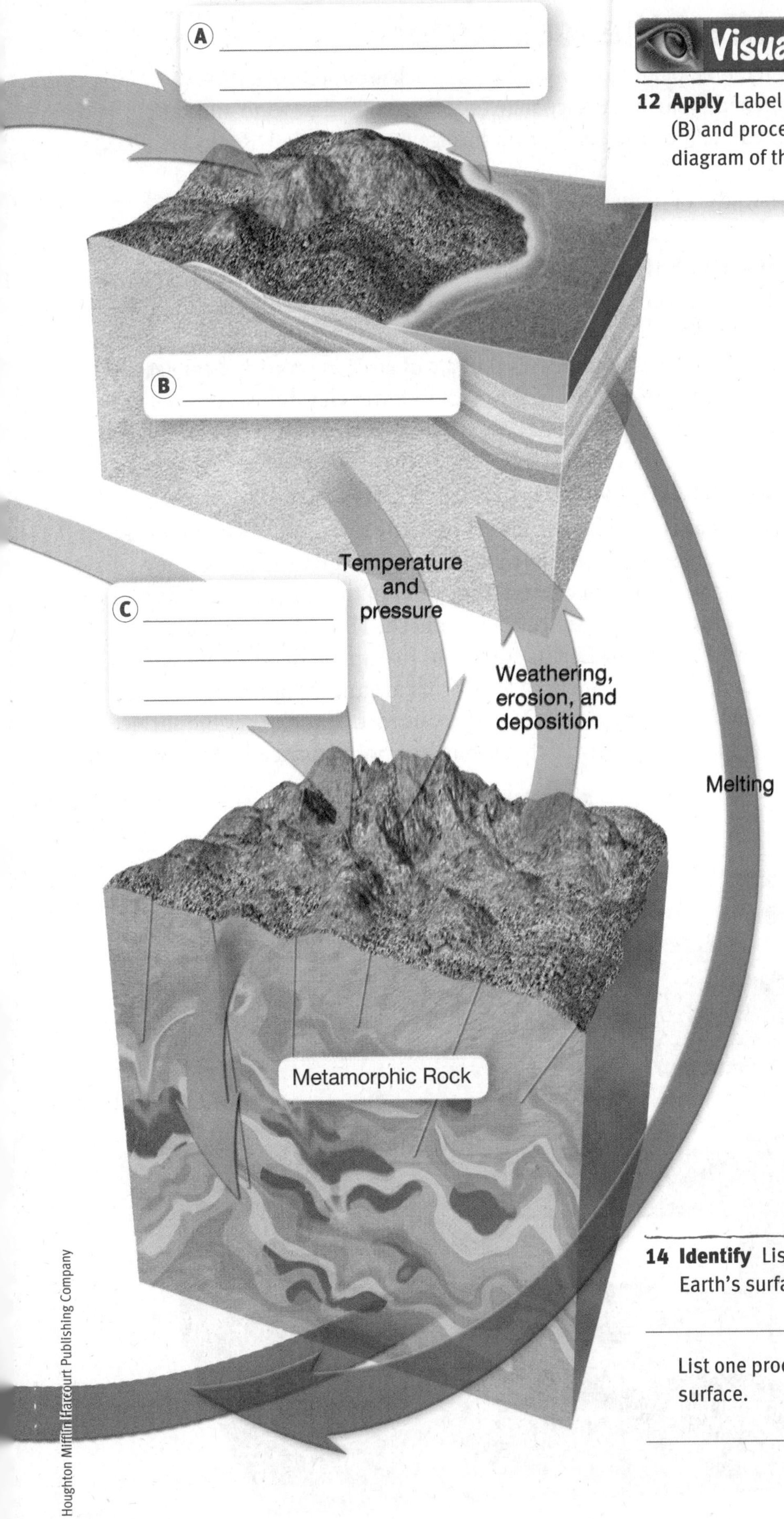

(A) _____
_____

Visualize It!

12 Apply Label the missing rock type (B) and processes (A and C) on the diagram of the rock cycle.

(B) _____

Temperature and pressure

(C) _____
_____
_____

Weathering, erosion, and deposition

Melting

Metamorphic Rock

Think Outside the Book

13 Apply Write a series of blog entries from the viewpoint of igneous rock that is changing into sedimentary rock.

14 Identify List one process that happens above Earth's surface.

_____

List one process that happens below Earth's surface.

_____

How do tectonic plate motions affect the rock cycle?

Tectonic plate motions can move rock around. Rock that was beneath Earth's surface may become exposed to wind and rain. Sediment or rock on Earth's surface may be buried. Rock can also be changed into metamorphic rock by tectonic plate collisions because of increased temperature and pressure.

By Moving Rock Up or Down

15 Compare How does uplift differ from subsidence?

_____

_____

_____

There are two types of vertical movements in Earth's crust: uplift and subsidence. **Uplift** is the rising of regions of the crust to higher elevations. Uplift increases the rate of erosion on rock. **Subsidence** is the sinking of regions of the crust to lower elevations. Subsidence leads to the formation of basins where sediment can be deposited.

By Pulling Apart Earth's Surface

A **rift zone** is an area where a set of deep cracks form. Rift zones are common between tectonic plates that are pulling apart. As they pull apart, blocks of crust in the center of the rift zone subside and the pressure on buried rocks is reduced. The reduction in pressure allows rock below Earth's surface to rise up. As the rock rises, it undergoes partial melting and forms magma. Magma can cool below Earth's surface to form igneous rock. If it reaches the surface, magma becomes lava, which can also cool to form igneous rock.

Visualize It! Inquiry

16 Predict Label uplift and subsidence on this diagram. What pathway in the rock cycle might rock take next if it is subjected to uplift? Explain.

_____

_____

_____

Before

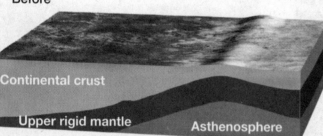

Continental crust

Upper rigid mantle   Asthenosphere

After   Rift Zone

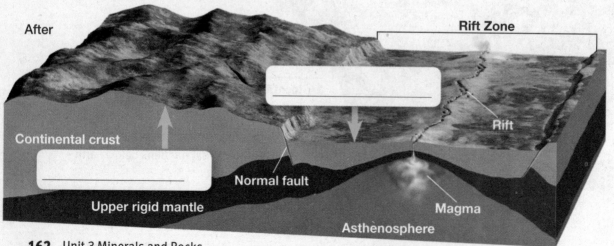

Continental crust

Normal fault   Rift

Upper rigid mantle   Magma

Asthenosphere

Cliff Dwellings

Can you imagine living on the side of a cliff? Some ancient peoples could! They created dwellings from cliff rock. They also decorated rock with art, as you can see in the pictographs shown below.

Cliff Palace
This dwelling in Colorado is called the Cliff Palace. It was home to the Ancient Puebloans from about 550 to 1300 CE.

Cliff Art
These pictographs are located at the Gila Cliff Dwellings in New Mexico.

A Palace in Rock
Ancient cliff dwellings are also found outside the United States. These dwellings from about 70 CE are located in Petra, Jordan.

© Houghton Mifflin Harcourt Publishing Company • Image Credits: (bkgd) ©George H.H. Huey/Corbis; (l) ©Greg Probst/Corbis; (r) ©Anders Blomqvist/Lonely Planet Images/Getty Images

Extend

Inquiry

17 Identify Describe how ancient people used rock to create shelter.

18 Research Find out how people lived in one of the cliff dwelling locations. How did living in a rock environment affect their daily lives?

19 Produce Illustrate how the people lived by doing one of the following: write a play, write a song, or create a graphic novel.

Visual Summary

To complete this summary, use what you know about the rock cycle to fill in the blanks below. Then use the key below to check your answers. You can use this page to review the main concepts of the lesson.

Each rock type can change into another of the three types.

20 When sediment is pressed together and cemented, the sediment becomes

_____

21 When lava cools and solidifies,

_____ forms.

22 Metamorphic rock can be altered by temperature and pressure to form a different type of

_____

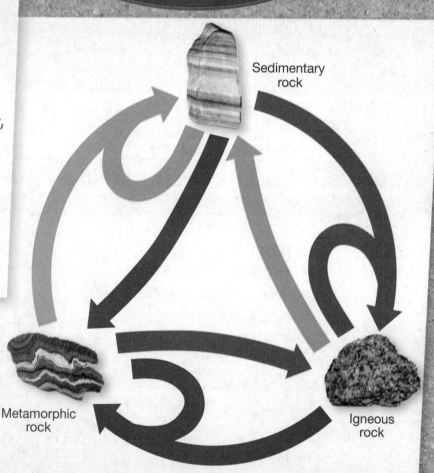

Rock Cycle

Sedimentary rock

Metamorphic rock

Igneous rock

23 Explain What factors and processes can affect the pathway that igneous rock takes in the rock cycle?

Lesson Review

Vocabulary

In your own words, define the following terms.

1 Rock cycle

_____

_____

2 Weathering

_____

3 Rift zone

_____

_____

Key Concepts

Use these photos to classify the rock as sedimentary, igneous, or metamorphic.

Example	Type of rock
4 Classify This rock is made up of the mineral calcite, and it formed from the remains of organisms that lived in water.	
5 Classify Through high temperature and pressure, this rock formed from a sedimentary rock.	
6 Classify This rock is made of tiny crystals that formed quickly when molten rock cooled at Earth's surface.	

7 Describe How can sedimentary rock become metamorphic rock?

_____

_____

_____

8 Explain How can subsidence lead to the formation of sedimentary rock?

_____

_____

9 Explain Why are rift zones common places for igneous rock to form?

_____

_____

_____

Critical Thinking

10 Hypothesize What would happen to the rock cycle if erosion did not occur?

_____

_____

11 Criticize A classmate states that igneous rock must always become sedimentary rock next, according to the rock cycle. Explain why this statement is not correct.

_____

_____

12 Predict Granite is an igneous rock that forms from magma cooled below Earth's surface. Why would granite have larger crystals than igneous rocks formed from lava cooled above Earth's surface?

_____

_____

My Notes

Analyzing Technology

Skills
Identify risks
Identify benefits
✔ Evaluate cost of technology
✔ Evaluate environmental impact
✔ Propose improvements
Propose risk reduction
✔ Compare technology
✔ Communicate results

Objectives
• Analyze the life cycle of an aluminum can.
• Analyze the life cycle of a glass bottle.
• Evaluate the cost of recycling versus disposal of technology.
• Analyze the environmental impact of technology.

Analyzing the Life Cycles of Aluminum and Glass

A life cycle analysis is a way to evaluate the real cost of a product. The analysis considers how much money an item costs to make. It also examines how making the product affects the economy and the environment through the life of the product. Engineers, scientists, and technologists use this information to improve processes and to compare products.

Costs of Production

Have you ever wondered where an aluminum soda can comes from? Have you wondered where the can goes when you are done with it? If so, you have started a life cycle analysis by asking the right questions. Aluminum is a metal found in a type of rock called *bauxite*. To get aluminum, first bauxite must be mined. The mined ore is then shipped to a processing plant. There, the bauxite is melted to get aluminum in a process called *smelting*. After smelting, the aluminum is processed. It may be shaped into bicycle parts or rolled into sheets to make cans. Every step in the production involves both financial costs and environmental costs that must be considered in a life cycle analysis.

Many bicycles are made of aluminum because it is lightweight and strong.

Costs of Disposal

After an aluminum can is used it can travel either to a landfill or to a recycling plant. The process of recycling an aluminum can does require the use of some energy. However, the financial and environmental costs of disposing of a can and mining ore are much greater than the cost of recycling a can. Additionally, smelting bauxite produces harmful wastes. A life cycle analysis of an aluminum can must include the cost and environmental effects of mining, smelting, and disposing of the aluminum can.

1 Analyze After a can is recycled, which steps are no longer part of the life cycle?

_____

_____

_____

_____

_____

Bauxite mining

Most bauxite mining occurs far away from where aluminum is used. Large ships or trains transport the ore before it is made into aluminum products.

Aluminum is one of the easiest materials to recycle. Producing a ton of aluminum by shredding and remelting uses about 5% of the energy needed to process enough bauxite to make a ton of aluminum.

Remelting

Shredding

Smelting

Fabrication

Recycling

Life Cycle of an Aluminum Can

Manufacturing

Consumer use

2 Evaluate In the life cycle shown here, which two steps could include an arrow to indicate disposal?

_____

_____

 You Try It!

Now it's your turn to analyze the life cycle of a product.

✋ You Try It!

Now, apply what you have learned about the life cycle of aluminum to analyze the life cycle of a glass bottle. Glass is made by melting silica from sand or from mineral deposits mined from the Earth. A kiln heats the silica until it melts to form a red-hot glob. Then, the glass is shaped and cooled to form useful items.

1 Evaluate Cost of Technology

As a group, discuss the steps that would be involved in making a glass bottle. List the steps in the space below. Start with mining and end at a landfill. Include as many steps in the process as you can think of. Beside each step, tell whether there would be financial costs, environmental costs, or both.

Life Cycle of a Glass Bottle

2 Evaluate Environmental Impact

Use the table below to indicate which of the steps listed above would have environmental costs, and what type of cost would be involved. A step can appear in more than one column.

Cause pollution	Consume energy	Damage habitat

③ Propose Improvements

In your group, discuss how you might improve the life cycle of a glass bottle and reduce the impact on the environment. Draw a life cycle that includes your suggestions for improvement.

④ Compare Technology

How does your improved process decrease the environmental effects of making and using glass bottles?

_____

_____

_____

_____

⑤ Communicate Results

Imagine that you are an accountant for a company that produces glass bottles. In the space below, write an argument for using recycled glass that is based on financial savings for your company.

_____

_____

_____

_____

Three Classes of Rock

ESSENTIAL QUESTION

How do rocks form?

By the end of this lesson, you should be able to describe the formation and classification of sedimentary, igneous, and metamorphic rocks.

Wind and water have eroded the softer rock surrounding Ship Rock, an igneous landform in New Mexico.

Lesson Labs

Quick Labs
• Stretching Out
• Observing Rocks

S.T.E.M. Lab
• Modeling Rock Formation

Engage Your Brain

1 Predict Check T or F to show whether you think each statement is true or false.

T   F

☐   ☐   All rocks form deep beneath Earth's surface.

☐   ☐   Some rocks are made up of materials from living things.

☐   ☐   Some rocks take millions of years to form.

☐   ☐   All rocks are made up of the same kinds of minerals.

☐   ☐   Some rocks form from particles of other rocks.

2 Identify How do you think rocks might form as a result of the volcanic activity shown here?

_____

_____

_____

_____

Active Reading

3 Apply Use context clues to write your own definition for the words *composition* and *texture*.

Example sentence:
The <u>composition</u> of the trail mix was 50% nuts, 30% dried fruit, and 20% granola.

composition:

_____

_____

Example sentence:
Because glass is smooth, flat, and shiny, it has a much different <u>texture</u> than wood does.

texture:

_____

_____

Vocabulary Terms

• rock   • texture
• composition

4 Apply As you learn the definition of each vocabulary term in this lesson, create your own definition or sketch to help you remember the meaning of the term.

A Rocky World

How are rocks classified?

Active Reading

5 Identify As you read, underline two properties that are used to classify rock.

A combination of one or more minerals or organic matter is called **rock**. Scientists divide rock into three classes based on how each class of rock forms. The three classes of rock are igneous, sedimentary, and metamorphic. Each class of rock can be further divided into more specific types of rock. For example, igneous rocks can be divided based on where they form. All igneous rock forms when molten rock cools and solidifies. However, some igneous rocks form on Earth's surface and others form within Earth's crust. Sedimentary and metamorphic rocks are also divided into more specific types of rock. How do scientists understand how to classify rocks? They observe their composition and texture.

By Mineral Composition

The minerals and organic matter a rock contains determine the **composition**, or makeup, of that rock, as shown below. Many rocks are made up mostly of the minerals quartz and feldspar, which contain a large amount of the compound silica. Other rocks have different compositions. The limestone rock shown below is made up mostly of the mineral calcite.

Do the Math

6 Graph Fill in the percentage grid on the right to show the amounts of calcite and aragonite in limestone.

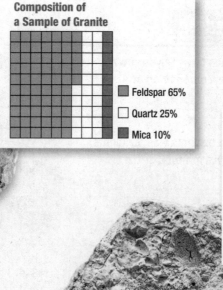

Composition of a Sample of Granite

- ▨ Feldspar 65%
- ☐ Quartz 25%
- ▪ Mica 10%

Composition of a Sample of Limestone

- ☐ Calcite 95%
- ▪ Aragonite 5%

Granite is made of silica minerals.

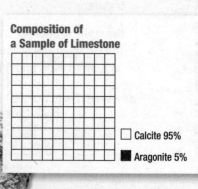

Limestone is made of carbonate minerals.

By Texture

The size, shape, and positions of the grains that make up a rock determine a rock's **texture**. Coarse-grained rock has large grains that are easy to see with your eyes. Fine-grained rock has small grains that can only be seen by using a hand lens or microscope. The texture of a rock may give clues as to how and where it formed. Igneous rock can be fine-grained or coarse-grained depending on the time magma takes to cool. The texture of metamorphic rock depends on the rock's original composition and the temperature and pressure at which the rock formed. The rocks shown below look different because they formed in different ways.

Visualize It!

7 Describe Observe the sedimentary rocks on this page and describe their texture as coarse-grained, medium-grained, or fine-grained.

This mudstone is made up of microscopic particles of clay.

B _____

_____

This sandstone formed from sand grains that once made up a sand dune.

A _____

_____

This breccia is composed of broken fragments of rock cemented together.

C _____

_____

The Furnace Below

What are two kinds of igneous rock?

Igneous rock forms when hot, liquid magma cools into solid rock. Magma forms when solid rock melts below Earth's surface. Magma flows through passageways up toward Earth's surface. Magma can cool and harden below Earth's surface, or it can make its way above Earth's surface and become lava.

Intrusive Igneous Rock

When magma does not reach Earth's surface, it cools in large chambers, in cracks, or between layers in the surrounding rock. When magma pushes into, or intrudes, surrounding rock below Earth's surface and cools, the rock that forms is called *intrusive igneous rock*. Magma that is well insulated by surrounding rock cools very slowly. The minerals form large, visible crystals. Therefore, intrusive igneous rock generally has a coarse-grained texture. Examples of intrusive igneous rock are granite and diorite. A sample of diorite is shown at the left.

8 Infer How can you tell that diorite is an intrusive igneous rock?

Diorite is an example of intrusive igneous rock.

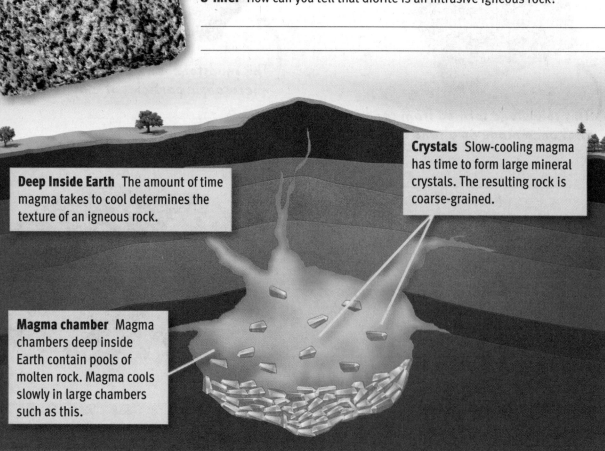

Deep Inside Earth The amount of time magma takes to cool determines the texture of an igneous rock.

Crystals Slow-cooling magma has time to form large mineral crystals. The resulting rock is coarse-grained.

Magma chamber Magma chambers deep inside Earth contain pools of molten rock. Magma cools slowly in large chambers such as this.

Extrusive Igneous Rock

Igneous rock that forms when lava erupts, or extrudes, onto Earth's surface is called *extrusive igneous rock*. Extrusive igneous rock is common around the sides and bases of volcanoes. Lava cools very quickly at Earth's surface. So, there is very little time for crystal formation. Because there is little time for crystals to form, extrusive rocks are made up of very small crystals and have a fine-grained texture. Obsidian (ahb•SID•ee•uhn) is an extrusive rock that cools so rapidly that no crystals form. Obsidian looks glassy, so it is often called *volcanic glass*. Other common extrusive igneous rocks are basalt and andesite.

Lava flows form when lava erupts from a volcano. The photo above shows an active lava flow. Sometimes lava erupts and flows from long cracks in Earth's crust called *fissures*. It also flows on the ocean floor at places where tension is causing Earth's crust to pull apart.

Active Reading **9 Explain** How does the rate at which magma cools affect the texture of igneous rock?

_____

_____

Basalt is an example of extrusive igneous rock.

10 Compare Use the Venn diagram to compare and contrast intrusive igneous rock and extrusive igneous rock.

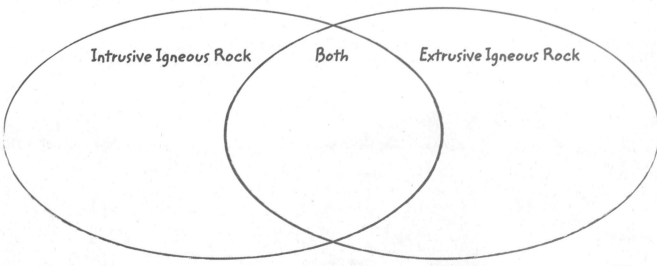

Intrusive Igneous Rock   Both   Extrusive Igneous Rock

Lay It On!

What are three types of sedimentary rock?

All the processes that form sedimentary rock occur mainly at or near the surface of Earth. Some of these processes include weathering, erosion, deposition, burial, and cementation. Based on the way that they form, scientists classify sedimentary rocks as clastic, chemical, and organic sedimentary rock.

Clastic Sedimentary Rock

Clastic sedimentary rock forms when sediments are buried, compacted, and cemented together by calcite or quartz. The size of the sediment, or clasts, that makes up the rock is used to classify clastic sedimentary rocks. Fine-grained sedimentary rocks, in which grains are too small to be seen, include mudstone, siltstone, and shale. Sandstone, which is shown at the left, is a medium-grained clastic sedimentary rock with visible grains. Breccia and conglomerate are coarse-grained clastic sedimentary rocks made of large particles, such as pebbles, cobbles, and boulders.

Chemical Sedimentary Rock

Chemical sedimentary rocks form when water, usually seawater, evaporates. Most water contains dissolved minerals. As water evaporates, the minerals in water become concentrated to the point that they precipitate out of solution and crystallize. Halite, or rock salt, is an example of chemical sedimentary rock. It is made of sodium chloride, $NaCl$. Halite forms when sodium ions and chlorine ions in shallow bodies of water become so concentrated that halite crystallizes from solution.

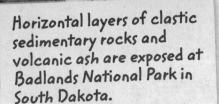

Horizontal layers of clastic sedimentary rocks and volcanic ash are exposed at Badlands National Park in South Dakota.

Sandstone

Visualize It!

11 Identify How would you describe the texture of the halite shown below?

_____

_____

The Bonneville Salt Flats near the Great Salt Lake in Utah are made largely of halite. The salt flats are the remains of an ancient lake bed.

Halite

© Houghton Mifflin Harcourt Publishing Company • Image Credits: (t) ©Dean Conger/Corbis; (c) ©David L. Brown/Design Pics/Corbis; (c) ©Andrew J. Martinez/Photo Researchers, Inc.; (bl) The Natural History Museum /Alamy; (br) ©Dean Conger/Corbis

The White Cliffs of Dover on the English sea coast are made up of the skeletons of the marine alga that is shown below.

Skeleton of a marine alga

Organic Sedimentary Rock

Organic sedimentary rock forms from the remains or fossils, of once-living plants and animals. Most limestone forms from the fosssils of organisms that once lived in the ocean. Over time, the skeletons of these marine organisms, which are made of calcium carbonate, collect on the ocean floor. These animal remains, together with sediment, are eventually buried, compacted, and cemented together to form *fossiliferous* [fahs•uh•LIF•er•uhs] limestone.

Coquina is a fossiliferous limestone that consists of the shells of marine mollusks that have been cemented together by calcite. Chalk is a soft, white limestone that is made up of the skeletons of microorganisms that collect in huge numbers on the floor of the deep ocean.

Coal is another type of organic sedimentary rock. It forms when plant material is buried and changes into coal as a result of increasing heat and pressure. This process occurs over millions of years.

Active Reading **12 Identify** What are two types of organic sedimentary rock?

_____

_____

13 Compare Use the table to compare and contrast clastic, chemical, and organic sedimentary rock.

Three Types of Sedimentary Rock

Clastic	Chemical	Organic

The Heat Is On!

Sedimentary shale

Slate

Phyllite

When shale is exposed to increasing temperature and pressure, different foliated metamorphic rocks form.

What are two types of metamorphic rock?

As a rock is exposed to high temperature and pressure, the crystal structures of the minerals in the rock change to form new minerals. This process results in the formation of metamorphic rock, which has either a foliated texture or a nonfoliated texture.

Foliated Metamorphic Rock

The metamorphic process in which mineral grains are arranged in planes or bands is called *foliation* (foh•lee•AY•shuhn). Foliation occurs when pressure causes the mineral grains in a rock to realign to form parallel bands.

Metamorphic rocks with a foliated texture include slate, phyllite, schist (SHIST), and gneiss (NYS). Slate and phyllite are commonly produced when shale, a fine-grained sedimentary rock, is exposed to an increase in temperature and pressure. The minerals in slate and phyllite are squeezed into flat, sheet-like layers. With increasing temperature and pressure, phyllite may become schist, a coarse-grained foliated rock. With further increases in temperature and pressure, the minerals in schist separate into alternating bands of light and dark minerals. Gneiss is a coarse-grained, foliated rock that forms from schist. Slate, phyllite, schist, and gneiss can all begin as shale, but they are very different rocks. Each rock forms under a certain range of temperatures and pressures, and contains different minerals.

Schist

Gneiss

14 Describe What happens to the minerals as gneiss forms from schist?

_____

_____

Nonfoliated Metamorphic Rock

Metamorphic rocks that do not have mineral grains that are aligned in planes or bands are called *nonfoliated*. Nonfoliated metamorphic rocks are commonly made of one or only a few minerals. During metamorphism, mineral grains or crystals may change size or shape, and some may change into another mineral.

Two common nonfoliated metamorphic rocks are quartzite and marble. Quartzite forms when quartz sandstone is exposed to high temperature and pressure. This causes the sand grains to grow larger and the spaces between the sand grains disappear. For that reason, quartzite is very hard and not easily broken down.

When limestone undergoes metamorphism, the limestone becomes marble. During the process of metamorphism, the calcite crystals in the marble grow larger than the calcite grains in the original limestone.

The mineral grains in quartzite (top) and crystals in marble (bottom) do not form bands.

Active Reading **15 Apply** What are two characteristics of nonfoliated metamorphic rocks?

_____

_____

Marble is a nonfoliated metamorphic rock that forms when limestone is metamorphosed. Marble is used to build monuments and statues.

Think Outside the Book **Inquiry**

16 Apply With a classmate, discuss how different types of rocks can be used as building or construction materials.

Visual Summary

To complete this summary, fill in the blanks. Then, use the key below to check your answers. You can use this page to review the main concepts of the lesson.

Sedimentary rock may form from layers of sediment that are cemented together.

17 Sedimentary rocks can be classified into three groups:

_____,

_____, and

_____

Three Classes of Rock

Igneous rock forms from magma or lava that has cooled and hardened.

18 Igneous rocks can be classified into two groups:

_____

and _____

Metamorphic rock forms under high temperature or pressure deep within Earth's crust.

19 Metamorphic rocks can be classified into two groups:

_____

and _____

Answers: 17 clastic, chemical, organic; 18 intrusive, extrusive; 19 foliated, nonfoliated

20 Synthesize While hiking in the mountains, you see a large outcrop of marble. Describe one process by which the metamorphic rock marble forms from the sedimentary rock limestone.

Lesson Review

Vocabulary

Fill in the blank with the term that best completes the following sentence.

1 Sedimentary rocks that are made up of large pebbles and stones have a coarse-grained

_____

2 Most granite has a _____ of quartz, mica, and feldspar.

3 _____ can be considered to be mixtures of minerals.

Key Concepts

4 Summarize How does the cooling rate of magma or lava affect the texture of the igneous rock that forms?

_____
_____
_____
_____
_____
_____
_____

5 Describe How does clastic sedimentary rock form?

_____
_____
_____
_____

6 Explain What is the difference between foliated and nonfoliated metamorphic rock?

_____
_____
_____
_____
_____
_____
_____

Critical Thinking

Use this photo to answer the following questions.

7 Identify What type of rock is shown here? How do you know?

_____
_____
_____

8 Describe How did this rock form?

_____
_____
_____

9 Infer Suppose this rock was exposed to high temperatures and pressure. What would most likely happen to it?

_____
_____

10 Infer What information can a foliated metamorphic rock provide you about the conditions under which it formed?

_____
_____
_____
_____
_____

My Notes

Unit 3 ⟨ Big Idea ⟩ Minerals and rocks are basic building blocks of Earth and can change over time from one type of mineral or rock to another.

Lesson 1

ESSENTIAL QUESTION
What are minerals, how do they form, and how can they be identified?

Describe the basic structures of minerals and identify different minerals by using their physical properties.

Lesson 2

ESSENTIAL QUESTION
What is the rock cycle?

Describe the series of processes and classes of rocks that make up the rock cycle.

Lesson 3

ESSENTIAL QUESTION
How do rocks form?

Describe the formation and classification of sedimentary, igneous, and metamorphic rocks.

Connect ESSENTIAL QUESTIONS
Lessons 1 and 3

1 Synthesize Describe a process by which one mineral can change into another mineral.

_____

_____

_____

_____

Think Outside the Book

2 Synthesize Choose one of these activities to help synthesize what you have learned in this unit.

☐ Using what you learned in lessons 1, 2, and 3, explain in a short essay how a chemical sedimentary rock formed, beginning with a lake full of dissolved gypsum minerals.

☐ Using what you learned in lessons 1, 2, and 3, create a poster presentation to describe the type and texture of a rock formed by an explosive volcanic event.

Unit 3 Review

Name _____

Vocabulary

Fill in each blank with the term that best completes the following sentences.

1 The _____ is a series of geologic processes in which rock can form, change from one type to another, be destroyed, and form again.

2 Changes in temperature or pressure, or chemical processes, can transform an existing rock into a _____ rock.

3 A _____ is a naturally occurring, solid combination of one or more minerals or organic matter.

4 The rising of regions of Earth's crust to higher elevations is called _____.

5 _____ is a physical property used to describe how the surface of a mineral reflects light.

Key Concepts

Read each question below, and circle the best answer.

6 The table below lists five classes of nonsilicate minerals.

Class	Description	Example
Carbonates	contain carbon and oxygen compounds	calcite
Halides	contain ions of chlorine, fluorine, iodine, and bromine	halite
Native elements	contain only one type of atom	gold
Oxides	contain oxygen compounds	hematite
Sulfides	contain sulfur compounds	pyrite

There are actually six classes of nonsilicate minerals. Which class is missing from this chart?

A feldspars

B micas

C silicates

D sulfates

7 Granite can form when magma cools within Earth. Basalt can form when lava cools on Earth's surface. What do granite and basalt have in common?

A They are igneous.

B They are old.

C They are fossils.

D They are intrusive.

8 A student is trying to identify a mineral in science class.

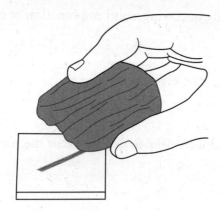

What property of the mineral is the student testing?

A cleavage

C luster

B color

D streak

9 Which one of the following statements about elements, atoms, and compounds is not true?

A Elements consist of one type of atom and can combine to form compounds.

B Compounds are smaller than atoms.

C Elements and compounds form the basis of all materials on Earth.

D Atoms cannot be broken down into smaller substances.

10 Which of the following best describes how sedimentary rock forms?

A Molten rock beneath the surface of Earth cools and becomes solid.

B Layers of sediment become compressed over time to form rock.

C Chemical processes or changes in pressure or temperature change a rock.

D Molten rock reaches the surface and cools to become solid rock.

Name _____

11 Study the diagram below.

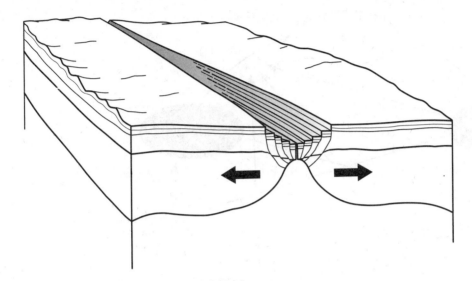

What process is occurring in this image?

A Two tectonic plates are moving toward each other, creating a syncline.

B Two tectonic plates are pulling away from each other, creating a rift zone.

C Two tectonic plates are moving toward each other, creating an anticline.

D Two tectonic plates are moving away from each other, creating a new mountain range.

12 Over time, repeated temperature changes can cause a rock to break down into smaller pieces. What is this an example of?

A subsidence   **C** deposition

B weathering   **D** erosion

Critical Thinking

Answer the following questions in the space provided.

13 You are standing by a cliff far away from the ocean. You see a sedimentary layer with shells in it. You are told the shells are from oceanic organisms. How do you think this layer formed?

_____

_____

_____

_____

14 The diagram below shows the rock cycle.

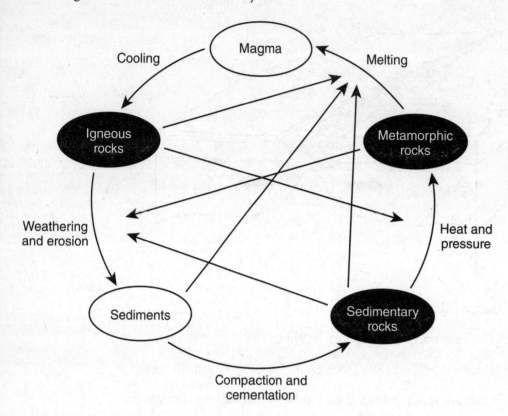

The rock cycle describes how rocks change. What conditions must be present for igneous or sedimentary rock to change into metamorphic rock? Name two ways that this could happen.

_____

_____

_____

Connect **ESSENTIAL QUESTIONS**
Lessons 1 and 3

Answer the following question in the space provided.

15 Explain a way that a sedimentary rock could form, then over time break down into smaller pieces, and become a sedimentary rock again in another location.

_____

_____

_____

_____

_____

The Restless Earth

Big Idea

The movement of tectonic plates accounts for important features of Earth's surface and for major geologic events.

The Cleveland volcano in Alaska erupts.

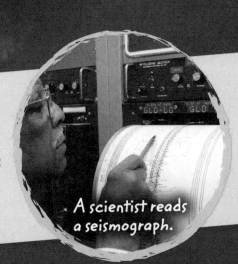

A scientist reads a seismograph.

What do you think?

Earth is continuously changing. Volcanoes and earthquakes are powerful forces of change. Volcanoes form new rock and reshape the land. Earthquakes move rocks. How did the landscape around you form?

Unit 4
The Restless Earth

Lesson 1
Earth's Layers 192

Lesson 2
Plate Tectonics 200

People in Science 214

Lesson 3
Mountain Building 216

Lesson 4
Volcanoes 226

Lesson 5
Earthquakes 238

Engineering and Technology ... 248

Lesson 6
Measuring Earthquake Waves .. 252

Unit Review 268

Stable Structures

The building on the right, located in San Francisco, was engineered to protect it from earthquakes.

1 Think About It

A People in different parts of the United States—and all over the world—need to make buildings earthquake-proof. Where would it be of most importance to have earthquake-proof buildings?

_____

_____

B The taller the building, the more difficult it is to make it safe during an earthquake. Why do you think this is?

_____

_____

C Some materials survive the shaking from an earthquake, while others crumble or crack. What materials might withstand an earthquake? Why?

_____

_____

_____

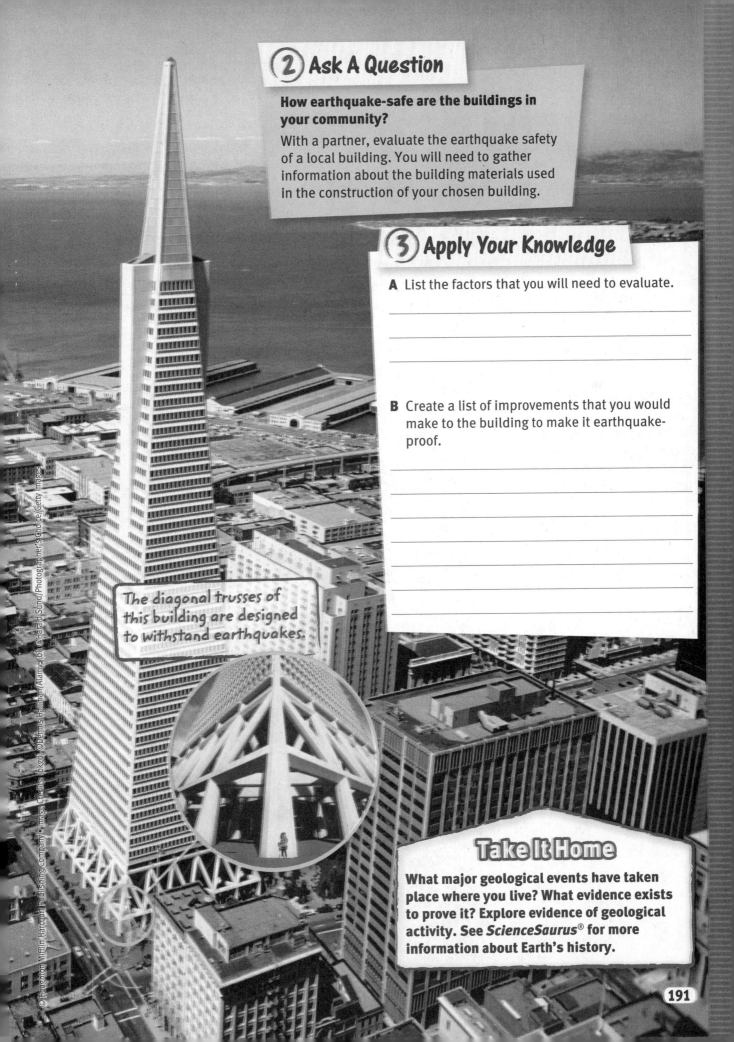

② Ask A Question

How earthquake-safe are the buildings in your community?

With a partner, evaluate the earthquake safety of a local building. You will need to gather information about the building materials used in the construction of your chosen building.

③ Apply Your Knowledge

A List the factors that you will need to evaluate.

_____

_____

_____

B Create a list of improvements that you would make to the building to make it earthquake-proof.

_____

_____

_____

_____

_____

_____

_____

The diagonal trusses of this building are designed to withstand earthquakes.

Take It Home

What major geological events have taken place where you live? What evidence exists to prove it? Explore evidence of geological activity. See *ScienceSaurus*® for more information about Earth's history.

Earth's Layers

ESSENTIAL QUESTION

What are Earth's layers?

By the end of this lesson, you should be able to identify Earth's compositional and physical layers and describe their properties.

If you could dig below this canyon, you would discover that Earth is made up of different layers below its surface.

© Houghton Mifflin Harcourt Publishing Company • Image Credits: ©Phil Schermeister/Corbis

 **Lesson Labs**

Quick Labs
• Layers of Earth
• Ordering Earth's Layers

S.T.E.M. Lab
• Models of Earth

Engage Your Brain

1 Predict Check T or F to show whether you think each statement is true or false.

T   F

☐   ☐   The outermost layer of solid Earth is sometimes called the crust.

☐   ☐   The crust is the densest layer.

☐   ☐   The mantle is the layer between the crust and the core.

☐   ☐   Earth's core is divided into five parts.

2 Describe If you were asked to describe this apple, how many layers would you say it has? How would you describe the layers?

_____

_____

_____

_____

_____

_____

Active Reading

3 Synthesize You can often define an unknown word if you know the meaning of its word parts. Use the word parts and sentence below to make an educated guess about the meaning of the word *mesosphere*.

Word part	Meaning
meso-	middle
-sphere	ball

Example sentence
The <u>mesosphere</u> is more than 2,000 km thick.

Vocabulary Terms

• crust
• mantle
• convection
• core
• lithosphere
• asthenosphere
• mesosphere

4 Apply As you learn the definition of each vocabulary term in this lesson, create your own definition or sketch to help you remember the meaning of the term.

Mesosphere: _____

_____

_____

_____

Peeling the Layers

What is inside Earth?

If you tried to dig to the center of Earth, what do you think you would find? Would Earth be solid or hollow? Would it be made of the same material throughout? Actually, Earth is made of several layers. The materials that make up each layer have characteristic properties that vary from layer to layer. Scientists think about Earth's layers in two ways—in terms of their chemical composition and in terms of their physical properties.

Think Outside the Book (Inquiry)

5 Apply With a classmate, discuss why scientists might have two ways for thinking about Earth's layers.

What are Earth's compositional layers?

Earth can be divided into three layers based on chemical composition. These layers are called the *crust*, the *mantle*, and the *core*. Each compositional layer is made up of a different mixture of chemicals.

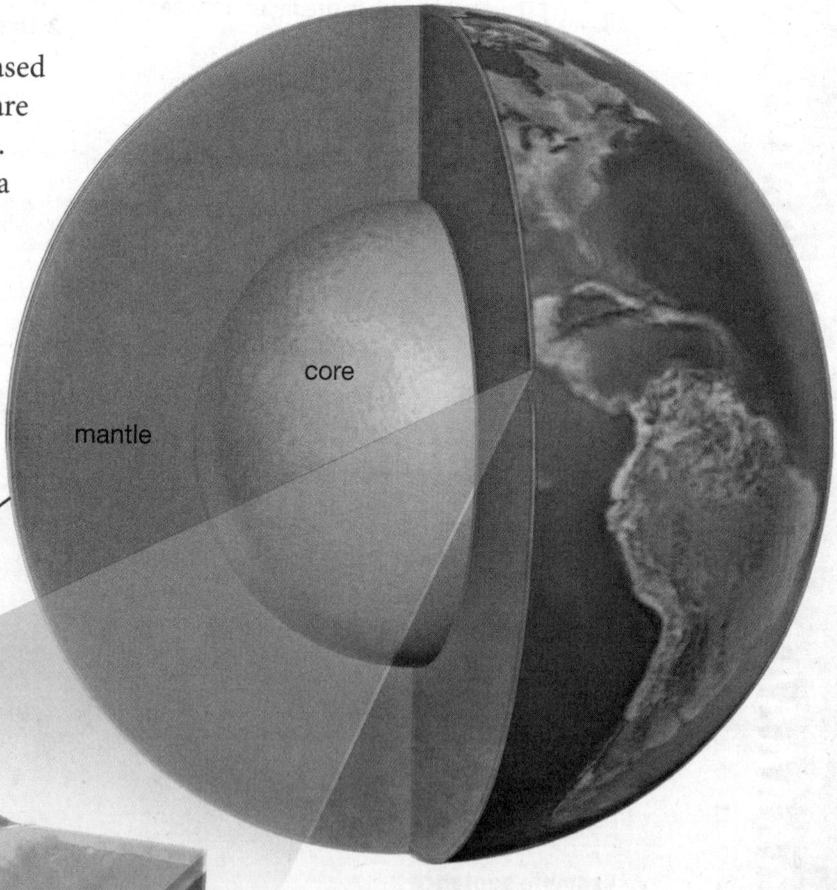

Earth is divided into three layers based on the chemical composition of each layer.

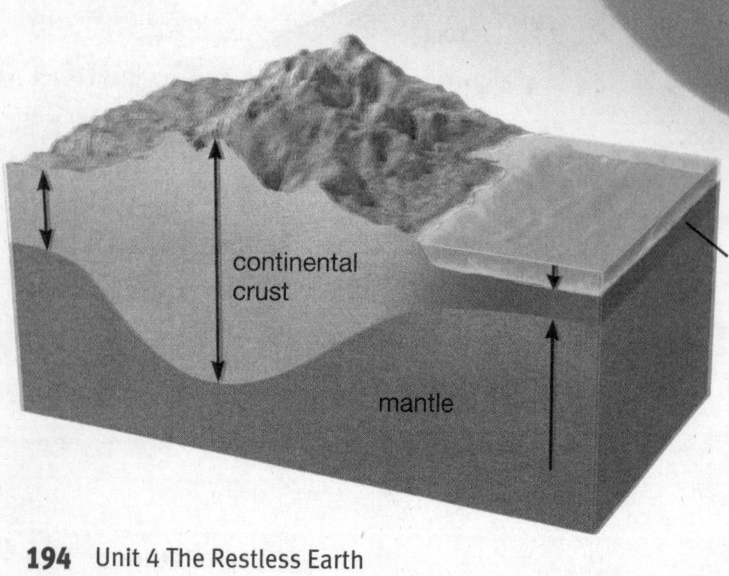

core

mantle

crust

continental crust

oceanic crust

mantle

Continental crust is thicker than oceanic crust.

Crust

The outermost solid layer of Earth is the **crust**. There are two types of crust—continental and oceanic. Both types are made mainly of the elements oxygen, silicon, and aluminum. However, the denser oceanic crust has almost twice as much iron, calcium, and magnesium. These elements form minerals that are denser than those in the continental crust.

Active Reading

6 Identify List the compositional layers in order of most dense to least dense.

_____

_____

_____

Mantle

The **mantle** is located between the core and the crust. It is a region of hot, slow-flowing, solid rock. When convection takes place in the mantle, cooler rock sinks and warmer rock rises. **Convection** is the movement of matter that results from differences in density caused by variations in temperature. Scientists can learn about the mantle by observing mantle rock that has risen to Earth's surface. The mantle is denser than the crust. It contains more magnesium and less aluminum and silicon than the crust does.

Core

The **core** extends from below the mantle to the center of Earth. Scientists think that the core is made mostly of iron and some nickel. Scientists also think that it contains much less oxygen, silicon, aluminum, and magnesium than the mantle does. The core is the densest layer. It makes up about one-third of Earth's mass.

Active Reading **7 Identify** What element makes up most of Earth's core? _____

© Houghton Mifflin Harcourt Publishing Company

What are Earth's physical layers?

Earth can also be divided into layers based on physical properties. The properties considered include whether the layer is solid or liquid, and how the layer moves or transmits waves. The five physical layers are the *lithosphere, asthenosphere, mesosphere, outer core,* and *inner core.*

Active Reading **8 Label** Write the names of the compositional layers shown below in the spaces provided.

Visualize It!

9 Analyze Which of Earth's compositional layers make up the lithosphere?

_____

_____

Lithosphere

The outermost, rigid layer of Earth is the **lithosphere.** The lithosphere is made of two parts—the crust and the rigid, upper part of the mantle. The lithosphere is divided into pieces called *tectonic plates.*

A

Asthenosphere

The **asthenosphere** is a layer of weak or soft mantle that is made of rock that flows slowly. Tectonic plates move on top of this layer.

Mesosphere

The strong, lower part of the mantle is called the **mesosphere.** Rock in the mesosphere flows more slowly than rock in the asthenosphere does.

B

Outer Core

The outer core is the liquid layer of Earth's core. It lies beneath the mantle and surrounds the inner core.

Inner Core

The inner core is the solid, dense center of our planet that extends from the bottom of the outer core to the center of Earth, which is about 6,380 km beneath the surface.

C

 **Do the Math** Sample Problem

Here's an example of how to find the percentage thickness of the core that is the outer core.

Physical	Compositional
Continental lithosphere (150 km)	Continental crust (30 km)
Asthenosphere (250 km)	Mantle (2,900 km)
Mesosphere (2,550 km)	
Outer core (2,200 km)	Core (3,430 km)
Inner core (1,230 km)	

Identify

A. What do you know?
    core = 3,430 km   outer core = 2,200 km

B. What do you want to find out?
    Percentage of core that is outer core

Plan

C. Write the formula:

   Percentage (%) of core that is outer core =

   $$\left(\frac{\text{thickness of outer core}}{\text{thickness of core}}\right) \times 100\%$$

D. Substitute into the formula:

   $$\% = \frac{(2,200)}{(3,430)} \times 100\%$$

Solve

E. Calculate and simplify:

   $$\% = 0.6414 \times 100\% = 64.14\%$$

Answer: 64.14%

 **Do the Math** You Try It

10 Calculate What percentage thickness of the continental lithosphere is continental crust?

Identify

A. What do you know?

B. What do you want to find out?

Plan

C. Write the formula:

D. Substitute into the formula:

Solve

E. Calculate and simplify:

Answer:

Visual Summary

To complete this summary, fill in the blanks with the correct word or phrase. Then, use the key below to check your answers. You can use this page to review the main concepts of the lesson.

Earth is divided into three compositional layers.

11 The outermost compositional layer of the Earth is the _____.

12 The _____ is denser than the crust and contains more magnesium.

Earth is divided into five physical layers.

13 The _____ is divided into pieces called tectonic plates.

14 The _____ core is the liquid layer of Earth's core.

Earth's Layers

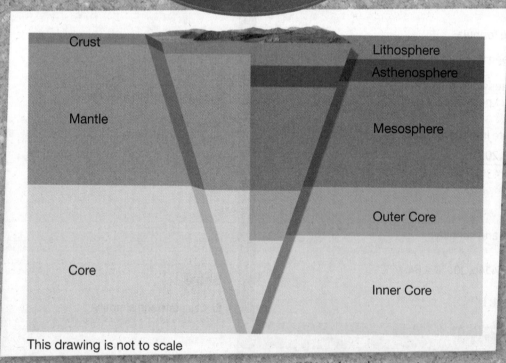

Crust

Mantle

Core

Lithosphere

Asthenosphere

Mesosphere

Outer Core

Inner Core

This drawing is not to scale

15 **Synthesize** Which physical layers correspond to which compositional layers?

Lesson Review

Vocabulary

Fill in the blank with the term that best completes the following sentence.

1 The _____ is a region of hot, slow-flowing, solid rock between the core and the crust.

2 The _____ is the densest compositional layer and makes up one-third of Earth's mass.

3 The _____ is the outermost, rigid physical layer of Earth.

Key Concepts

Use this diagram to answer the following questions.

4 Identify Which model of Earth's interior does this image show?

_____

5 Identify Which of these layers is made mostly of iron and nickel?

_____

6 Compare Explain the differences between the inner core and the outer core.

_____

_____

_____

Critical Thinking

7 Compare Explain the difference between the lithosphere and the crust.

_____

_____

_____

_____

8 Hypothesizing Scientists find dense rock on Earth's surface that is made of magnesium and smaller amounts of aluminum and silicon. What layer of Earth might this rock help scientists study? Explain your answer.

_____

_____

_____

_____

_____

_____

9 Apply In a model of Earth's layers that is determined by physical properties, how might the atmosphere be classified? Would it be part of the lithosphere, or a separate layer? Explain your answer.

_____

_____

_____

_____

_____

_____

_____

_____

_____

_____

_____

My Notes

Plate Tectonics

ESSENTIAL QUESTION

What is plate tectonics?

By the end of this lesson, you should be able to explain the theory of plate tectonics, to describe how tectonic plates move, and to identify geologic events that occur because of tectonic plate movement.

The San Andreas Fault is located where two tectonic plates slide past each other.

The course of this river has been shifted as a result of tectonic plate motion.

Lesson Labs

Quick Labs
- Tectonic Ice Cubes
- Mantle Convection
- Reconstructing Land Masses

Exploration Lab
- Seafloor Spreading

Engage Your Brain

1 Identify Check T or F to show whether you think each statement is true or false.

T   F

☐   ☐   Earth's surface is all one piece.

☐   ☐   Scientists think the continents once formed a single landmass.

☐   ☐   The sea floor is smooth and level.

☐   ☐   All tectonic plates are the same.

2 Predict Imagine that ice cubes are floating in a large bowl of punch. If there are enough cubes, they will cover the surface of the punch and bump into one another. Parts of the cubes will be below the surface of the punch and will displace the punch. Will some cubes displace more punch than others? Explain your answer.

_____

_____

_____

_____

_____

_____

Active Reading

3 Apply Many scientific words, such as *divergent* and *convergent,* also have everyday meanings or are related to words with everyday meanings. Use context clues to write your own definition for each underlined word.

Example sentence
They argued about the issue because their opinions about it were <u>divergent</u>.

divergent:

_____

_____

Example sentence

The two rivers <u>converged</u> near the town.

convergent:

_____

_____

Vocabulary Terms
- Pangaea
- sea-floor spreading
- plate tectonics
- tectonic plates
- convergent boundary
- divergent boundary
- transform boundary
- convection

4 Identify This list contains key terms you'll learn in this lesson. As you read, underline the definition of each term.

Puzzling Evidence

What evidence suggests that continents move?

Have you ever looked at a map and noticed that the continents look like they could fit together like puzzle pieces? In the late 1800s, Alfred Wegener proposed his hypothesis of continental drift. He proposed that the continents once formed a single landmass, broke up, and drifted. This idea is supported by several lines of evidence. For example, fossils of the same species are found on continents on different sides of the Atlantic Ocean. These species could not have crossed the ocean. The hypothesis is also supported by the locations of mountain ranges and rock formations and by evidence of the same ancient climatic conditions on several continents.

Geologic evidence supports the hypothesis of continental drift.

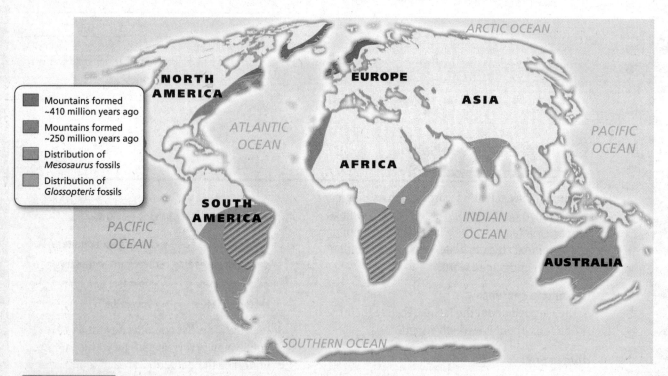

Mountains formed ~410 million years ago

Mountains formed ~250 million years ago

Distribution of *Mesosaurus* fossils

Distribution of *Glossopteris* fossils

Visualize It! **5 Summarize** Using the map and its key, complete the table to describe evidence that indicates each continent pair was once joined.

	Fossil evidence	Mountain evidence
South America and Africa		
North America and Europe		

What is Pangaea?

Active Reading 6 **Identify** As you read, underline the description of how North America formed from Pangaea.

Using evidence from many scientific fields, scientists can construct a picture of continental change throughout time. Scientists think that about 245 million years ago, the continents were joined in a single large landmass they call **Pangaea** (pan•JEE•uh). As the continents collided to form Pangaea, mountains formed. A single, large ocean called Panthalassa surrounded Pangaea.

About 200 million years ago, a large rift formed and Pangaea began to break into two continents—*Laurasia* and *Gondwana*. Then, Laurasia began to drift northward and rotate slowly, and a new rift formed. This rift separated Laurasia into the continents of North America and Eurasia. The rift eventually formed the North Atlantic Ocean. At the same time, Gondwana also broke into two continents. One continent contained land that is now the continents of South America and Africa. The other continent contained land that is now Antarctica, Australia, and India.

About 150 million years ago, a rift between Africa and South America opened to form the South Atlantic Ocean. India, Australia, and Antarctica also began to separate from each other. As India broke away from Australia and Antarctica, it started moving northward, toward Eurasia.

As India and the other continents moved into their present positions, new oceans formed while others disappeared. In some cases, continents collided with other continents. About 50 million years ago, India collided with Eurasia, and the Himalaya Mountains began to form. Mountain ranges form as a result of these collisions, because a collision welds new crust onto the continents and uplifts some of the land.

The Breakup of Pangaea

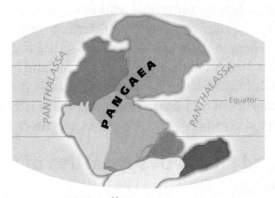

245 million years ago

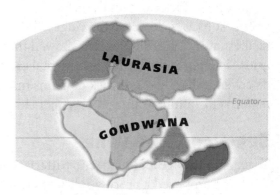

200 million years ago

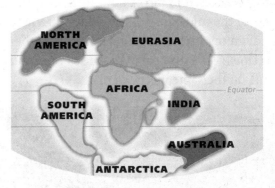

65 million years ago

3 million years ago

What discoveries support the idea of continental drift?

Wegener's ideas of continental drift were pushed aside for many years because scientists could not determine how continents moved. Then, in the mid-1900s, scientists began mapping the sea floor. They expected the floor to be smooth and level. Instead, they found huge under-water mountain ranges called *mid-ocean ridges*. The discovery of mid-ocean ridges eventually led to the theory of plate tectonics, which built on some of Wegener's ideas.

7 Summarize Why would many scientists not accept the hypothesis of continental drift?

Age and Magnetic Properties of the Sea Floor

Scientists learned that the mid-ocean ridges form along cracks in the crust. Rock samples from the sea floor revealed that the youngest rock is closest to the ridge, while the oldest rock is farthest away. The samples also showed that even the oldest ocean crust is young compared to continental crust. Scientists also discovered that sea-floor rock contains magnetic patterns. These patterns form mirror images on either side of a mid-ocean ridge.

Sea-Floor Spreading

To explain the age and magnetic patterns of sea-floor rocks, scientists proposed a process called **sea-floor spreading**. In this process, molten rock from inside Earth rises through the cracks in the ridges, cools, and forms new oceanic crust. The old crust breaks along the mid-point of the ridge and the two pieces of crust move away in opposite directions from each other. In this way, the sea floor slowly spreads apart. As the sea floor moves, so do the continents on the same piece of crust.

This map shows where mid-ocean ridges are located.

Ocean Trenches

If the sea floor has been spreading for millions of years, why is Earth not getting larger? Scientists discovered the answer when they found huge trenches, like deep canyons, in the sea floor. At these sites, dense oceanic crust is sinking into the asthenosphere as shown in the diagram below. Older crust is being destroyed at the same rate new crust is forming. Thus, Earth remains the same size.

With this new information about the sea floor, sea-floor spreading, and ocean trenches, scientists could begin to understand how continents were able to move.

8 Identify Why is Earth not getting larger if the sea floor is spreading?

_____

_____

_____

Visualize It!

9 Provide Label the youngest rock and the oldest rock on this diagram of sea-floor spreading.

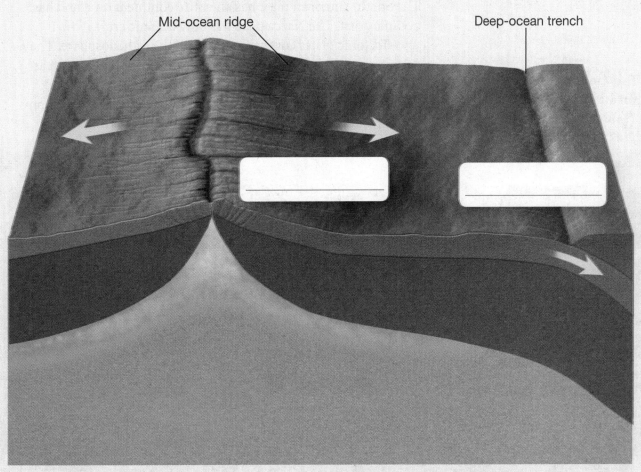

Sea-floor spreading takes place at mid-ocean ridges.

Mid-ocean ridge

Deep-ocean trench

A Giant Jigsaw

What is the theory of plate tectonics?

As scientists' understanding of continental drift, mid-ocean ridges, and sea-floor spreading grew, scientists formed a theory to explain these processes and features. **Plate tectonics** describes large-scale movements of Earth's lithosphere, which is made up of the crust and the rigid, upper part of the mantle. Plate tectonics explains how and why features in Earth's crust form and continents move.

What is a tectonic plate?

The lithosphere is divided into pieces called **tectonic plates.** These plates move around on top of the asthenosphere. The plates are moving in different directions and at different speeds. Each tectonic plate fits together with the plates that surround it. The continents are located on tectonic plates and move around with them. The major tectonic plates include the Pacific, North American, Nazca, South American, African, Australian, Eurasian, Indian, and Antarctic plates. Not all tectonic plates are the same. The South American plate has an entire continent on it and has oceanic crust. The Nazca plate has only oceanic crust.

Tectonic plates cover the surface of the asthenosphere. They vary in size, shape, and thickness. Thick tectonic plates, such as those with continents, displace more asthenosphere than thin oceanic plates do. But, oceanic plates are much more dense than continental plates are.

The Andes Mountains formed where the South American plate and Nazca plate meet.

12 Locate Which letter marks where the Andes Mountains are located on the map of tectonic plates, A, B, or C? _____

The tectonic plates fit together like the pieces of a jigsaw puzzle.

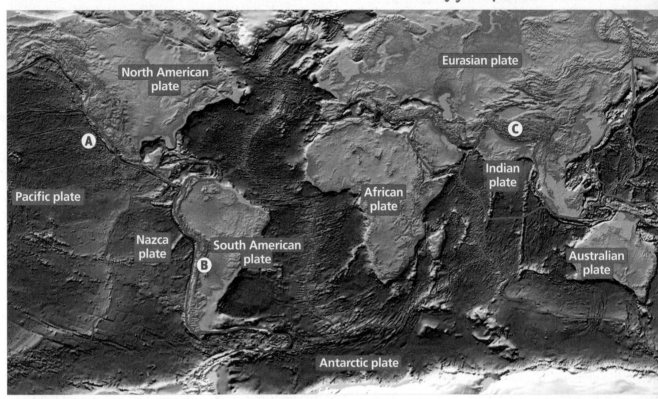

The thickest part of the South American plate is the continental crust. The thinnest part of this plate is in the Atlantic Ocean.

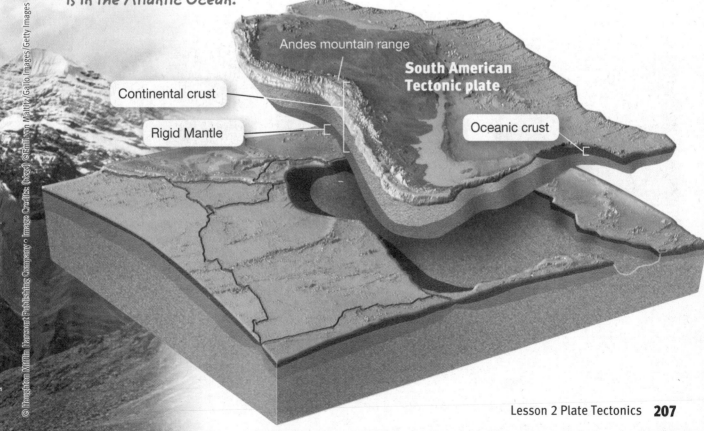

Boundaries

What are the three types of plate boundaries?

The most dramatic changes in Earth's crust occur along plate boundaries. Plate boundaries may be on the ocean floor, around the edges of continents, or even within continents. There are three types of plate boundaries: divergent boundaries, convergent boundaries, and transform boundaries. Each type of plate boundary is associated with characteristic landforms.

Active Reading

13 Identify As you read, underline the locations where plate boundaries may be found.

Convergent Boundaries

Convergent boundaries form where two plates collide. Three types of collisions can happen at convergent boundaries. When two tectonic plates of continental lithosphere collide, they buckle and thicken, which pushes some of the continental crust upward. When a plate of oceanic lithosphere collides with a plate of continental lithosphere, the denser oceanic lithosphere sinks into the asthenosphere. Boundaries where one plate sinks beneath another plate are called subduction zones. When two tectonic plates of oceanic lithosphere collide, one of the plates subducts, or sinks, under the other plate.

14 Infer Why do you think the denser plate subducts in a collision?

_____

_____

_____

Continent-Continent Collisions
When two plates of continental lithosphere collide, they buckle and thicken. This causes mountains to form.

Continent-Ocean Collisions
When a plate of oceanic lithosphere collides with a plate of continental lithosphere, the oceanic lithosphere subducts because it is denser.

Ocean-Ocean Collisions
When two plates of oceanic lithosphere collide, the older, denser plate subducts under the other plate.

Divergent Boundaries

At a **divergent boundary**, two plates move away from each other. This separation allows the asthenosphere to rise toward the surface and partially melt. This melting creates magma, which erupts as lava. The lava cools and hardens to form new rock on the ocean floor.

As the crust and the upper part of the asthenosphere cool and become rigid, they form new lithosphere. This lithosphere is thin, warm, and light. This warm, light rock sits higher than the surrounding sea floor because it is less dense. It forms mid-ocean ridges. Most divergent boundaries are located on the ocean floor. However, rift valleys may also form where continents are separated by plate movement.

At divergent boundaries, plates separate.

Transform Boundaries

A boundary at which two plates move past each other horizontally is called a **transform boundary**. However, the plate edges do not slide along smoothly. Instead, they scrape against each other in a series of sudden slippages of crustal rock that are felt as earthquakes. Unlike other types of boundaries, transform boundaries generally do not produce magma. The San Andreas Fault in California is a major transform boundary between the North American plate and the Pacific plate. Transform motion also occurs at divergent boundaries. Short segments of mid-ocean ridges are connected by transform faults called fracture zones.

At transform boundaries, plates slide past each other horizontally.

Active Reading

15 Contrast How are transform boundaries different from convergent and divergent boundaries?

_____

_____

_____

_____

Hot Plates

What causes tectonic plates to move?

Scientists have proposed three mechanisms to explain how tectonic plates move over Earth's surface. Mantle convection drags plates along as mantle material moves beneath tectonic plates. Ridge push moves plates away from mid-ocean ridges as rock cools and becomes more dense. Slab pull tugs plates along as the dense edge of a plate sinks beneath Earth's surface.

Active Reading

16 Identify As you read, underline three mechanisms scientists have proposed to explain plate motion.

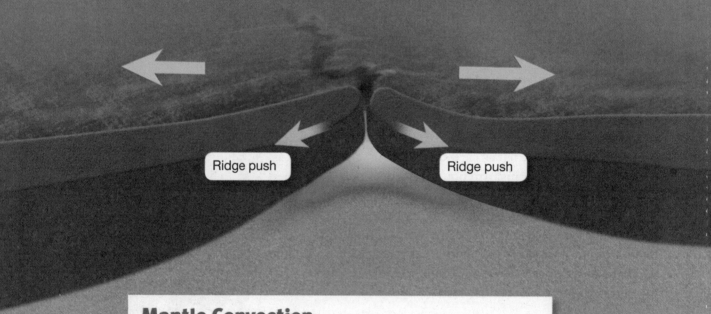

Ridge push   Ridge push

Mantle Convection

As atoms in Earth's core and mantle undergo radioactive decay, energy is released as heat. Some parts of the mantle become hotter than others parts. The hot parts rise as the sinking of cooler, denser material pushes the heated material up. This kind of movement of material due to differences in density is called **convection**. It was thought that as the mantle convects, or moves, it would drag the overlying tectonic plates along with it. However, this hypothesis has been criticized by many scientists because it does not explain the huge amount of force that would be needed to move plates.

© Houghton Mifflin Harcourt Publishing Company

Ridge Push

Newly formed rock at a mid-ocean ridge is warm and less dense than older, adjacent rock. Because of its lower density, the new rock rests at a higher elevation than the older rock. The older rock slopes downward away from the ridge. As the newer, warmer rock cools, it also becomes more dense. These cooling and increasingly dense rocks respond to gravity by moving down the slope of the asthenosphere, away from the ridge. This force, called ridge push, pushes the rest of the plate away from the mid-ocean ridge.

Slab Pull

At subduction zones, a denser tectonic plate sinks, or subducts, beneath another, less dense plate. The leading edge of the subducting plate is colder and denser than the mantle. As it sinks, the leading edge of the plate pulls the rest of the plate with it. This process is called slab pull. In general, subducting plates move faster than other plates do. This evidence leads many scientists to think that slab pull may be the most important mechanism driving tectonic plate motion.

Slab pull

17 Compare Complete the chart with brief descriptions to compare and contrast mantle convection, ridge push, and slab pull.

Mechanisms

Mantle convection	Ridge push	Slab pull

Visual Summary

To complete this summary, fill in the blanks to complete the label or caption. Then use the key below to check your answers. You can use this page to review the main concepts of the lesson.

Plate Tectonics

The continents were joined in a single landmass.

18 Scientists call the landmass _____

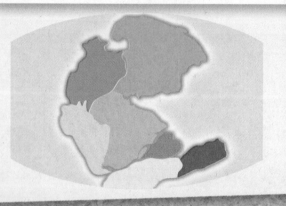

Tectonic plates differ in size and composition.

19 The United States lies on the _____ plate.

There are three types of plate boundaries: convergent, divergent, and transform.

20 This image shows a _____ boundary.

Three mechanisms may drive plate motion. These are mantle convection, slab pull, and ridge push.

21 The mechanism that scientists think is most important is _____

Answers: 18 Pangaea; 19 North American; 20 transform; 21 slab pull

22 **Synthesize** How does the flow of energy as heat in Earth's interior contribute to the movement of tectonic plates? Explain what would happen if Earth were not a convecting system.

Lesson Review

Vocabulary

Fill in the blanks with the term that best completes the following sentences.

1 The lithosphere is divided into pieces called

_____

2 The theory that describes large-scale movements of Earth's lithosphere is called

_____

3 The movement of material due to differences in density that are caused by differences in temperature is called _____

_____

Key Concepts

Use this diagram to answer the following questions.

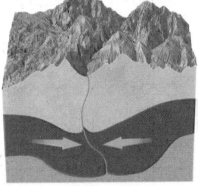

4 **Identify** What type of plate boundary is shown?

_____

5 **Identify** Which types of lithosphere are colliding at this boundary?

_____

_____

6 **Identify** What landforms are likely to form at this boundary?

_____

_____

7 **Describe** How is continental lithosphere different from oceanic lithosphere?

_____

_____

_____

8 **Compare** How are convergent boundaries different from divergent boundaries?

_____

_____

_____

Critical Thinking

9 **Analyze** Explain why cool rock material sinks when convection takes place in the mantle.

_____

_____

_____

_____

_____

_____

10 **Defend** A classmate states that continental drift could not be possible because it would take far too much force to move tectonic plates. Describe the hypotheses scientists use to explain the movement of tectonic plates. Which hypothesis do many scientists think may explain the great force needed to move plates?

_____

_____

_____

_____

_____

_____

_____

My Notes

Estella Atekwana

GEOPHYSICIST

Dr. Estella Atekwana studies changes on Earth's surface. Some of the changes may tell us how life on Earth developed. Others may help us to detect whether life exists somewhere else in the universe.

Some of Dr. Atekwana's work takes her to Botswana and Zambia in Africa. There she is studying the formation of a new rift valley. Rift valleys are places where continents break apart. (For example, long ago a rift valley formed, and Africa broke apart from South America.) Studying this rift valley, Dr. Atekwana hopes to learn more about how new landmasses form. Further, the ground reveals the remains of plants and animals that once lived there. These remains can tell us more about the climate that existed there millions of years ago.

Currently, Dr. Atekwana is doing brand new research in a new field of geology known as biogeophysics. She is looking at the effects that microorganisms have on rocks. She is using new technologies to study how rock changes after microorganisms have mixed with it. This research may one day help scientists detect evidence of life on other planets. Looking for the same geophysical changes in the rocks on Mars might be a way of detecting whether life ever existed on that planet. If the rocks show the same changes as the rocks on Earth, it could be because microorganisms once lived in them.

Dr. Atekwana's research included this visit to Victoria Falls on the Zambezi River in Africa.

Social Studies Connection

Dr. Atekwana studies rift valleys—areas where the tectonic plates are pulling apart. Research to find out where else in the world scientists have located rift valleys.

JOB BOARD

Surveying and Mapping Technicians

What You'll Do: Help surveyors take measurements of outdoor areas. Technicians hold measuring tapes and adjust instruments, take notes, and make sketches.

Where You Might Work: Outdoors and indoors entering measurements into a computer.

Education: Some post-secondary education to obtain a license.

Other Job Requirements: Technicians must be able to visualize objects, distances, sizes, and shapes. They must be able to work with great care, precision, and accuracy because mistakes can be expensive. They must also be in good physical condition.

Petroleum Technician

What You'll Do: Measure and record the conditions in oil or gas wells to find out whether samples contain oil and other minerals.

Where You Might Work: Outdoors, sometimes in remote locations and sometimes in your own town or city.

Education: An associate's degree or a certificate in applied science or science-related technology.

Other Job Requirements: You need to be able to take accurate measurements and keep track of many details.

Geologist

What You'll Do: Study the history of Earth's crust. Geologists work in many different businesses. You may explore for minerals, oil, or gas. You may find and test ground water supplies. You may work with engineers to make sure ground is safe to build on.

Where You Might Work: In the field, where you collect samples, and in the office, where you analyze them. Geologists work in mines, on oil rigs, on the slopes of volcanoes, in quarries, and in paleontological digs.

Education: A four-year bachelor's degree in science.

Other Job Requirements: Geologists who work in the field must be in good physical condition. Most geologists do field training. Geologists need strong math skills, analytical skills, and computer skills. They also need to be able to work well with other members of a team.

Mountain Building

ESSENTIAL QUESTION

How do mountains form?

By the end of this lesson, you should be able to describe how the movement of Earth's tectonic plates causes mountain building.

The highest peak in the Alps mountain range is Mont Blanc at just over 4,800 m tall.

 Lesson Labs

Quick Labs
- What Happens When Objects Collide?
- Modeling Mountains
- Modeling Geological Processes

Engage Your Brain

1 Predict Check T or F to show whether you think each statement is true or false.

T   F

☐ ☐ Mountains can originate from a level surface that is folded upward.

☐ ☐ Rocks can be pulled apart by the movement of tectonic plates.

☐ ☐ All mountains are created by volcanoes.

☐ ☐ A mountain range can form only at the edge of a tectonic plate.

2 Hypothesize The Appalachian Mountains were once taller than the Rocky Mountains. What do you think happened to the mountains? Explain.

_____

_____

_____

Rocky Mountains

Appalachian Mountains

Active Reading

3 Compare The terms *compression* and *tension* have opposite meanings. Compare the two sentences below, then write your own definition for *compression* and *tension*.

Vocabulary	Sentence
compression	The stack of books on Jon's desk caused the bottom book to be flattened by <u>compression</u>.
tension	Keisha pulled the piece of string so hard, the <u>tension</u> caused the string to break.

compression:

_____

_____

tension:

_____

_____

Vocabulary Terms

- deformation
- folding
- fault
- shear stress
- tension
- compression

4 Apply As you learn the definition of each vocabulary term in this lesson, create your own definition or sketch to help you remember the meaning of the term.

Lesson 3 Mountain Building **217**

© Houghton Mifflin Harcourt Publishing Company • Image Credits: (bkgd) ©Guido Baviera/Grand Tour/Corbis; (t) ©John E. Marriott/All Canada Photos/Getty Images; (b) ©Kenneth Murray/Photo Researchers, Inc.

Stressed Out

How can tectonic plate motion cause deformation?

The movement of tectonic plates places stress on rocks. A tectonic plate is a block of lithosphere that consists of crust and the rigid outermost part of the mantle. *Stress* is the amount of force per unit area that is placed on an object. Rocks can bend or break under stress. In addition, low temperatures make materials more brittle, or easily broken. High temperatures can allow rock to bend.

When a rock is placed under stress, it deforms, or changes shape. **Deformation** (dee•fohr•MAY•shuhn) is the process by which rocks change shape when under stress. Rock can bend if it is placed under high temperature and pressure for long periods of time. If the stress becomes too great, or is applied quickly, rock can break. When rocks bend, folds form. When rocks break, faults form.

Active Reading

5 Identify As you read, list some objects near you that can bend or break from deformation.

_____

_____

_____

_____

_____

By applying stress, the boy is causing the spaghetti to deform. Similarly, stress over a long period of time can cause rock to bend.

Like the spaghetti, stress over a short period of time or great amounts of stress can cause rock to break.

Visualize It!

6 Correlate How can the same material bend in one situation but break in another?

_____

_____

_____

_____

What are two kinds of folds?

Folded rock layers appear bent or buckled. **Folding** occurs when rock layers bend under stress. The bends are called *folds*. Scientists assume that all rock layers start out as horizontal layers deposited on top of each other over time. Sometimes, different layers of rocks can still be seen even after the rocks have been folded. When scientists see a fold, they know that deformation has happened. Two common types of folds are synclines and anticlines.

Synclines and Anticlines

Folds are classified based on the age of the rock layers. In a *syncline* (SIN•klyn), the youngest layers of rock are found at the core of a fold. The oldest layers are found on the outside of the fold. Synclines usually look like rock layers that are arched upward, like a bowl. In an *anticline* (AN•tih•klyn), the oldest layers of rock are found at the core of the fold. The youngest layers are found on the outside of the fold. Anticlines often look like rock layers that are arched downwards and high in the middle. Often, both types of folds will be visible in the same rock layers, as shown below.

The hinge is the middle point of the bend in a syncline or anticline.

Visualize It!

8 Identify Rock layers are labeled on the image below. Which rock layers are the youngest and oldest?

_____

_____

How do you know? _____

_____

_____

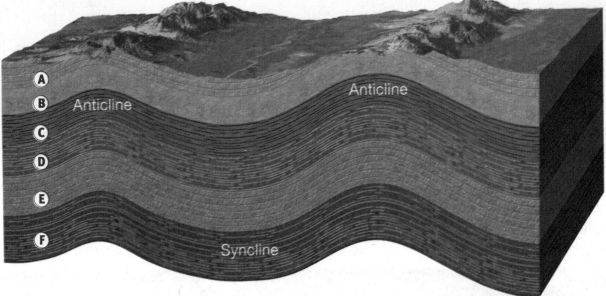

© Houghton Mifflin Harcourt Publishing Company • Image Credits: (t) ©Robert Harding Picture Library Ltd/Alamy

Faulted

What are the three kinds of faults?

Rock can be under so much stress that it cannot bend and may break. The crack that forms when large blocks of rock break and move past each other is called a **fault**. The blocks of rock on either side of the fault are called *fault blocks*. The sudden movement of fault blocks can cause earthquakes.

Any time there is a fault in Earth's crust, rocks tend to move in predictable ways. Earth has three main kinds of faults: strike-slip faults, normal faults, and reverse faults. Scientists classify faults based on the way fault blocks move relative to each other. The location where two fault blocks meet is called the *fault plane*. A fault plane can be oriented horizontally, vertically, or at any angle in between. For any fault except a perfectly vertical fault, the block above the fault plane is called the *hanging wall*. The block below the fault plane is the *footwall*.

The movement of faults can create mountains and other types of landforms. At any tectonic plate boundary, the amount of stress on rock is complex. Therefore, any of the three types of faults can occur at almost all plate boundaries.

Active Reading

9 Identify As you read, underline the direction of movement of the fault blocks in each type of fault.

Strike-Slip Faults

In a strike-slip fault, the fault blocks move past each other horizontally. Strike-slip faults form when rock is under shear stress. **Shear stress** is stress that pushes rocks in parallel but opposite directions as seen in the image. As rocks are deformed deep in Earth's crust, energy builds. The release of this energy can cause earthquakes as the rocks slide past each other. Strike-slip faults are common along transform boundaries, where tectonic plates move past each other. The San Andreas fault system in California is an example of a strike-slip fault.

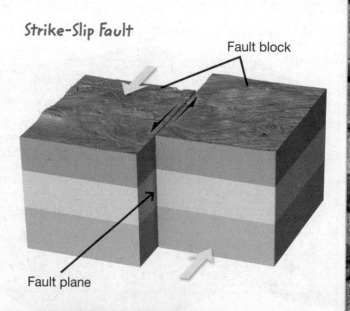

Strike-Slip Fault

Fault block

Fault plane

Normal Faults

In the normal fault shown on the right, the hanging wall moves down relative to the footwall. The faults are called normal because the blocks move in a way that you would *normally* expect as a result of gravity. Normal faults form when the rock is under tension. **Tension** (TEN•shun) is stress that stretches or pulls rock apart. Therefore, normal faults are common along divergent boundaries. Earth's crust can also stretch in the middle of a tectonic plate. The Basin and Range area of the southwestern United States is an example of a location with many normal fault structures.

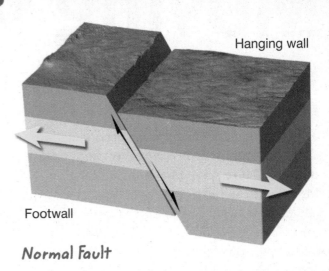

Hanging wall

Footwall

Normal Fault

Reverse Faults

In the reverse fault shown on the right, the hanging wall moves up relative to the footwall. The faults are called reverse because the hanging blocks move up, which is the reverse of what you would expect as a result of gravity. Reverse faults form when rocks undergo compression. **Compression** (kuhm•PRESH•uhn) is stress that squeezes or pushes rock together. Reverse faults are common along convergent boundaries, where two plates collide. The San Gabriel Mountains in the United States are caused by reverse faults.

Reverse Fault

👁 Visualize It!

10 Identify Label the fault plane, hanging wall, and footwall on the reverse fault to the right.

Think Outside the Book Inquiry

11 Compile Create a memory matching game of the types of faults. Create as many cards as you can with different photos, drawings, or written details about the types of faults. Use the cards to quiz yourself and your classmates.

Moving On Up

What are the three kinds of mountains?

The movement of energy as heat and material in Earth's interior contribute to tectonic plate motions that result in mountain building. Mountains can form through folding, volcanism, and faulting. *Uplift,* a process that can cause land to rise can also contribute to mountain building. Because tectonic plates are always in motion, some mountains are constantly being uplifted.

Active Reading **12 Identify** As you read, underline examples of folded, volcanic, and fault-block mountains.

Folded Mountains

Folded mountains form when rock layers are squeezed together and pushed upward. They usually form at convergent boundaries, where plates collide. For example, the Appalachian Mountains (ap•uh•LAY•chun) formed from folding and faulting when the North American plate collided with the Eurasian and African plates millions of years ago.

In Europe, the Pyrenees (PIR•uh•neez) are another range of folded mountains, as shown below. They are folded over an older, pre-existing mountain range. Today, the highest peaks are over 3,000 m tall.

The Pyrenees Mountains are folded mountains that separate France from Spain.

Visualize It!

13 Identify What evidence do you see that the Pyrenees Mountains are folded mountains?

_____

_____

_____

Volcanic Mountains

Volcanic mountains form when melted rock erupts onto Earth's surface. Many major volcanic mountains are located at convergent boundaries. Volcanic mountains can form on land or on the ocean floor. Volcanoes on the ocean floor can grow so tall that they rise above the surface of the ocean, forming islands. Most of Earth's active volcanoes are concentrated around the edge of the Pacific Ocean. This area is known as the Ring of Fire. Many volcanoes, including Mt. Griggs in the image to the right, are located on the Northern rim of the Pacific plate in Alaska.

Mt. Griggs volcano on the Alaskan Peninsula is 2,317 m high.

The Teton Mountains in Wyoming are fault-block mountains.

Fault-Block Mountains

Fault-block mountains form when tension makes the lithosphere break into many normal faults. Along the faults, pieces of the lithosphere drop down compared with other pieces. The pieces left standing form fault-block mountains. The Teton Mountains (TEE•tuhn) and the Sierra Nevadas are fault-block mountains.

14 Identify Draw a simple version of each type of mountain below.

Folded	Volcanic	Faulted

Visual Summary

To complete this summary, fill in the blanks with the correct word or phrase. Then use the key below to check your answers. You can use this page to review the main concepts of the lesson.

Mountain Building

Rocks can bend or break under stress.

15 The process by which rocks change shape under stress is called _____

Folds occur when rock layers bend.

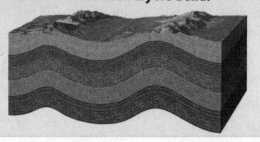

16 A rock structure with the oldest rocks at the core of the fold is called a/an _____

Faults occur when rock layers break.

Footwall

Hanging wall

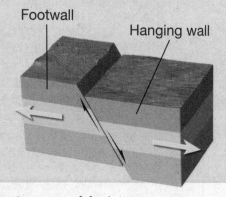

17 The type of fault pictured is a _____ fault.

Mountains form through folding, volcanism, and faulting.

18 The type of mountains pictured are _____ mountains.

Answers: 15 deformation; 16 anticline; 17 normal; 18 fault-block

19 **Synthesize** The middle of tectonic plates tend to have fewer mountains than locations near tectonic plate boundaries. What might be one possible explanation for this?

Lesson Review

Vocabulary

Fill in the blank with the term that best completes the following sentences.

1 A normal fault is a result of a type of stress known as _____

2 A strike-slip fault is a result of _____ stress.

3 A reverse fault is caused by a type of stress known as _____

Key Concepts

Fill in the table below by identifying the type of mountain described in the example question.

Example	Type of Mountain
4 Identify The Basin and Range province is characterized by many normal faults.	
5 Identify The Cascade Range in the United States has many eruptive mountains.	
6 Identify The Pyrenees Mountains have many syncline and anticline structures.	

7 Describe How does the movement of tectonic plates cause deformation in rock?

_____
_____
_____

8 Compare How do folded, volcanic, and fault-block mountains differ?

_____
_____
_____
_____

Critical Thinking

Use the diagram below to answer the following questions.

9 Correlate What type of stress caused the fault shown in the image?

_____

10 Apply Along which type of tectonic plate boundary would this fault be common? How do you know?

_____
_____
_____

11 Analyze Can rock undergo compression, tension, and shear stress all at once? Explain.

_____
_____
_____
_____

12 Conclude Imagine you are walking along a roadway and see a syncline. What can you conclude about the formation of that fold?

_____
_____
_____
_____

My Notes

Volcanoes

ESSENTIAL QUESTION

How do volcanoes change Earth's surface?

By the end of this lesson, you should be able to describe what the various kinds of volcanoes and eruptions are, where they occur, how they form, and how they change Earth's surface.

The Arenal volcano in Costa Rica has been active since 1968. The volcano has erupted on and off for over 7,000 years.

✋ Lesson Labs

Quick Labs
- Modeling an Explosive Eruption
- Volcano Mapping

Exploration Lab
- Modeling Lava Viscosity

🧠 Engage Your Brain

1 Predict Check T or F to show whether you think each statement is true or false.

T	F	
☐	☐	Volcanoes create new landforms such as mountains.
☐	☐	Tectonic plate boundaries are the only locations where volcanoes form.
☐	☐	Volcanic eruptions are often accompanied by earthquakes.
☐	☐	Volcanoes form new rocks and minerals.

2 Hypothesize You are a news reporter assigned to cover a story about the roadway in the image below. Describe what you think happened in this photo.

_____

_____

_____

✏️ Active Reading

3 Synthesize You can often define an unknown word if you know the meaning of its word parts. Use the word parts and sentence below to make an educated guess about the meaning of the word *pyroclastic*.

Word part	Meaning
pyro-	heat or fire
-clastic	pieces

Example sentence

<u>Pyroclastic</u> material was ejected into the atmosphere with explosive force during the eruption of the volcano.

pyroclastic:

_____

_____

Vocabulary Terms
- volcano
- magma
- lava
- vent
- tectonic plate
- hot spot

4 Apply As you learn the definition of each vocabulary term in this lesson, create your own definition or sketch to help you remember the meaning of the term.

Magma MAGIC

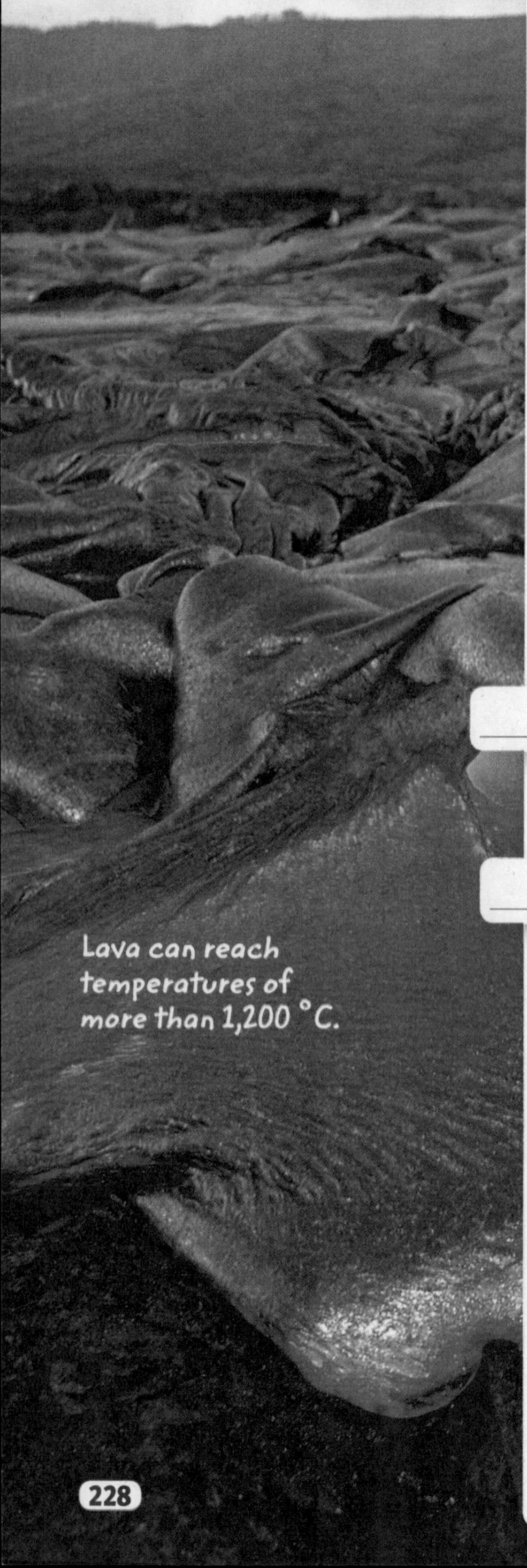

What is a volcano?

What do volcanoes look like? Most people think of a steep mountain with smoke coming out of the top. In fact, a **volcano** is any place where gas, ash, or melted rock come out of the ground. A volcano can be a tall mountain, as shown below, or a small crack in the ground. Volcanoes occur on land and underwater. There are even volcanoes on other planets. Not all volcanoes actively erupt. Many are *dormant,* meaning an eruption has not occurred in a long period of time.

Volcanoes form as rock below the surface of Earth melts. The melted rock, or **magma**, is less dense than solid rock, so it rises toward the surface. **Lava** is magma that has reached Earth's surface. Lava and clouds of ash can erupt from a **vent**, or opening of a volcano.

Visualize It!

5 Identify Label the parts of the volcano. Include the following terms: *magma, lava, vent, ash cloud.*

Lava can reach temperatures of more than 1,200 °C.

What are the kinds of volcanic landforms?

The location of a volcano and the composition of magma determine the type of volcanic landforms created. Shield volcanoes, cinder cones, composite volcanoes, lava plateaus, craters, and calderas are all types of volcanic landforms.

Volcanic Mountains

Materials ejected from a volcano may build up around a vent to create volcanic mountains. *Viscosity* (vyz•SKAHZ•ih•tee) is the resistance of a liquid material, such as lava, to flow. The viscosity of lava determines the explosiveness of an eruption and the shape of the resulting volcanic mountain. Low-viscosity lava flows easily, forms low slopes, and erupts without large explosions. High-viscosity lava does not flow easily, forms steep slopes, and can erupt explosively. *Pyroclastic materials* (py•roh•KLAHZ•tyk), or hot ash and bits of rock, may also be ejected into the atmosphere.

Active Reading

7 Identify As you read, underline the main features of each type of volcanic mountain.

Think Outside the Book **Inquiry**

6 Apply Small fragments of rock material that are ejected from a volcano are known as *volcanic ash*. Volcanic ash is a form of pyroclastic material. The material does not dissolve in water and is very abrasive, meaning it can scratch surfaces. Ash can build up to great depths in locations around a volcano. Write a cleanup plan for a town that explains how you might safely remove and dispose of volcanic ash.

- **Shield Volcanoes** Volcanoes with a broad base and gently sloping sides are *shield volcanoes*. Shield volcanoes cover a wide area and generally form from mild eruptions. Layers of lava flow out from the vent, harden, and slowly build up to form the cone. The Hawaiian Islands are shield volcanoes.

Layers of lava
Magma

- **Cinder Cones** Sometimes, ash and pieces of lava harden in the air and can fall to the ground around a small vent. The hardened pieces of lava are called cinders. The cinders and ash build up around the vent and form a steep volcano called a *cinder cone*. A cinder cone can also form at a side vent on other volcanic mountains, such as on shield or composite volcanoes.

Pyroclastic material
Ash and cinders
Conduit

- **Composite Volcanoes** Alternating layers of hardened lava flows and pyroclastic material create *composite volcanoes* (kuhm•PAHZ•iht). During a mild eruption, lava flows cover the sides of the cone. During an explosive eruption, pyroclastic material is deposited around the vent. Composite volcanoes commonly develop into large and steep volcanic mountains.

Pyroclastic material
Lava and ash layers

Fissures and Lava Plateaus

Fissure eruptions (FIH•shohr ee•RUHP•shuhnz) happen when lava flows from giant cracks, or *fissures*, in Earth's surface. The fissures are found on land and on the ocean floor. A fissure eruption has no central opening. Lava flows out of the entire length of the fissure, which can be many kilometers long. As a result, a thick and mostly flattened layer of cooled lava, called a *lava plateau* (plah•TOH), can form. One example of a lava plateau is the Columbia Plateau Province in Washington, Oregon, and Idaho, as shown to the right.

The Palouse Falls in Washington plunge deep into exposed layers of the Columbia lava plateau.

Craters and Calderas

A *volcanic crater* is an opening or depression at the top of a volcano caused by eruptions. Inside the volcano, molten rock can form an expanded area of magma called a *magma chamber*, as shown to the right. When the magma chamber below a volcano empties, the roof of the magma chamber may collapse and leave an even larger, basin-shaped depression called a *caldera* (kahl•DAHR•uh). Calderas can form from the sudden drain of a magma chamber during an explosive eruption or from a slowly emptied magma chamber. More than 7,000 years ago, the cone of Mount Mazama in Oregon collapsed to form a caldera. The caldera later filled with water and is now called Crater Lake.

A caldera can be more than 100 km in diameter.

Visualize It!

8 Describe How does the appearance of land surfaces change before and after a caldera forms?

_____

_____

_____

Before

Expanded magma chamber

After

Collapsed magma chamber

ERUPTION!

Where do volcanoes form?

Volcanoes can form at plate boundaries or within the middle of a plate. Recall that **tectonic plates** are giant sections of lithosphere on Earth's surface. Volcanoes can form at *divergent plate boundaries* where two plates are moving away from each other. Most fissure eruptions occur at divergent boundaries. Shield volcanoes, fissure eruptions, and cinder cones can also occur away from plate boundaries within a plate at *hot spots*. The type of lava normally associated with these volcanoes has a relatively low viscosity, few trapped gases, and is usually not explosive.

Composite volcanoes are most common along *convergent plate boundaries* where oceanic plates subduct. In order for the rock to melt, it must be hot and the pressure on it must drop, or water and other fluids must be added to it. Extra fluids from ocean water form magma of higher viscosity with more trapped gases. Thus, composite volcanoes produce the most violent eruptions. The *Ring of Fire* is a name used to describe the numerous explosive volcanoes that form on convergent plate boundaries surrounding the Pacific Ocean.

Active Reading

9 Identify As you read, underline three locations where volcanoes can form.

Plate Tectonic Boundaries and Volcano Locations Worldwide

Visualize It!

10 Describe How do the locations of volcanoes relate to tectonic plate boundaries?

_____

_____

_____

At Divergent Boundaries

At divergent boundaries, plates move away from each other. The lithosphere stretches and gets thinner, so the pressure on the mantle rock below decreases. As a result, the asthenosphere bulges upward and magma forms. This magma rises through fissures in the lithosphere, out onto the land or the ocean floor.

Most divergent boundaries are on the ocean floor. When eruptions occur in these areas, undersea volcanoes develop. These volcanoes and other processes lead to the formation of a long, underwater mountain range known as a *mid-ocean ridge*. Two examples of mid-ocean ridges are the East Pacific Rise in the Pacific Ocean and the Mid-Atlantic Ridge in the Atlantic Ocean. The youngest rocks in the ocean are located at mid-ocean ridges.

Shield volcanoes and cinder cones are common in Iceland, where the Mid-Atlantic Ridge runs through the country. As the plates move away from each other, new crust forms. When a divergent boundary is located in the middle of a continent, the crust stretches until a rift valley is formed, as shown below.

Active Reading **11 Identify** What types of volcanic landforms occur at divergent plate boundaries?

_____

_____

_____

Divergent plate boundaries create fissure eruptions and shield volcanoes.

Fissure

The Great Rift Valley in Africa is a location where the crust is stretching and separating.

Tectonic plates move away from each other at divergent boundaries.

At Convergent Boundaries

At convergent boundaries, two plates move toward each other. In most cases, one plate sinks beneath the other plate. As the sinking plate dives into the mantle, fluids in the sinking plate become super heated and escape. These escaping fluids cause the rock above the sinking plate to melt and form magma. This magma rises to the surface and erupts to form volcanoes.

The magma that forms at convergent boundaries has a high concentration of fluids. As the magma rises, decreasing pressure causes the fluid trapped in the magma to form gas bubbles. But, because the magma has a high viscosity, these bubbles cannot escape easily. As the bubbles expand, the magma rises faster. Eventually, the magma can erupt explosively, forming calderas or composite volcanoes. Gas, ash, and large chunks of rock can be blown out of the volcanoes. The Cascade Range is a chain of active composite volcanoes in the northwestern United States, as shown to the right. In 1980, Mt. St. Helens erupted so violently that the entire top of the mountain was blown away.

© Houghton Mifflin Harcourt Publishing Company • Image Credits: (tr) ©NASA/Science Source/Photo Researchers, Inc.

Visualize It!

12 Identify Draw two arrows in the white boxes to indicate the direction of motion of the plates that formed the Cascade volcanoes.

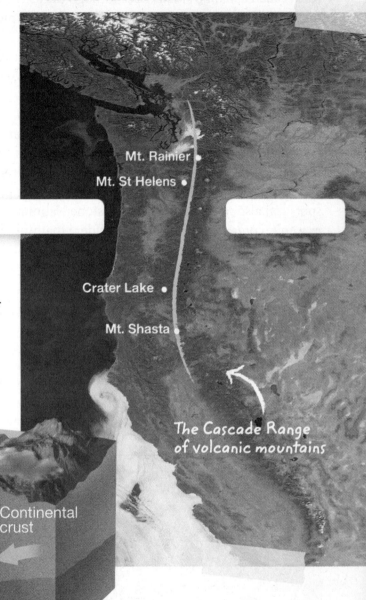

Mt. Rainier

Mt. St Helens

Crater Lake

Mt. Shasta

The Cascade Range of volcanic mountains

Tectonic plates move toward each other at convergent boundaries.

Oceanic crust

Continental crust

13 Summarize List the characteristics of divergent-boundary volcanoes and convergent-boundary volcanoes below.

Volcanoes at divergent boundaries	Volcanoes at convergent boundaries

At Hot Spots

Volcanoes can form within a plate, away from the plate boundaries. A **hot spot** is a location where a column of extremely hot mantle rock, called a *mantle plume*, rises through the asthenosphere. As the hot rock reaches the base of the lithosphere, it melts partially to form magma that can rise to the surface and form a volcano. Eruptions at a hot spot commonly form shield volcanoes. As tectonic plates move over a mantle plume, chains of volcanic mountains can form, as shown below.

The youngest Hawaiian island, the Big Island, is home to Kilauea (kih•loh•AY•uh). The Kilauea volcano is an active shield volcano located over a mantle plume. To the north and west of Kilauea is a chain of progressively-older shield volcanoes. These volcanoes were once located over the same mantle plume. Hot spots can also occur on land. Yellowstone National Park, for example, contains a huge volcanic caldera that was formed by the same mantle plume that created the Columbia Plateau.

Visualize It!

14 Analyze Which location, *A*, *B*, or *C*, do you think is the oldest volcano? How do you know?

_____

_____

_____

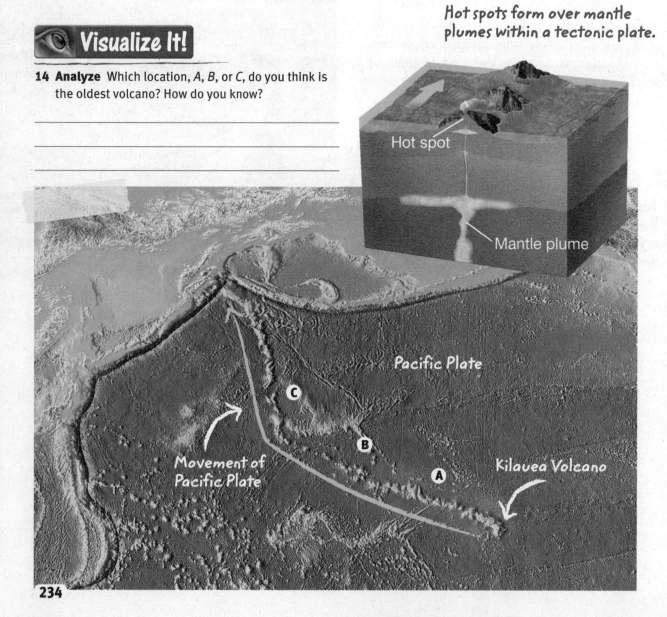

Hot spots form over mantle plumes within a tectonic plate.

Hot spot

Mantle plume

Pacific Plate

Movement of Pacific Plate

Kilauea Volcano

C

B

A

Living Near a Volcano

Volcanoes occur around the world. Many people live near volcanoes because the soils around a volcano can be very rich with essential minerals. These minerals make the soils fertile for growing a variety of crops. Living near a volcano also has its hazards. Sudden and unexpected eruptions can cause people to lose their homes and their lives.

Not All Bad

Volcanic rocks are used in jewelry, in making concrete, and in water filtration systems. Even cat litter and facial scrubs can contain volcanic rock.

Destruction

Earthquakes, fires, ash, and lava flows during an eruption can destroy entire cities.

Ash in the Air

Volcanic ash can cause breathing problems, bury crops, and damage engines. The weight of falling ash can cause buildings to collapse.

Extend

Inquiry

15 Identify Are all characteristics of volcanoes dangerous?

16 Apply Research the eruption of a specific volcano of your choice. Describe how the volcano affected the environment and the people near the volcano.

17 Design Create a poster that outlines a school safety plan for events that can occur before, during, and after a volcanic eruption.

Visual Summary

To complete this summary, check the box that indicates true or false. Then, use the key below to check your answers. You can use this page to review the main concepts of the lesson.

Lava and magma are different.

T F
18 ☐ ☐ Lava is inside Earth's crust and may contain trapped gases.

The three types of volcanic mountains are shield volcanoes, cinder cones, and composite volcanoes.

T F
19 ☐ ☐ The type of volcano shown is a shield volcano.

Volcanoes

Volcanoes can form at tectonic plate boundaries.

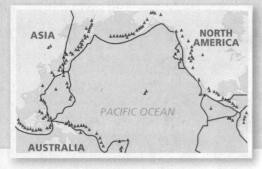

ASIA

NORTH AMERICA

PACIFIC OCEAN

AUSTRALIA

T F
20 ☐ ☐ At divergent plate boundaries, plates move toward each other.

Volcanoes can form at hot spots.

Hot spot

Mantle plume

T F
21 ☐ ☐ Hot spots are restricted to tectonic plate boundaries.

Answers: 18 False; 19 True; 20 False; 21 False

---

22 Explain How do volcanoes contribute to the formation of new landforms?

Lesson Review

Vocabulary

Write 1 or 2 sentences that describe the differences between the two terms.

1 magma   lava

_____

_____

_____

2 volcano   vent

_____

_____

_____

3 tectonic plate   hot spot

_____

_____

_____

Key Concepts

Use the image to answer the following question.

4 Identify How did the composite volcano in the image get its layered interior?

_____

_____

_____

5 Analyze Is pyroclastic material likely to form from low-viscosity lava or high-viscosity lava? Explain.

_____

_____

_____

_____

Describe the location and characteristics of the types of volcanic landforms in the table below.

Volcanic landform	Description
6 Hot-spot volcanoes	
7 Cinder cones	
8 Calderas	

Critical Thinking

9 Hypothesize In Iceland, the Mid-Atlantic Ridge runs through the center of the country. What can you conclude about the appearance of Iceland many thousands of years from now?

_____

_____

_____

_____

_____

10 Analyze Why do you think the location surrounding the Pacific Ocean is known as the Ring of Fire?

_____

_____

_____

_____

My Notes

Lesson 5

Earthquakes

ESSENTIAL QUESTION

Why do earthquakes happen?

By the end of this lesson, you should be able to describe the causes of earthquakes and to identify where earthquakes happen.

The 1995 Kobe earthquake in Japan destroyed more than 200,000 buildings and structures including this railroad track.

Engage Your Brain

1 Predict Fill in any words or numbers that you think best complete each of the statements below.

Each year there are approximately _____ earthquakes detected around the world.

In the United States, the state with the most earthquakes on average is _____

Every year, earthquakes cause _____ of dollars in damages in the United States.

Most earthquakes only last for several _____ of time.

2 Analyze Using the image, list in column 1 some of the hazards that can occur after an earthquake. In column 2, explain why you think these items or situations would be hazardous.

Hazards	Why?

Active Reading

3 Synthesize You can often define an unknown word if you know the meaning of its word parts. Use the word parts and sentence below to make an educated guess about the meaning of the word *epicenter*.

Word part	Meaning
epi-	on, upon, or over
-center	the middle

Example sentence
The epicenter of the earthquake was only 3 km from our school.

epicenter:

_____

_____

Vocabulary Terms

- earthquake
- focus
- epicenter
- tectonic plate boundary
- fault
- deformation
- elastic rebound

4 Apply As you learn the definition of each vocabulary term in this lesson, create your own definition or sketch to help you remember the meaning of the term.

Let's Focus

5 Identify As you read, underline the definitions of *focus* and *epicenter*.

What is an earthquake?

Earthquakes can cause extreme damage and loss of life. **Earthquakes** are ground movements that occur when blocks of rock in Earth move suddenly and release energy. The energy is released as seismic waves which cause the ground to shake and tremble.

Earthquake waves can be tracked to a point below Earth's surface known as the focus. The **focus** is a place within Earth along a fault at which the first motion of an earthquake occurs. Motion along a fault causes stress. When the stress on the rock is too great, the rock will rupture and cause an earthquake. The earthquake releases the stress. Directly above the focus on Earth's surface is the **epicenter** (EP•i•sen•ter). Seismic waves flow outward from the focus in all directions.

Visualize It!

6 Identify Label the epicenter, focus, and fault on the diagram.

Seismic waves

What causes earthquakes?

Most earthquakes occur near the boundaries of tectonic plates. A **tectonic plate boundary** is where two or more tectonic plates meet. As tectonic plates move, pressure builds up near the edges of the plates. These movements break Earth's crust into a series of faults. A **fault** is a break in Earth's crust along which blocks of rock move. The release of energy that accompanies the movement of the rock along a fault causes an earthquake.

Elastic Rebound

When rock is put under tremendous pressure, stress may deform, or change the shape of, the rock. **Deformation** (dee•for•MAY•shun) is the process by which rock becomes deformed and changes shape due to stress. As stress increases, the amount of energy that is stored in the rock increases, as seen in image B to the right.

Stress can change the shape of rock along a fault. Once the stress is released, rock may return to its original shape. When rock returns to nearly the same shape after the stress is removed, the process is known as *elastic deformation*. Imagine an elastic band that is pulled tight under stress. Once stress on the elastic band is removed, there is a *snap!* The elastic band returns to its original shape. A similar process occurs during earthquakes.

Similar to an elastic band, rock along tectonic plate boundaries can suddenly return to nearly its original shape when the stress is removed. The sudden *snap* is an earthquake. The return of rock to its original shape after elastic deformation is called **elastic rebound**. Earthquakes accompany the release of energy during elastic rebound. When the rock breaks and rebounds, it releases energy as seismic waves. The seismic wave energy radiates from the focus of the earthquake in all directions. This energy causes the ground to shake for a short time. Most earthquakes last for just a few seconds.

Visualize It!

7 Compare Did an earthquake occur between images A and B or between images B and C? How do you know?

_____

_____

_____

Along a fault, rocks are pushed or pulled in different directions and at different speeds.

As stress increases and energy builds within the rock, the rock deforms but remains locked in place.

Too much stress causes the rock to break and rebound to its original shape, releasing energy.

Unstable Ground

📖 **Active Reading**

8 Identify As you read, underline the locations where earthquakes occur.

Where do earthquakes happen?

Each year, approximately 500,000 earthquakes are detected worldwide. The map below shows some of these earthquakes. Movement of material and energy in the form of heat in Earth's interior contribute to plate motions that result in earthquakes.

Most earthquakes happen at or near tectonic plate boundaries. Tectonic plate boundaries are areas where Earth's crust experiences a lot of stress. This stress occurs because the tectonic plates are colliding, separating, or grinding past each other horizontally. There are three main types of tectonic plate boundaries: divergent, convergent, and transform. The movement and interactions of the plates causes the crust to break into different types of faults. Earthquakes happen along these faults.

Plate Tectonic Boundaries and Earthquake Locations Worldwide

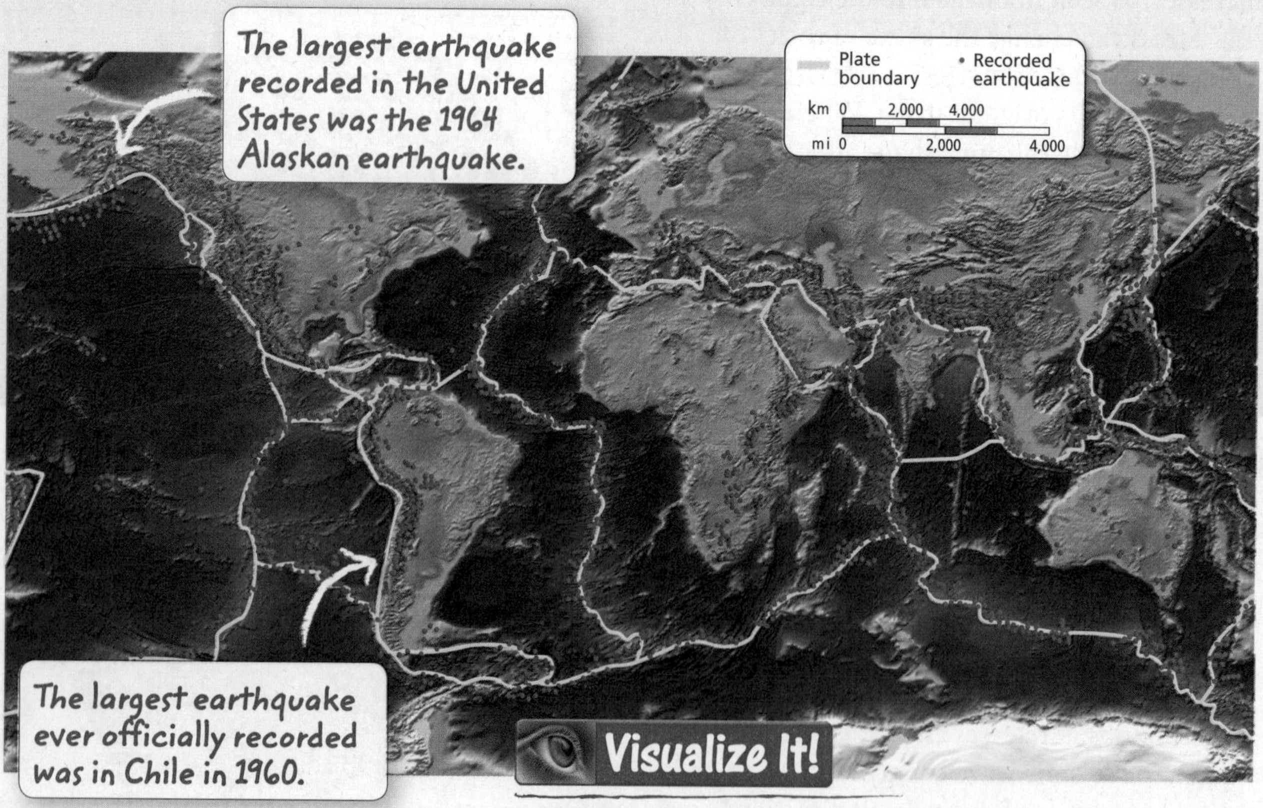

The largest earthquake recorded in the United States was the 1964 Alaskan earthquake.

The largest earthquake ever officially recorded was in Chile in 1960.

👁 **Visualize It!**

9 Identify Where are most of Earth's earthquakes located? How do you know?

_____

_____

_____

10 Correlate In the caption for each diagram, write in the type of fault that is common at each of the types of tectonic plate boundaries.

At Divergent Boundaries

At a divergent boundary, plates pull apart, causing the crust to stretch. Stress that stretches rock and makes rock thinner is called *tension*. Normal faults commonly result when tension pulls rock apart.

Most of the crust at divergent boundaries is thin, so the earthquakes tend to be shallow. Most earthquakes at divergent boundaries are no more than 20 km deep. A mid-ocean ridge is an example of a divergent boundary where earthquakes occur.

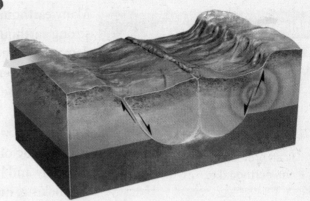

At divergent boundaries, earthquakes are common along _____ faults.

At Convergent Boundaries

Convergent plate boundaries occur when plates collide, causing rock to be squeezed. Stress that shortens or squeezes an object is known as *compression*. Compression causes the formation of reverse faults. Rocks are thrust over one another at reverse faults.

When two plates come together, both plates may crumple up to form mountains. Or one plate can subduct, or sink, underneath the other plate and into the mantle. The earthquakes that happen at convergent boundaries can be very strong. Subduction zone earthquakes occur at depths of up to 700 km.

At convergent boundaries, earthquakes are common along _____ faults.

At Transform Boundaries

A transform boundary is a place where two tectonic plates slide past each other horizontally. Stress that distorts a body by pushing different parts of the body in opposite directions is called *shear stress*. As the plates move, rocks on both sides of the fault are sheared, or broken, as they grind past one another in opposite directions.

Strike–slip faults are common at transform boundaries. Most earthquakes along the faults at transform boundaries are relatively shallow. The earthquakes are generally within the upper 50 km of the crust.

At transform boundaries, earthquakes are common along _____ faults.

What are some effects of earthquakes?

Many earthquakes do not cause major damage. However, some strong earthquakes can cause billions of dollars in property damage. Earthquakes may even cause human injuries and loss of life. In general, areas closest to the epicenter of an earthquake experience the greatest damage.

Danger to People and Structures

The shaking of an earthquake can cause structures to move vertically and horizontally. When structures cannot withstand the shaking, major destruction can occur. Following the release of seismic waves, buildings can shake so violently that a total or partial collapse can happen, as shown below.

Much of the injury and loss of life that happen during and after earthquakes is caused by structures that collapse. In addition, fires, gas leaks, floods, and polluted water supplies can cause secondary damages following an earthquake. The debris left after an earthquake can take weeks or months to clean up. Bridges, roadways, homes, and entire cities can become disaster zones.

Tsunamis

An earthquake under the ocean can cause a vertical movement of the sea floor that displaces an enormous amount of water. This displacement may cause a tsunami to form. A *tsunami* (sue•NAH•mee) is a series of extremely long waves that can travel across the ocean at speeds of up to 800 km/h. Tsunami waves travel outward in all directions from the point where the earthquake occurred. As the waves approach a shoreline, the size of the waves increases. The waves can be taller than 30 m. Tsunami waves can cause major destruction and take many lives as they smash and wash away anything in their path. Many people may drown during a tsunami. Floods, polluted water supplies, and large amount of debris are common in the aftermath.

12 Identify List some of the hazards associated with earthquakes on land and underwater.

On Land	Underwater

Why It Matters

Killer Quake

Imagine losing half the people in your city. On December 26, 2004, a massive tsunami destroyed approximately one-third of the buildings in Banda Aceh, Indonesia, and wiped out half the population.

Before

How Tsunamis Form
In the ocean, tsunami waves are fast but not very tall. As the waves approach a coast, they slow down and get much taller.

Before the Earthquake
The Banda Aceh tsunami resulted from a very strong earthquake in the ocean. Banda Aceh was very close to the epicenter.

Major Damages
The destruction to parts of Asia were so massive that geographers had to redraw the maps of some of the countries.

After

Extend

Inquiry

13 Identify In what ocean did the earthquake occur?

14 Research Investigate one other destructive tsunami and find out where the earthquake that caused it originated.

15 Debate Many of the people affected by the tsunami were poor. Why might earthquakes be more damaging in poor areas of the world?

Visual Summary

To complete this summary, fill in the correct word. Then use the key below to check your answers. You can use this page to review the main concepts of the lesson.

Earthquakes

Earthquakes occur along faults.

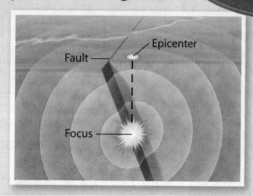

16 The epicenter of an earthquake is directly above the _____

Rocks break and snap back to their original shape in an earthquake.

17 Earthquakes happen when rocks bend and snap back in a process called _____

Earthquakes usually happen along plate boundaries.

18 The three types of plate boundaries are

_____

_____

_____

Earthquakes can cause a lot of damage.

19 An example of the dangers of earthquakes is _____

20 **Hypothesize** Can earthquakes be prevented?

Lesson Review

Vocabulary

In your own words, define the following terms.

1 Elastic rebound

_____
_____
_____

2 Focus

_____
_____
_____

3 Fault

_____
_____
_____

Key Concepts

Example	Type of Boundary
4 Identify Most of the earthquakes in Japan are a result of one plate sinking under another.	
5 Identify The African Rift Valley is a location where plates are moving apart.	
6 Identify The San Andreas fault is a location where tectonic plates move horizontally past each other.	

7 Explain What causes an earthquake?

_____
_____
_____
_____

Critical Thinking

Use the image to answer the following questions.

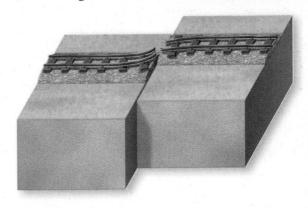

8 Analyze How does the image demonstrate that deformation has taken place?

_____
_____
_____
_____

9 Apply How does Earth's surface and the structures on the surface change as a result of an earthquake?

_____
_____
_____
_____
_____
_____

10 Hypothesize Why do you think there is often only a short amount of time to evacuate an area before an earthquake?

_____
_____
_____
_____
_____

My Notes

Engineering Design Process

Skills
Identify a need
Conduct research
✓ Brainstorm solutions
✓ Select a solution
Design a prototype
✓ Build a prototype
✓ Test and evaluate
✓ Redesign to improve
✓ Communicate results

Objectives
• Explain how scientists measure the energy of earthquakes.
• Design a model seismometer to measure motion.
• Test and modify a prototype to achieve a desired result.

Building a Seismometer

An earthquake occurs when rocks beneath the ground move suddenly. The energy of this movement travels through Earth in waves. Sometimes the shaking is detected hundreds or thousands of miles away from the origin of the earthquake. Scientists can learn about earthquakes by measuring the earthquake waves.

Measuring Motion

A seismometer is a device for measuring the motion of the ground beneath it. To develop seismometers, scientists had to solve a problem: How do you keep one part of the device from moving when the ground moves? The solution can be seen in the design shown here. A spring separates a heavy weight from the frame of the seismometer. Attached to the weight is a pen. The tip of the pen touches the surface of a circular drum that is covered in paper and slowly turning. When the ground moves, the frame and the rotating drum move along with it. The spring absorbs the ground's movement, so the weight and pen do not move. The pen is always touching the paper on the rotating drum. When the ground is not moving, the pen draws a straight line. When the ground moves, the pen draws this movement.

Waves move the instrument, but the spring and weight keep the pen still.

1 Infer This instrument measures the up-and-down motion of earthquake waves. How would you have to change the instrument to measure side-to-side motion of an earthquake?

_____

_____

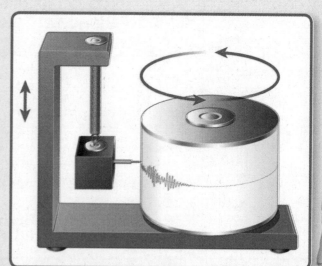

2 Infer In the oval below, write *moves* or *still* to indicate whether the labeled part moves during an earthquake or remains still.

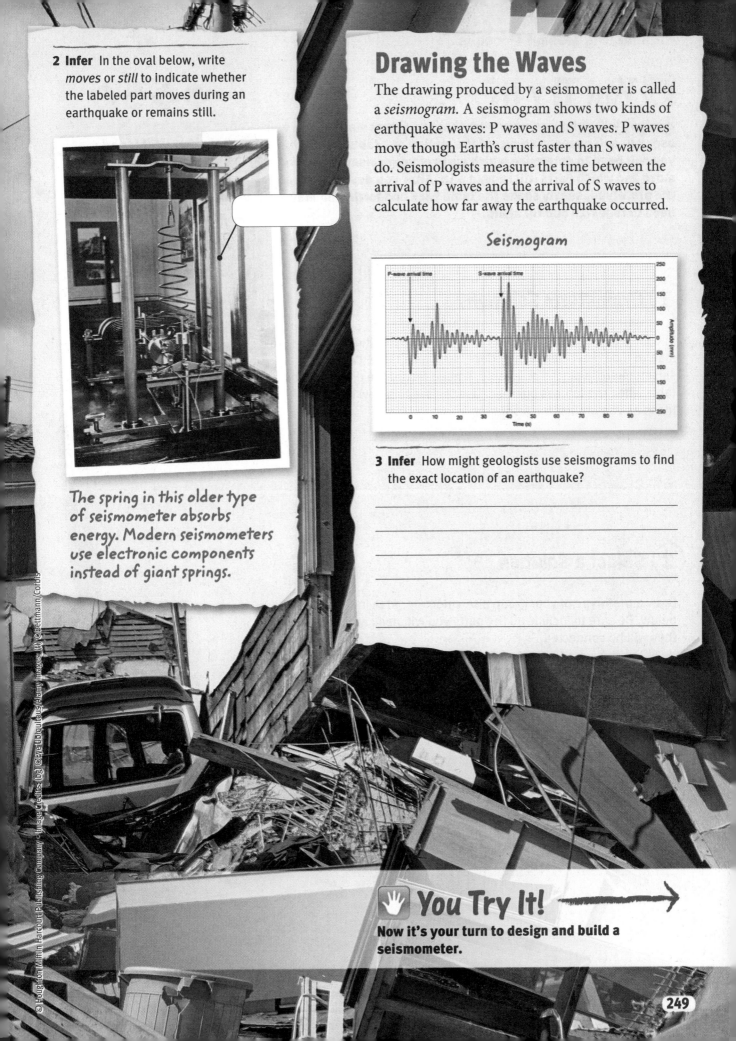

The spring in this older type of seismometer absorbs energy. Modern seismometers use electronic components instead of giant springs.

Drawing the Waves

The drawing produced by a seismometer is called a *seismogram*. A seismogram shows two kinds of earthquake waves: P waves and S waves. P waves move though Earth's crust faster than S waves do. Seismologists measure the time between the arrival of P waves and the arrival of S waves to calculate how far away the earthquake occurred.

Seismogram

3 Infer How might geologists use seismograms to find the exact location of an earthquake?

_____

_____

_____

_____

_____

_____

✋ **You Try It!** ⟶

Now it's your turn to design and build a seismometer.

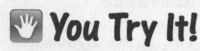 # You Try It!

Now you will build a seismometer that can detect motion. You will use your seismometer to record the motion of a table. To do this, you will need to determine which parts of your seismometer will move and which parts will remain still. After you design and build the prototype, slowly shake the table back and forth. You may need to redesign and try again.

You Will Need

✔ large square wooden frame

✔ metal weights

✔ string

✔ fine point felt tip pen

✔ long strips or roll of paper

✔ tape

✔ various hooks and hardware

1 Brainstorm Solutions

In your group, brainstorm ideas for a seismometer that will measure side-to-side movement of a surface, such as a table. When the seismometer is placed on a table, it must record the motion of the table when the table is bumped. Use the space below to record ideas as you brainstorm a solution.

_____

_____

_____

_____

2 Select a Solution

Draw a prototype of your group's seismometer idea in the space below. Be sure to include all the parts you will need and show how they will be connected.

③ Build a Prototype

In your group, build the seismometer. As the group builds it, are there some aspects of the design that cannot be assembled as predicted? What did the group have to revise in the prototype?

_____

_____

_____

_____

④ Test and Evaluate

Bump or shake the table under the seismometer. Did the prototype record any motion on the paper strip? If not, what can you revise?

_____

_____

_____

_____

⑤ Redesign to Improve

Choose one aspect to revise, and then test again. Keep making revisions, one at a time, until your seismometer records the motion of the table. How many revisions did the group make?

_____

_____

⑥ Communicate Results

Report your observations about the prototype seismometer. Include changes that improved its performance or decreased its performance. Propose ways that you could have built a more accurate seismometer. Describe what additional materials you would need and what they would be used for.

_____

_____

_____

_____

_____

_____

Measuring Earthquake Waves

ESSENTIAL QUESTION

How are seismic waves used to study earthquakes?

By the end of this lesson, you should be able to understand how seismic waves are useful in determining the strength, location, and effects of an earthquake.

This map shows the ground movement and shaking intensity of the 1906 earthquake that struck San Francisco. The areas that suffered the most damage are shown in red. The areas shown in green suffered the least damage.

Lesson Labs

Quick Labs
• Earthquakes and Buildings
• Locating an Earthquake's Epicenter

S.T.E.M. Lab
• Use a Seismograph to Determine the Amount of Energy in an Earthquake

Engage Your Brain

1 Predict Check T or F to show whether you think each statement is true or false.

T F

☐ ☐ Earthquakes often occur along faults.

☐ ☐ Earthquakes produce two main kinds of seismic waves.

☐ ☐ More than one kind of scale can be used to measure the magnitude of an earthquake.

☐ ☐ Older buildings tend to withstand earthquakes better than newer buildings.

2 Describe This graph shows the progression of an earthquake. How might this graph indicate the strength of an earthquake?

_____

_____

_____

_____

Active Reading

3 Synthesize Many English words have their roots in other languages. Use the Greek words below to make a guess about the meaning of the words *seismometer* and *seismogram*.

Greek word	Meaning
seismos	earthquake
metron	measure
gramma	writing

Example sentence
The <u>seismometer</u> recorded a series of weak earthquakes.

seismometer:

_____

Example sentence
The <u>seismogram</u> printout indicated that a small earthquake had just occurred.

seismogram:

_____

Vocabulary Terms

• focus
• epicenter
• seismic waves
• seismogram
• magnitude
• intensity

4 Apply As you learn the definition of each vocabulary term in this lesson, create your own definition or sketch to help you remember the meaning of the term.

Shake, Rattle, and Roll

What happens during an earthquake?

Have you ever felt the ground move under your feet? Many people have. Every day, somewhere in the world, earthquakes happen. An earthquake occurs when blocks of rock move suddenly and release energy. This energy travels through rock as waves.

Movement Takes Place Along a Fault

Earth's lithosphere (LITH•uh•sfir) is the rocky outer layer of Earth that includes the crust. The lithosphere is made up of large plates. These plates pull apart, push together, or move past one another. As plates move, stress on rocks at or near the edges of the plates increases. This stress causes faults to form. A *fault* is a break in a body of rock along which one block moves relative to another. Stress along faults causes the rocks to deform, or change from their original shape. If this stress becomes too great, rocks along a fault will break and move along the fault. Once rocks break, the pieces of broken rock return to an undeformed shape. When rocks along a fault break and move along a fault, energy is released into the surrounding rock in the form of waves. This process is what causes earthquakes.

![Active Reading]

5 Identify As you read, underline the definition of a fault.

6 Sequence Fill in the cause-and-effect chain for earthquakes.

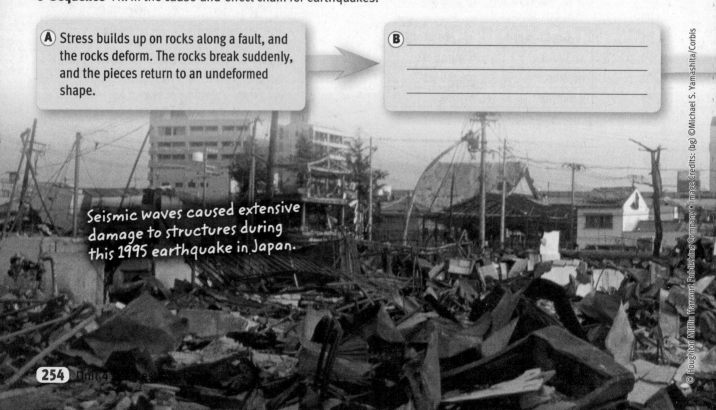

A Stress builds up on rocks along a fault, and the rocks deform. The rocks break suddenly, and the pieces return to an undeformed shape.

B _____

Seismic waves caused extensive damage to structures during this 1995 earthquake in Japan.

Energy Is Released as Seismic Waves

As stress builds up in rocks along a fault, the energy that is stored in the deforming rock increases. When the rock breaks, the rocks on either side of the fault slip past one another and return to an undeformed state. The location along a fault at which the first motion of an earthquake takes place is called the **focus**. The **epicenter** is the point on Earth's surface directly above an earthquake's starting point or focus. A large amount of stored energy is released when rocks along a fault slip. This energy travels away from the focus and through Earth in all directions as seismic (SYZ•mik) waves. **Seismic waves** are vibrations that cause different types of ground motion. The strength of an earthquake is based on the energy that is released as rocks break and return to an undeformed shape.

Energy moves outward from the water drop as ripples on the water.

Visualize It!

7 Compare How are the ripples that are moving through the water in this pond similar to seismic waves that travel through Earth? How are they different?

_____

_____

_____

Ⓒ Seismic waves travel through Earth and along Earth's surface.

Ⓓ _____

_____

_____

Waves of Motion

What are two kinds of seismic waves?

Earthquakes are the result of the movement of energy through Earth as seismic waves. There are two kinds of seismic waves, body waves and surface waves. Each kind of wave travels through Earth in different ways and at different speeds. The speed of a seismic wave depends on the material through which the wave travels.

Body Waves

You are probably familiar with ocean waves or sound waves. Like all waves, seismic waves carry energy. *Body waves* are seismic waves that travel through Earth's interior. P waves, or pressure waves, are the fastest body waves. P waves are also called *primary waves* because they are always the first seismic waves to be detected by instruments that monitor earthquakes. P waves can travel through solids, liquids, and gases. They cause rock to move back and forth in the direction the wave is traveling.

S waves, or shear waves, are a second kind of body wave. S waves move rock from side to side. Unlike P waves, S waves cannot travel through the completely liquid parts of Earth. Also, S waves are slower than P waves. Thus, another name for S waves is *secondary waves*.

© Houghton Mifflin Harcourt Publishing Company

Visualize It!

9 Identify Fill in the labels to identify each type of seismic wave.

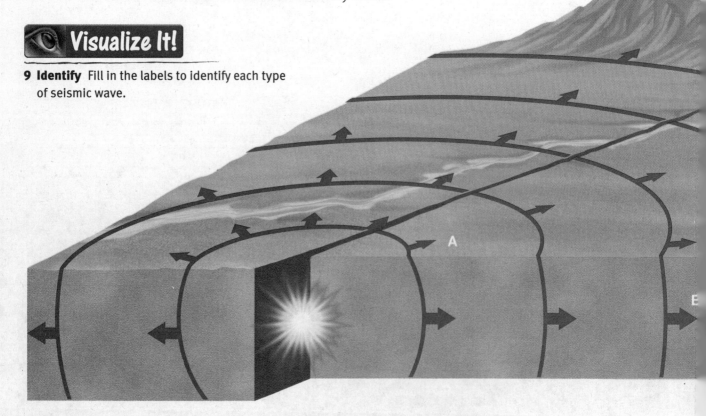

A

E

Surface Waves

Seismic waves that travel along the surface of Earth rather than through it are called *surface waves*. Surface waves produce motion only on Earth's surface. Surface waves are slower than both P and S waves. However, because their energy is focused on Earth's surface, surface waves cause more damage than these body waves.

Surface waves produce two types of ground motion as they move along Earth's surface. The first is a rolling, up-and-down motion that dies out with depth. This motion occurs in the same direction as the direction in which the wave is traveling. Surface waves also produce a back-and-forth motion. This motion is perpendicular to the direction in which the wave is traveling.

10 Compare How do surface waves differ from body waves?

_____

_____

_____

A _____ are the slowest type of wave. They move the ground both up and down, as shown here, and back and forth.

B _____ are the second-fastest type of wave. They cause rock to move side to side.

C _____ are the fastest type of wave. They cause rock to move back and forth.

Wave Action!

How are seismic waves measured?

Imagine walls shaking, windows rattling, and glasses and dishes clinking. After only seconds, the vibrating stops. Within minutes, news reports give information about the strength and the location of the earthquake. How could scientists learn this information so quickly? Scientists use instruments called *seismometers* to record the seismic waves generated by earthquakes. Seismometers are located at seismometer stations that are arranged in networks. When seismic waves reach a seismometer, the seismometer produces a seismogram. A **seismogram** is a tracing of earthquake motion. Seismograms also record the arrival times of seismic waves at a seismometer station. Seismograms are plotted on a graph like the one shown below. Scientists use the graph to pinpoint the location of an earthquake's epicenter.

Seismometers located at seismometer stations produce seismograms that make a tracing of earthquake motion.

 **Do the Math** You Try It

P waves travel faster than S waves and are the first waves to be recorded at a seismometer station. The difference between the arrival times of P waves and S waves is called *lag time*. Lag time increases as the waves travel farther from their point of origin. Lag time can be used to find the distance to an earthquake's epicenter.

Identify

11 Calculate What are the lag times for each of the locations A, B, and C?

Plotting Seismograms on a Time-Distance Graph

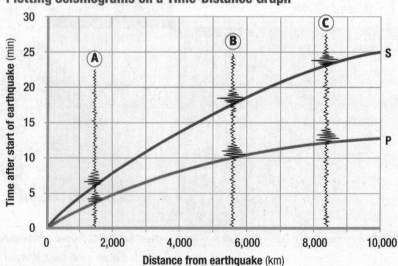

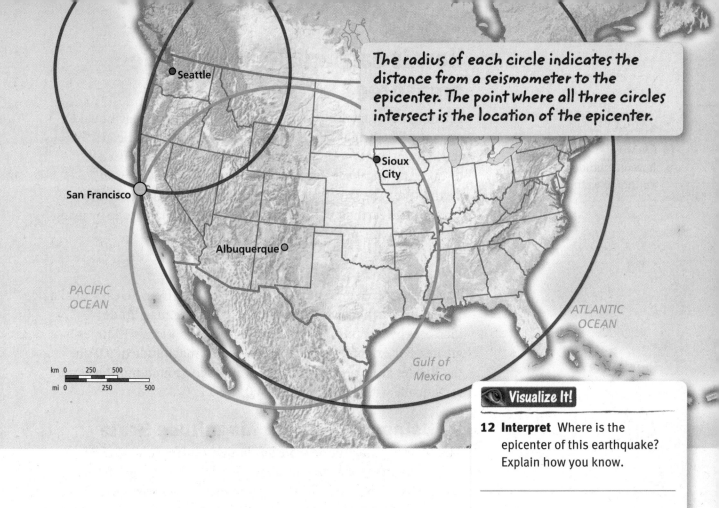

The radius of each circle indicates the distance from a seismometer to the epicenter. The point where all three circles intersect is the location of the epicenter.

Seattle

Sioux City

San Francisco

Albuquerque

PACIFIC OCEAN

ATLANTIC OCEAN

Gulf of Mexico

km 0 250 500
mi 0 250 500

Visualize It!

12 Interpret Where is the epicenter of this earthquake? Explain how you know.

_____

_____

_____

How is an earthquake's epicenter located?

Scientists use the data from seismograms to find an earthquake's epicenter. The S-P time method is an easy way to locate the epicenter of an earthquake. The method is based on the differences in arrival times of P and S waves, called lag time, at different seismometer stations. Lag time tells scientists how far waves have traveled from the epicenter. The epicenter of the earthquake can then be located by drawing circles around at least three seismometer stations on a map, as shown above. The radius of each circle is equal to the distance from that seismometer station to the earthquake's epicenter. The point at which all of the circles intersect is the epicenter. This process is called *triangulation*. Today, computers perform these calculations.

Active Reading **13 Identify** What is the name of the process used to locate an earthquake's epicenter?

_____

_____

Think Outside the Book **Inquiry**

14 Research With a classmate, research recent earthquake activity in your state. Present your findings in an oral report.

How is earthquake magnitude measured?

Seismograms can also provide information about an earthquake's strength. The height of the waves on a seismogram indicates the amount of ground motion. Ground motion can be used to calculate **magnitude**, the measure of energy released by an earthquake. The larger the magnitude of an earthquake is, the stronger the earthquake. Seismologists express magnitude by using the Richter scale or the Moment Magnitude scale.

By Using the Richter Scale

The Richter scale measures the ground motion from an earthquake to find the earthquake's strength. Each time the magnitude increases by one unit, the measured ground motion is 10 times greater. For example, an earthquake with a magnitude of 5.0 on the Richter scale produces 10 times as much ground motion as an earthquake with a magnitude of 4.0.

By Using the Moment Magnitude Scale

The Moment Magnitude scale has largely replaced the Richter scale. Moment magnitude measures earthquake strength based on the size of the area of the fault that moves, the average distance that the fault moves, and the rigidity of the rocks in the fault. The Moment Magnitude scale is more accurate for large earthquakes than the Richter scale is. The moment magnitude of an earthquake is expressed by a number. The larger the number is, the stronger the earthquake was. The largest earthquake ever recorded took place in Chile and registered a moment magnitude of 9.5.

Active Reading

15 Identify As you read, underline how magnitude is related to earthquake strength.

16 Identify After the Chilean earthquake in 1960, which has been the strongest earthquake in the last 100 years?

The 1964 earthquake on Kodiak Island, Alaska, measured 9.2 on the Moment Magnitude scale.

Year	Location	Moment Magnitude
2011	Tōhoku, Japan	9.0
2010	Port-au-Prince, Haiti	7.0
1994	Northridge, California	6.7
1964	Prince William Sound, Alaska	9.2
1960	Southern Chile	9.5

How is earthquake intensity measured?

The effects of an earthquake and how the earthquake is felt by people are known as the earthquake's **intensity**. An earthquake's magnitude is different from its intensity. Magnitude measures how much energy is released by an earthquake. Intensity measures the effects of an earthquake at Earth's surface.

The Modified Mercalli scale is used to describe an earthquake's intensity. The scale ranges from I to XII. Earthquakes that have an intensity value of I are barely noticeable. Earthquakes that have an intensity value of XII cause total destruction. Intensity values vary from place to place and are usually highest near the epicenter of the earthquake.

 Visualize It!

17 Infer Describe the damage that you see in the photograph.

_____

_____

_____

Intensity	Description
I	felt by very few people under especially favorable conditions
II	felt by few people at rest; some suspended items may swing
III	felt by most people indoors; vibrations feel like passing trucks
IV	felt by many people; windows or dishes rattle
V	felt by nearly everyone; some objects are broken or overturned
VI	felt by all people; heavy objects are moved; slight damage to structures
VII	causes slight to moderate damage to buildings; chimneys may topple
VIII	causes considerable damage to ordinary buildings; some partial collapse
IX	causes considerable damage to earthquake-resistant buildings
X	destroys many structures, including foundations; rails are bent
XI	destroys most structures; bridges destroyed; rails are bent
XII	causes total destruction; objects tossed through the air

Not all earthquakes result in catastrophic damage. During this earthquake, only moderate damage occurred.

Damage Control

What factors determine the effects of an earthquake?

The effects of an earthquake can vary over a wide area. Four factors determine the effects of an earthquake on a given area. These factors are magnitude, the local geology, the distance from the epicenter, and the type of construction used in an area.

Magnitude

Recall that an earthquake's magnitude is directly related to its strength. Stronger earthquakes cause more ground motion and, thus, cause more damage than weaker earthquakes. As an earthquake's magnitude increases, the intensity of an earthquake is commonly higher.

Local Geology

The amount of damage caused by an earthquake also depends on the material through which seismic waves travel. In general, solid rock is not likely to increase an earthquake's intensity. However, seismic waves can become more dangerous when they travel through loose soils and sediments that are saturated with water. When water-saturated soil or sediment is shaken by seismic waves, the soil and sediment particles become completely surrounded by water. This process, which is shown below, is called *liquefaction*. Liquefaction can intensify ground shaking or cause the ground to settle. Settling can cause structures to tilt or collapse.

18 Apply Why would it be potentially dangerous to build a home or building on loose soil or sediment?

_____

_____

_____

Grains in silty or sandy soils are normally in contact with one another, which gives the soil strength and stiffness.

When ground shaking occurs, the grains lose contact with one another, and the strength of the soil decreases.

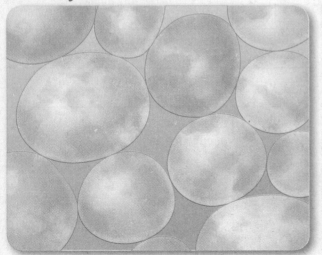

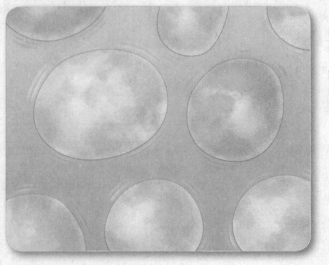

© Houghton Mifflin Harcourt Publishing Company • Image Credits:

Distance from the Epicenter

Surface waves, which move along Earth's surface, are the most destructive of all seismic waves. The more energy a surface wave carries, the stronger the ground motion will be and the more damage the wave will cause. However, surface waves decrease in size and energy the farther that they travel from the epicenter of an earthquake. Therefore, the farther an area is located from the epicenter, the less damage it will suffer.

Building Construction

The materials with which structures are built also determine the amount of earthquake damage. Flexible structures are more likely to survive strong ground shaking. Structures that are made of brick or concrete are not very flexible and are easily damaged. Wood and steel are more flexible. Taller buildings are more susceptible to damage than shorter buildings. This diagram shows technologies in use that control how much tall buildings sway during earthquakes. Other technologies are designed to prevent seismic waves from moving through buildings.

 Visualize It!

19 Apply How are mass dampers and active tendon systems similar in the way they protect a building from earthquake damage?

_____

_____

_____

_____

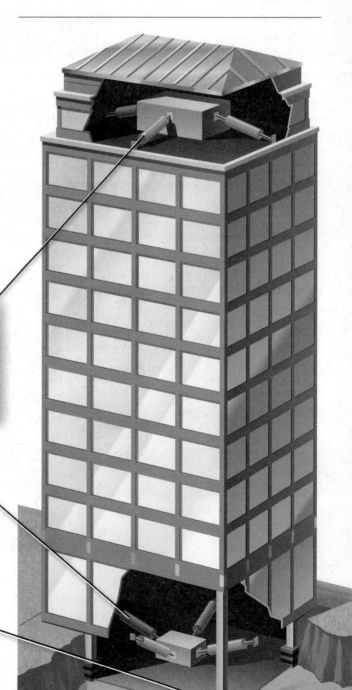

A **mass damper** is a weight placed in the roof of a building. Motion sensors detect building movement during an earthquake and send messages to a computer. The computer then signals controls in the roof to shift the mass damper to counteract the building's movement.

The **active tendon system** works much like the mass damper system in the roof. Sensors notify a computer that the building is moving. Then the computer activates devices to shift a large weight to counteract the movement.

Base isolators act as shock absorbers during an earthquake. They are made of layers of rubber and steel wrapped around a lead core. Base isolators absorb seismic waves and prevent the waves from traveling through the building.

Visual Summary

To complete this summary, fill in the blanks. Then use the key below to check your answers. You can use this page to review the main concepts of the lesson.

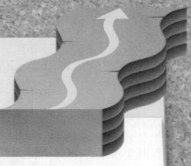

Seismic waves are vibrations that cause ground motion during earthquakes.

20 Seismic waves are caused by
_____
traveling through rock.

Magnitude is a measure of the energy released by an earthquake.

21 An earthquake's magnitude can be measured using the
_____

and the
_____
_____

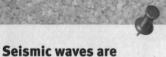

Measuring Earthquake Waves

Seismic waves are measured by instruments.

22 Instruments called
_____
are used to record the arrival times of P waves and S waves.

Different factors determine the effects of earthquakes.

23 The effects of an earthquake are determined by the earthquake's magnitude, _____,
distance from the _____,
and _____

Answers: 20 energy; 21 Richter scale, Moment Magnitude scale; 22 seismometers;
23 local geology, epicenter, building construction

24 **Evaluate** How many seismometers are needed to determine the location of the epicenter of an earthquake? Explain.

Lesson Review

Vocabulary

Fill in the blank with the term that best completes the following sentences.

1 The tracings of seismometers are called

_____

2 An earthquake's _____ is located directly above its _____

3 The _____ of an earthquake is a measure of its strength.

Key Concepts

4 Summarize What causes an earthquake?

_____

_____

_____

_____

5 Contrast How is the motion of P waves different from the motion of S waves?

_____

_____

_____

_____

6 Compare What is the difference between earthquake magnitude and intensity?

_____

_____

_____

_____

_____

7 Explain How is distance from the epicenter related to the amount of earthquake damage?

_____

_____

_____

_____

Critical Thinking

Use the time-distance graph to answer the following questions.

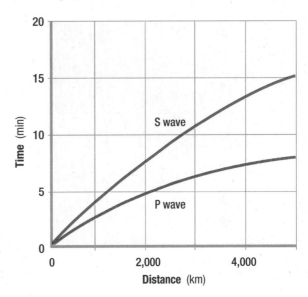

8 Identify What is the lag time at 2,000 km from the earthquake's epicenter?

_____

9 Calculate The average speed of P waves is 6.1 km/s, and the average speed of S waves is 4.1 km/s. Use the following equation to calculate how long each wave type takes to travel 100 km: 100 km ÷ average speed of the wave = time.

_____

_____

_____

10 Calculate Find the lag time for earthquake waves at 100 km by subtracting the time P waves take to travel 100 km from the time S waves take to travel 100 km.

_____

_____

11 Assess Why would surface waves be more damaging to buildings than P waves or S waves?

_____

_____

_____

_____

My Notes

Unit 4 ⟨Big Idea⟩ The movement of tectonic plates accounts for important features of Earth's surface and for major geologic events.

Lesson 1
ESSENTIAL QUESTION
What are Earth's layers?

Identify Earth's compositional and physical layers and describe their properties.

Lesson 4
ESSENTIAL QUESTION
How do volcanoes change Earth's surface?

Describe what the various kinds of volcanoes and eruptions are, where they occur, how they form, and how they change Earth's surface.

Lesson 2
ESSENTIAL QUESTION
What is plate tectonics?

Explain the theory of plate tectonics and plate movement, and identify the geologic events caused by this.

Lesson 5
ESSENTIAL QUESTION
Why do earthquakes happen?

Describe the causes of earthquakes and identify where earthquakes happen.

Lesson 3
ESSENTIAL QUESTION
How do mountains form?

Describe how the movement of Earth's tectonic plates causes mountain building.

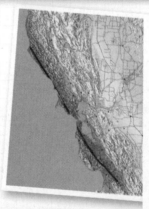

Lesson 6
ESSENTIAL QUESTION
How are seismic waves used to study earthquakes?

Understand how seismic waves are useful in determining the strength, location, and effects of an earthquake.

Connect ESSENTIAL QUESTIONS
Lessons 2 and 5

1 Synthesize Explain why tectonic plate boundaries are areas of intense geological activity.

_____

_____

_____

_____

Think Outside the Book

2 Synthesize Choose one of these activities to help synthesize what you have learned in this unit.

☐ Using what you learned in lessons 2, 3, 4, and 5, prepare a poster presentation that summarizes plate tectonic activity at convergent boundaries.

☐ Using what you learned in lessons 2, 3, and 5 prepare a poster presentation that summarizes plate tectonics at divergent boundaries.

Name _____

Vocabulary

Fill in each blank with the term that best completes the following sentences.

1 The hot, convecting _____ is the layer of rock between the Earth's crust and core.

2 _____ is the theory that explains how large pieces of Earth's outermost layer move and change shape.

3 _____ is the bending of rock layers due to stress.

4 A(n) _____ is a vent or fissure in the Earth's surface through which magma and gases are expelled.

5 A(n) _____ is a movement or trembling of the ground that is caused by a sudden release of energy when rocks move along a fault.

Key Concepts

Read each question below, and circle the best answer.

6 What is the difference between lava and magma?

A Magma is found above Earth's surface and lava is found below Earth's surface.

B Lava is a solid material and magma is a liquid material.

C Magma is found below Earth's surface and lava is found above Earth's surface.

D Magma only erupts in the ocean and lava only erupts on land.

7 Tectonic plates are made of continental crust, oceanic crust, or a combination of the two. Besides their locations, how else are these two kinds of crust different?

A Tectonic plates made of continental crust are larger than plates made of oceanic crust.

B Tectonic plates made of continental crust are smaller than plates made of oceanic crust.

C Continental crust is thicker than oceanic crust.

D Continental crust is thinner than oceanic crust.

8 In the diagram below, an earthquake is taking place.

Cross Section of Lithosphere during an Earthquake

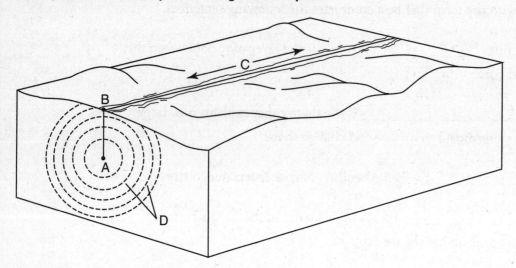

Where is the focus of the earthquake located?

A Point A

B Point B

C along the line labeled C

D along the series of circles labeled D

9 Volcanic eruptions can have many characteristics. They can be slow, fast, calm, explosive, or a combination of these. Which type of eruption is associated with the release of pyroclastic materials?

A a calm eruption

B an explosive eruption

C a fast eruption

D a slow eruption

10 What happens at a divergent tectonic plate boundary?

A Two tectonic plates move horizontally past one another.

B Two tectonic plates pull away from each other, forming a rift valley or mid-ocean ridge.

C Two tectonic plates come together to form one plate.

D Two tectonic plates collide, causing subduction.

11 A major tsunami occurred in the Indian Ocean on December 26, 2004 resulting in the loss of thousands of lives. The tsunami was caused by a major earthquake that originated below the point on the map on the ocean floor. The dashed lines on the map indicate the path of the tsunami's waves.

December 2004 Tsunami

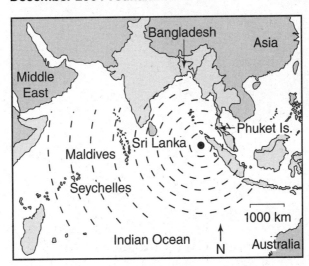

What term refers to the point on the ocean's surface indicated by the dot at the center of the waves?

A fault boundary

C earthquake epicenter

B earthquake focus

D tectonic plate boundary

12 Which of the following is a major difference between Earth's inner core and Earth's outer core?

A The inner core is liquid and the outer core is solid.

B The inner core is solid and the outer core is liquid.

C The inner core is gas and the outer core is solid.

D The inner core is solid and the outer core is gas.

13 Volcanic islands can form over hot spots. The Hawaiian Islands started forming over a hot spot in the Pacific Ocean millions of years ago. What process causes the hot, solid rock to rise through the mantle at these locations?

A condensation

C convection

B conduction

D radiation

14 Earth's three compositional layers are the mantle, core, and crust.

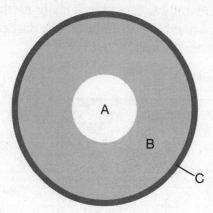

Which statement below is correct?

A A is the crust, B is the core, and C is the mantle.

B A is the core, B is the mantle, and C is the crust.

C A is the inner core, B is the outer core, and C is the mantle.

D A is the core, B is the crust, and C is the mantle.

15 Earth can be divided into five layers: lithosphere, asthenosphere, mesosphere, outer core, and inner core. Which properties are used to make these divisions?

A compositional properties   **C** chemical properties

B physical properties   **D** elemental properties

16 This diagram shows the formation of a fault-block mountain. Arrows outside of the blocks show the directions of force. Arrows inside the blocks show the directions of movement. The blocks *K* and *L* move along a line marked *J*.

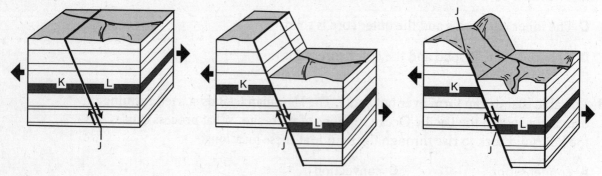

What does the line marked by the letter *J* represent?

A a river   **C** the fault line

B a rock layer   **D** the focus

17 The map below shows the epicenters of some major earthquakes of 2003.

Locations of Major Earthquakes in 2003

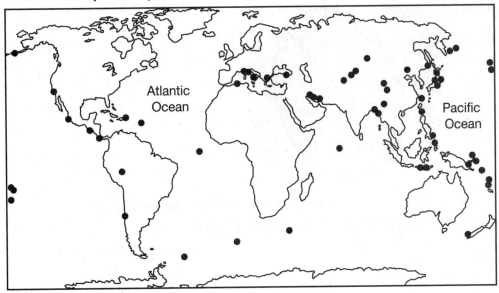

What is the most likely reason that there were no major earthquakes recorded in the interior of the continent of Africa?

A There are no faults in Africa.

B The landmass of Africa is too large to be affected by earthquakes.

C The plate boundary inside Africa is too small to form earthquakes.

D No major plate boundaries cut through the continent of Africa.

Critical Thinking

Answer the following questions in the space provided.

18 Explain how a convergent boundary is different from a transform boundary. Then, name one thing that commonly occurs along both convergent boundaries and transform boundaries.

_____

_____

_____

_____

_____

_____

19 The diagram below shows the five physical layers of Earth.

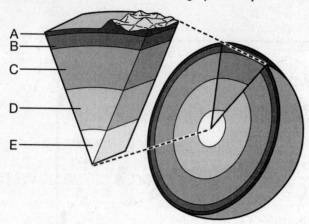

Identify the physical layers A, B, and C. Describe the relationship between these layers and how it is important to understanding plate tectonics.

_____

_____

_____

_____

20 Explain the difference between the Richter scale and the Moment Magnitude scale. Why might measurements from the Richter Scale be misleading to someone who does not know how it works?

_____

_____

_____

_____

Connect **ESSENTIAL QUESTIONS**
Lessons 3 and 4

Answer the following question in the space provided.

21 Explain how forces from tectonic plate movement can build these three types of mountains: folded mountains, fault-block mountains, and volcanic mountains.

_____

_____

_____

_____

_____

⟨Technology⟩
and ⟨Coding⟩

This breathtaking image of Earth was taken from the International Space Station, an international laboratory orbiting Earth. The operation of the International Space Station is controlled by 52 computers and millions of lines of computer code. Its many high-tech features include solar panels that power the laboratory and a human-like robotic astronaut.

This is Robonaut 2, a robot designed to do routine maintenance at the International Space Station.

Data Driven

What is computer science?

If you like computer technology and learning about how computers work, computer science might be for you. *Computer science* is the study of computer technology and how data is processed, stored, and accessed by computers. Computer science is an important part of many other areas, including science, math, engineering, robotics, medicine, game design, and 3D animation.

Computer technology is often described in terms of *hardware*, which are the physical components, and *software*, which are the programs or instructions that a computer runs. Computer scientists must understand how hardware and software work together. Computer scientists may develop new kinds of useful computer software. Or they may work with engineers to improve existing computer hardware.

The first electronic computer, the computer ENIAC (Electronic Numerical Integrator And Computer) was developed at the University of Pennsylvania in 1946.

The integrated circuit (IC), first developed in the 1950s, was instrumental in the development of small computer components.

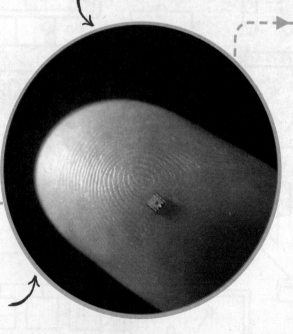

The development of the IC made it possible to reduce the overall size of computers and their components and to increase their processing speed.

How has computer technology changed over time?

Modern digital computer technology is less than 100 years old. Yet in that short amount of time, it has advanced rapidly. The earliest digital computers could perform only a limited number of tasks and were the size of an entire room. Over the decades, engineers continued to develop smaller, faster, and more powerful computers. Today's computers can process hundreds of millions of instructions per second!

Computer scientists and engineers think about what people want or need from computer technology. The most advanced hardware is not useful if people do not know how to use it. So computer scientists and engineers work to create software that is reliable, useful, and easy to use. Today's tablet computers, cell phones, and video game consoles can be used without any special training.

Advances in digital computer technology have help make computers cheaper and easier to operate, which has allowed many more people to work and play with them.

1 **Compare** Are modern computers simpler or more complex than early computers? Explain.

_____

_____

Computer Logic

What do computer scientists do?

Many people enjoy developing computer technology for fun. Learning how to create mobile phone games or Internet-enabled gadgets can be rewarding hobbies. For some people, that hobby may one day become a career in computer science. Working in computer science is a bit like solving a puzzle. Applying knowledge of how computers work to solve real-world problems requires collaboration, creativity, and logical step-by-step thinking.

This is a kayak folded up.

They collaborate across many disciplines

Computers are valuable tools in math and science because they can perform complex calculations very quickly. Computers are useful to many other fields, too. For example, animators use computer technology to create realistic lighting effects in 3D animated films. Mechanics use computers to diagnose problems in car systems. For every field that relies on special software or computer technology, there is an opportunity for computer scientists and engineers to collaborate and develop solutions for those computing needs. Computer scientists must be able to define and understand the problems presented to them and to communicate and work with experts in other fields to develop the solutions.

Computational origami is a computer program used to model the ways in which different materials, including paper, can be folded. It combines computer science and the art of paper folding to create new technologies, such as this kayak.

Tracking software helps biologists study animal behavior.

satellite

satellite data receiving center

satellite data processing center

transmitter

They help solve real-world problems

Some computer scientists carry out theoretical research. Others apply computer science concepts to develop software. Theoretical computer science and practical software development help solve real-world problems. For example, biologists need ways to safely and accurately track endangered animals. Computer science theories on artificial intelligence and pattern recognition have been applied to advanced animal-tracking technologies, such as satellite transmitters and aerial cameras. New kinds of image processing software now allow biologists to analyze the collected data in different ways.

They use logical, step-by-step thinking

Computers perform tasks given to them, and they do this very well. But in order to get the results they expect, computer scientists and programmers must write very accurate instructions. Computer science and programming requires logical thinking, deductive reasoning, and a good understanding of cause-and-effect relationships. When designing software, computer scientists must consider every possible user action and how the computer should respond to each action.

2 Explain How is computer science helping this scientist do her research?

_____

_____

_____

_____

Transmitters can be attached to animals to help track their movements.

Up to <Code>

How is computer software created?

Imagine that you are using a computer at the library to learn more about the history of electronic music. You use the library's database application to start searching for Internet resources. You also do a search to look for audio recordings. Finally, you open a word processor to take notes on the computer. Perhaps without realizing it, you've used many different pieces of software. Have you ever wondered how computer software is created?

Computer software is designed to address a need

Computer software can help us to learn more about our world. It can be useful to business. Or it can simply entertain us. Whatever its purpose, computer software should fulfill some human want or need. The first steps in creating software are precisely defining the need or want being addressed and planning how the software will work.

Computer software source code is written in a programming language

The instructions that tell a computer how to run video games, word processors, and other kinds of software are not written in a human language. They are written in a special programming language, or *code*. Javascript, C++, and Python are examples of programming languages. Programming languages—like human languages—must follow certain rules in order to be understood by the computer. A series of instructions written in a programming language is called *source code*.

Identifying what need a computer program addresses is one of the first development steps.

Source code is revised

Sometimes, programmers make mistakes in their code. Many programming environments have a feature that alerts the programmer to certain errors, such as spelling mistakes in commands, missing portions of code, or logical errors in the sequence of instructions. However, many mistakes go undetected, too. Some errors may cause the program to function incorrectly or not at all. When this happens, the programmer must identify the error, correct it, and test the software again.

Computer software is user tested, and revised

Once the software is created, it must be tested thoroughly to make sure it does not fail or behave in unexpected ways. It must also be tested to ensure that it meets users' needs. The creators of a piece of software might observe how people use it. Or they might ask users to provide feedback on certain features and test the software again.

3 Identify This source code contains an error. Infer where the error is located. What does this code "tell" the computer to do? Write your answers below.

_____

_____

_____

_____

```
13
14   # Scores are not tied, so check
15   # which player wins the round
16 ▾ if player1_score > player2_score:
17       print ("Player 1 wins!")
18 ▾ else:
19       prnt ("Player 2 wins!")
20


! Syntax error, line 19
```

Test running a program is important for finding and fixing errors in the code.

Play it Safe

How should I work with computers?

It is easy to lose track of time when you're sitting in front of a computer or game console. It's also easy to forget that things you say or do online can be seen and shared by many different people. Here are some tips for using computers safely and responsibly.

✓ Maintain good posture

Time can pass by quickly when you are working on a computer or another device. Balance computer time with other activities, including plenty of physical activity. When you are sitting at a computer, sit upright with your shoulders relaxed. Your eyes should be level with the top of the monitor and your feet should be flat on the ground.

✓ Observe electrical safety

Building your own electronics projects can be fun, but it's important to have an understanding of circuits and electrical safety first. Otherwise, you could damage your components or hurt yourself. The potential for an electrical shock is real when you open up a computer, work with frayed cords or, use ungrounded plugs or attempt to replace parts without understanding how to do so safely. Ask an adult for help before starting any projects. Also, avoid using a connected computer during thunderstorms.

head and neck in a straight, neutral position

shoulders are relaxed

wrists are straight

feet are flat on the ground

Good posture will help you avoid the aches and injuries related to sitting in front of a computer for a long time.

✓ Handle and maintain computers properly

Be cautious when handling and transporting electronic devices. Dropping them or spilling liquids on them could cause serious damage. Keep computers away from dirt, dust, liquids, and moisture. Never use wet cleaning products unless they are specifically designed for use on electronics. Microfiber cloths can be used to clear smudges from device screens. Spilled liquids can cause circuits to short out and hardware to corrode. If a liquid spills on a device, unplug it and switch it off immediately, remove the battery and wipe up as much of the liquid inside the device as possible. Don't switch the device back on until it is completely dry.

✓ Do not post private information online

Talk to your family about rules for Internet use. Do not use the Internet to share private information such as photographs, your phone number, or your address. Do not respond to requests for personal details from people you do not know.

✓ Treat yourself and others with respect

It is important to treat others with respect when on the Internet. Don't send or post messages online that you wouldn't say to someone in person. Unfortunately, not everyone acts respectfully while online. Some people may say hurtful things to you or send you unwanted messages. Do not reply to unwanted messages. Alert a trusted adult to any forms of contact, such as messages or photos, that make you feel uncomfortable.

4 Apply Fill in the chart below with a suitable response to each scenario.

SCENARIO	YOUR RESPONSE
You receive a text message from an online store asking for your home address.	
You've been lying down in front of a laptop, and you notice that your neck is feeling a little sore.	
You need to take a laptop computer with you on your walk to school.	
You want to try assembling a robotics kit with a friend.	
Someone posts unfriendly comments directed at you.	

Career in Computing:
Game Programmer

What do video game programmers do?

Creating your own universe with its own set of rules is fun. Just ask a programmer who works on video games!

What skills are needed in game programming?

A programmer should know how to write code, but there are other important skills a programmer needs as well. An understanding of physics and math is important for calculating how objects move and interact in a game. Game programmers usually work on a team with other people, such as artists, designers, writers, and musicians. They must be able to communicate effectively, and ideally, the programmer should understand the other team members' roles.

How can I get started with game development?

You don't need a big budget or years of experience to try it out. There are books, videos, and websites that can help you get started. When you're first experimenting with game development, start small. Try making a very simple game like Tic-Tac-Toe. Once you've mastered that, you can try something more complex.

5 Brainstorm Why would working on a team be important to the game development process?

_____

_____

_____

Look It Up!

References R2
Mineral Properties R2
Geologic Time Scale R4
Star Charts for the Northern Hemisphere R6
World Map R8
Classification of Living Things R10
Periodic Table of the Elements R12
Physical Science Refresher R14
Physical Laws and Useful Equations R16

Reading and Study Skills R18
A How-To Manual for Active Reading R18
Using Graphic Organizers to Take Notes R20
Using Vocabulary Strategies R24

Science Skills R26
Safety in the Lab R26
Designing, Conducting, and Reporting an Experiment R28
Using a Microscope R35
Measuring Accurately R36
Using the Metric System and SI Units R39

Math Refresher R41
Performing Calculations R41
Making and Interpreting Graphs R46

References

Mineral Properties

Here are five steps to take in mineral identification:

1 Determine the color of the mineral. Is it light-colored, dark-colored, or a specific color?

2 Determine the luster of the mineral. Is it metallic or non-metallic?

3 Determine the color of any powder left by its streak.

4 Determine the hardness of your mineral. Is it soft, hard, or very hard? Using a glass plate, see if the mineral scratches it.

5 Determine whether your sample has cleavage or any special properties.

TERMS TO KNOW	DEFINITION
adamantine	a non-metallic luster like that of a diamond
cleavage	how a mineral breaks when subject to stress on a particular plane
luster	the state or quality of shining by reflecting light
streak	the color of a mineral when it is powdered
submetallic	between metallic and nonmetallic in luster
vitreous	glass-like type of luster

Silicate Minerals					
Mineral	**Color**	**Luster**	**Streak**	**Hardness**	**Cleavage and Special Properties**
Beryl	deep green, pink, white, bluish green, or yellow	vitreous	white	7.5–8	1 cleavage direction; some varieties fluoresce in ultraviolet light
Chlorite	green	vitreous to pearly	pale green	2–2.5	1 cleavage direction
Garnet	green, red, brown, black	vitreous	white	6.5–7.5	no cleavage
Hornblende	dark green, brown, or black	vitreous	none	5–6	2 cleavage directions
Muscovite	colorless, silvery white, or brown	vitreous or pearly	white	2–2.5	1 cleavage direction
Olivine	olive green, yellow	vitreous	white or none	6.5–7	no cleavage
Orthoclase	colorless, white, pink, or other colors	vitreous	white or none	6	2 cleavage directions
Plagioclase	colorless, white, yellow, pink, green	vitreous	white	6	2 cleavage directions
Quartz	colorless or white; any color when not pure	vitreous or waxy	white or none	7	no cleavage

Nonsilicate Minerals

Mineral	Color	Luster	Streak	Hardness	Cleavage and Special Properties
Native Elements					
Copper	copper-red	metallic	copper-red	2.5–3	no cleavage
Diamond	pale yellow or colorless	adamantine	none	10	4 cleavage directions
Graphite	black to gray	submetallic	black	1–2	1 cleavage direction
Carbonates					
Aragonite	colorless, white, or pale yellow	vitreous	white	3.5–4	2 cleavage directions; reacts with hydrochloric acid
Calcite	colorless or white to tan	vitreous	white	3	3 cleavage directions; reacts with weak acid; double refraction
Halides					
Fluorite	light green, yellow, purple, bluish green, or other colors	vitreous	none	4	4 cleavage directions; some varieties fluoresce
Halite	white	vitreous	white	2.0–2.5	3 cleavage directions
Oxides					
Hematite	reddish brown to black	metallic to earthy	dark red to red-brown	5.6–6.5	no cleavage; magnetic when heated
Magnetite	iron-black	metallic	black	5.5–6.5	no cleavage; magnetic
Sulfates					
Anhydrite	colorless, bluish, or violet	vitreous to pearly	white	3–3.5	3 cleavage directions
Gypsum	white, pink, gray, or colorless	vitreous, pearly, or silky	white	2.0	3 cleavage directions
Sulfides					
Galena	lead-gray	metallic	lead-gray to black	2.5–2.8	3 cleavage directions
Pyrite	brassy yellow	metallic	greenish, brownish, or black	6–6.5	no cleavage

References

Geologic Time Scale

Geologists developed the geologic time scale to represent the 4.6 billion years of Earth's history that have passed since Earth formed. This scale divides Earth's history into blocks of time. The boundaries between these time intervals (shown in millions of years ago or mya in the table below), represent major changes in Earth's history. Some boundaries are defined by mass extinctions, major changes in Earth's surface, and/or major changes in Earth's climate.

The four major divisions that encompass the history of life on Earth are Precambrian time, the Paleozoic era, the Mesozoic era, and the Cenozoic era. The largest divisions are eons. **Precambrian time** is made up of the first three eons, over 4 billion years of Earth's history.

The **Paleozoic era** lasted from 542 mya to 251 mya. All major plant groups, except flowering plants, appeared during this era. By the end of the era, reptiles, winged insects, and fishes had also appeared. The largest known mass extinction occurred at the end of this era.

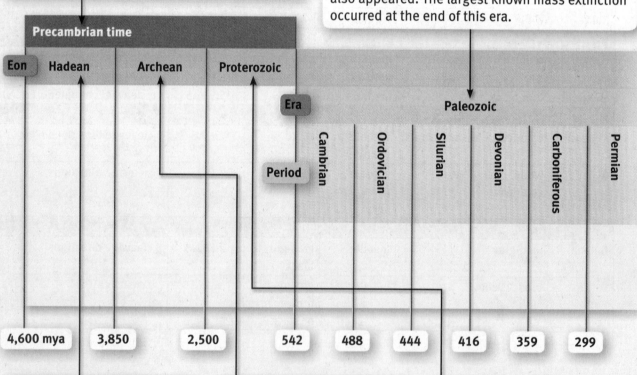

The **Hadean eon** lasted from about 4.6 billion years ago (bya) to 3.85 bya. It is described based on evidence from meteorites and rocks from the moon.

The **Archean eon** lasted from 3.85 bya to 2.5 bya. The earliest rocks from Earth that have been found and dated formed at the start of this eon.

The **Proterozoic eon** lasted from 2.5 bya to 542 mya. The first organisms, which were single-celled organisms, appeared during this eon. These organisms produced so much oxygen that they changed Earth's oceans and Earth's atmosphere.

Divisions of Time

The divisions of time shown here represent major changes in Earth's surface and when life developed and changed significantly on Earth. As new evidence is found, the boundaries of these divisions may shift. The Phanerozoic eon is divided into three eras. The beginning of each of these eras represents a change in the types of organisms that dominated Earth. And, each era is commonly characterized by the types of organisms that dominated the era. These eras are divided into periods, and periods are divided into epochs.

The **Mesozoic era** lasted from 251 mya to 65.5 mya. During this era, many kinds of dinosaurs dominated land, and giant lizards swam in the ocean. The first birds, mammals, and flowering plants also appeared during this time. About two-thirds of all land species went extinct at the end of this era.

The **Phanerozoic eon** began 542 mya. We live in this eon.

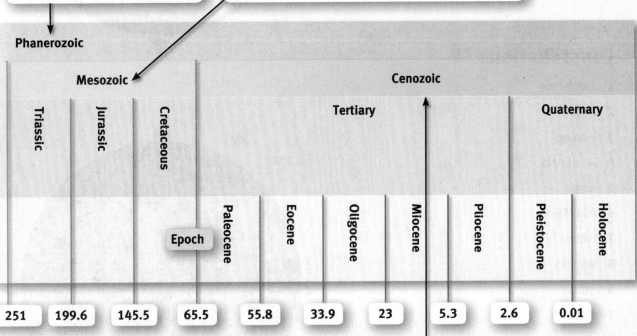

Phanerozoic

Mesozoic | Cenozoic

Triassic | Jurassic | Cretaceous | Tertiary | Quaternary

Epoch | Paleocene | Eocene | Oligocene | Miocene | Pliocene | Pleistocene | Holocene

251 | 199.6 | 145.5 | 65.5 | 55.8 | 33.9 | 23 | 5.3 | 2.6 | 0.01

The **Cenozoic era** began 65.5 mya and continues today. Mammals dominate this era. During the Mesozoic era, mammals were small in size but grew much larger during the Cenozoic era. Primates, including humans, appeared during this era.

References

Star Charts for the Northern Hemisphere

A star chart is a map of the stars in the night sky. It shows the names and positions of constellations and major stars. Star charts can be used to identify constellations and even to orient yourself using Polaris, the North Star.

Because Earth moves through space, different constellations are visible at different times of the year. The star charts on these pages show the constellations visible during each season in the Northern Hemisphere.

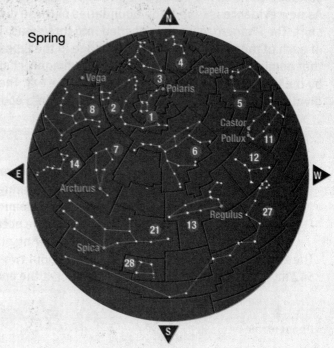

Spring

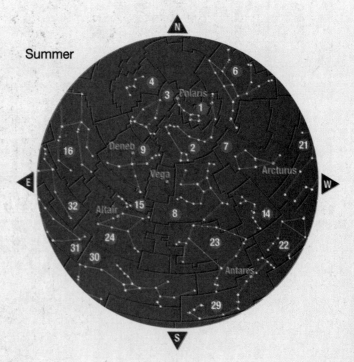

Summer

Constellations

1 Ursa Minor

2 Draco

3 Cepheus

4 Cassiopeia

5 Auriga

6 Ursa Major

7 Boötes

8 Hercules

9 Cygnus

10 Perseus

11 Gemini

12 Cancer

13 Leo

14 Serpens

15 Sagitta

16 Pegasus

17 Pisces

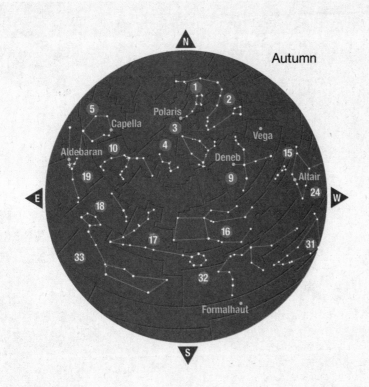

Autumn

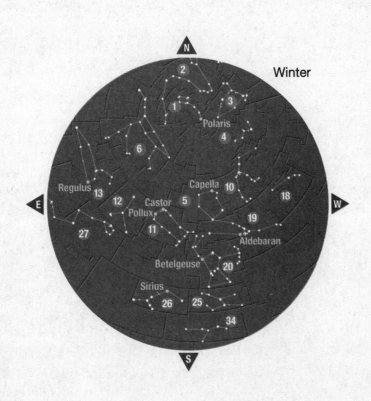

Winter

Constellations

18 Aries

19 Taurus

20 Orion

21 Virgo

22 Libra

23 Ophiuchus

24 Aquila

25 Lepus

26 Canis Major

27 Hydra

28 Corvus

29 Scorpius

30 Sagittarius

31 Capricornus

32 Aquarius

33 Cetus

34 Columba

World Map

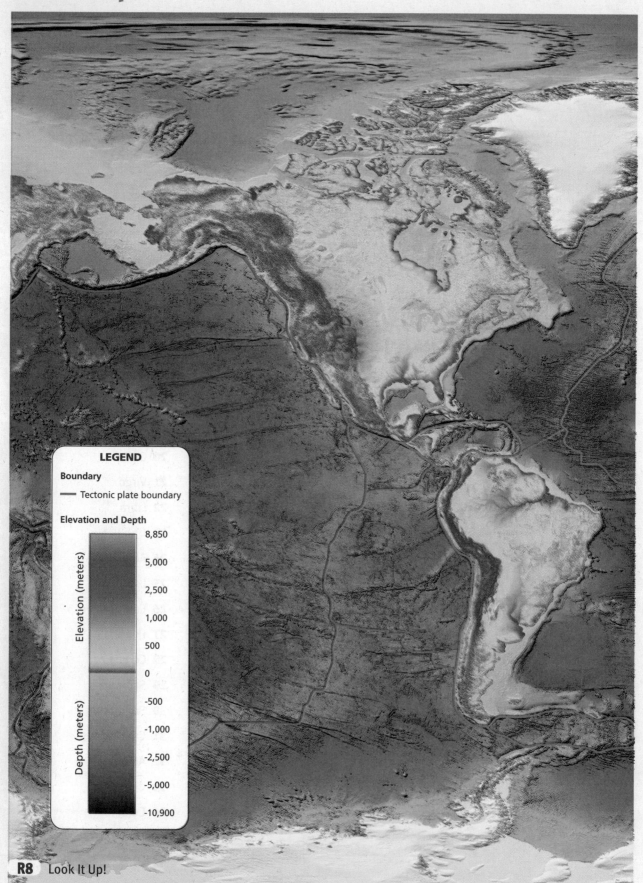

LEGEND

Boundary

—— Tectonic plate boundary

Elevation and Depth

Elevation (meters)

8,850
5,000
2,500
1,000
500
0

Depth (meters)

-500
-1,000
-2,500
-5,000
-10,900

References

Classification of Living Things

Domains and Kingdoms

All organisms belong to one of three domains: Domain Archaea, Domain Bacteria, or Domain Eukarya. Some of the groups within these domains are shown below. (Remember that genus names are italicized.)

Domain Archaea

The organisms in this domain are single-celled prokaryotes, many of which live in extreme environments.

Archaea		
Group	**Example**	**Characteristics**
Methanogens	*Methanococcus*	produce methane gas; can't live in oxygen
Thermophiles	*Sulpholobus*	require sulphur; can't live in oxygen
Halophiles	*Halococcus*	live in very salty environments; most can live in oxygen

Domain Bacteria

Organisms in this domain are single-celled prokaryotes and are found in almost every environment on Earth.

Bacteria		
Group	**Example**	**Characteristics**
Bacilli	*Escherichia*	rod shaped; some bacilli fix nitrogen; some cause disease
Cocci	*Streptococcus*	spherical shaped; some cause disease; can form spores
Spirilla	*Treponema*	spiral shaped; cause diseases such as syphilis and Lyme disease

Domain Eukarya

Organisms in this domain are single-celled or multicellular eukaryotes.

Kingdom Protista Many protists resemble fungi, plants, or animals, but are smaller and simpler in structure. Most are single celled.

Protists		
Group	**Example**	**Characteristics**
Sarcodines	*Amoeba*	radiolarians; single-celled consumers
Ciliates	*Paramecium*	single-celled consumers
Flagellates	*Trypanosoma*	single-celled parasites
Sporozoans	*Plasmodium*	single-celled parasites
Euglenas	*Euglena*	single celled; photosynthesize
Diatoms	*Pinnularia*	most are single celled; photosynthesize
Dinoflagellates	*Gymnodinium*	single celled; some photosynthesize
Algae	*Volvox*	single celled or multicellular; photosynthesize
Slime molds	*Physarum*	single celled or multicellular; consumers or decomposers
Water molds	powdery mildew	single celled or multicellular; parasites or decomposers

Kingdom Fungi Most fungi are multicellular. Their cells have thick cell walls. Fungi absorb food from their environment.

Fungi		
Group	**Examples**	**Characteristics**
Threadlike fungi	bread mold	spherical; decomposers
Sac fungi	yeast; morels	saclike; parasites and decomposers
Club fungi	mushrooms; rusts; smuts	club shaped; parasites and decomposers
Lichens	British soldier	a partnership between a fungus and an alga

Kingdom Plantae Plants are multicellular and have cell walls made of cellulose. Plants make their own food through photosynthesis. Plants are classified into divisions instead of phyla.

Plants		
Group	**Examples**	**Characteristics**
Bryophytes	mosses; liverworts	no vascular tissue; reproduce by spores
Club mosses	*Lycopodium;* ground pine	grow in wooded areas; reproduce by spores
Horsetails	rushes	grow in wetland areas; reproduce by spores
Ferns	spleenworts; sensitive fern	large leaves called fronds; reproduce by spores
Conifers	pines; spruces; firs	needlelike leaves; reproduce by seeds made in cones
Cycads	*Zamia*	slow growing; reproduce by seeds made in large cones
Gnetophytes	*Welwitschia*	only three living families; reproduce by seeds
Ginkgoes	*Ginkgo*	only one living species; reproduce by seeds
Angiosperms	all flowering plants	reproduce by seeds made in flowers; fruit

Kingdom Animalia Animals are multicellular. Their cells do not have cell walls. Most animals have specialized tissues and complex organ systems. Animals get food by eating other organisms.

Animals		
Group	**Examples**	**Characteristics**
Sponges	glass sponges	no symmetry or specialized tissues; aquatic
Cnidarians	jellyfish; coral	radial symmetry; aquatic
Flatworms	planaria; tapeworms; flukes	bilateral symmetry; organ systems
Roundworms	*Trichina;* hookworms	bilateral symmetry; organ systems
Annelids	earthworms; leeches	bilateral symmetry; organ systems
Mollusks	snails; octopuses	bilateral symmetry; organ systems
Echinoderms	sea stars; sand dollars	radial symmetry; organ systems
Arthropods	insects; spiders; lobsters	bilateral symmetry; organ systems
Chordates	fish; amphibians; reptiles; birds; mammals	bilateral symmetry; complex organ systems

References

Periodic Table of the Elements

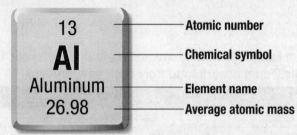

13	Atomic number
Al	Chemical symbol
Aluminum	Element name
26.98	Average atomic mass

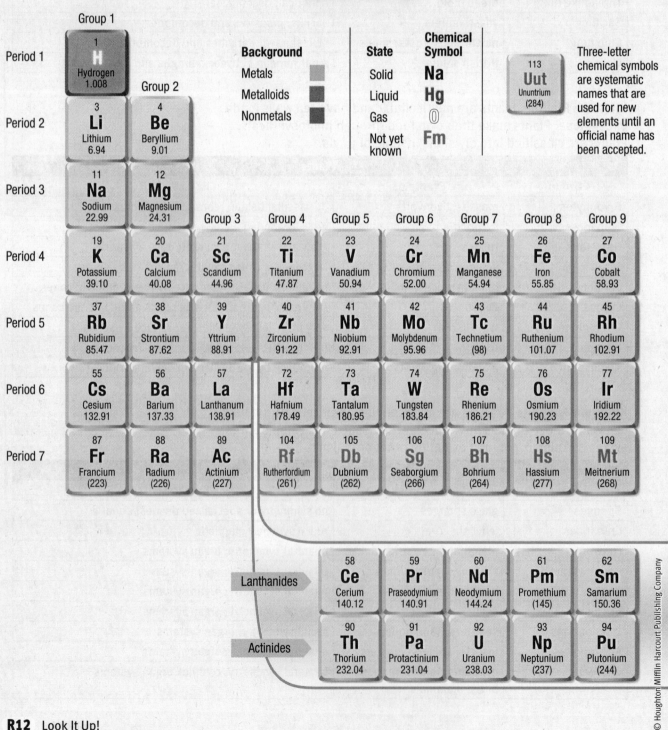

Background
- Metals
- Metalloids
- Nonmetals

State | **Chemical Symbol**
- Solid — **Na**
- Liquid — **Hg**
- Gas — Ⓞ
- Not yet known — **Fm**

113 **Uut** Ununtrium (284)

Three-letter chemical symbols are systematic names that are used for new elements until an official name has been accepted.

Group 1

Period 1
1 **H** Hydrogen 1.008

Group 2

Period 2
3 **Li** Lithium 6.94 | 4 **Be** Beryllium 9.01

Period 3
11 **Na** Sodium 22.99 | 12 **Mg** Magnesium 24.31

Group 3	Group 4	Group 5	Group 6	Group 7	Group 8	Group 9

Period 4
19 **K** Potassium 39.10 | 20 **Ca** Calcium 40.08 | 21 **Sc** Scandium 44.96 | 22 **Ti** Titanium 47.87 | 23 **V** Vanadium 50.94 | 24 **Cr** Chromium 52.00 | 25 **Mn** Manganese 54.94 | 26 **Fe** Iron 55.85 | 27 **Co** Cobalt 58.93

Period 5
37 **Rb** Rubidium 85.47 | 38 **Sr** Strontium 87.62 | 39 **Y** Yttrium 88.91 | 40 **Zr** Zirconium 91.22 | 41 **Nb** Niobium 92.91 | 42 **Mo** Molybdenum 95.96 | 43 **Tc** Technetium (98) | 44 **Ru** Ruthenium 101.07 | 45 **Rh** Rhodium 102.91

Period 6
55 **Cs** Cesium 132.91 | 56 **Ba** Barium 137.33 | 57 **La** Lanthanum 138.91 | 72 **Hf** Hafnium 178.49 | 73 **Ta** Tantalum 180.95 | 74 **W** Tungsten 183.84 | 75 **Re** Rhenium 186.21 | 76 **Os** Osmium 190.23 | 77 **Ir** Iridium 192.22

Period 7
87 **Fr** Francium (223) | 88 **Ra** Radium (226) | 89 **Ac** Actinium (227) | 104 **Rf** Rutherfordium (261) | 105 **Db** Dubnium (262) | 106 **Sg** Seaborgium (266) | 107 **Bh** Bohrium (264) | 108 **Hs** Hassium (277) | 109 **Mt** Meitnerium (268)

Lanthanides
58 **Ce** Cerium 140.12 | 59 **Pr** Praseodymium 140.91 | 60 **Nd** Neodymium 144.24 | 61 **Pm** Promethium (145) | 62 **Sm** Samarium 150.36

Actinides
90 **Th** Thorium 232.04 | 91 **Pa** Protactinium 231.04 | 92 **U** Uranium 238.03 | 93 **Np** Neptunium (237) | 94 **Pu** Plutonium (244)

The International Union of Pure and Applied Chemistry (IUPAC) has determined that, because of isotopic variance, the average atomic mass is best represented by a range of values for each of the following elements: hydrogen, lithium, boron, carbon, nitrogen, oxygen, silicon, sulfur, chlorine, and thallium. However, the values in this table are appropriate for everyday calculations.

Elements with atomic numbers of 95 and above are not known to occur naturally, even in trace amounts. They have only been synthesized in the lab. The physical and chemical properties of elements with atomic numbers 100 and above cannot be predicted with certainty. The states for elements with atomic numbers 100 and above are therefore shown as not yet known.

Group 18
2
He
Helium
4.003

Group 13	Group 14	Group 15	Group 16	Group 17
5	6	7	8	9	10
B	C	N	O	F	Ne
Boron	Carbon	Nitrogen	Oxygen	Fluorine	Neon
10.81	12.01	14.01	16.00	19.00	20.18
13	14	15	16	17	18
Al	Si	P	S	Cl	Ar
Aluminum	Silicon	Phosphorus	Sulfur	Chlorine	Argon
26.98	28.09	30.97	32.06	35.45	39.95

Group 10	Group 11	Group 12					
28	29	30	31	32	33	34	35	36
Ni	Cu	Zn	Ga	Ge	As	Se	Br	Kr
Nickel	Copper	Zinc	Gallium	Germanium	Arsenic	Selenium	Bromine	Krypton
58.69	63.55	65.38	69.72	72.63	74.92	78.96	79.90	83.80
46	47	48	49	50	51	52	53	54
Pd	Ag	Cd	In	Sn	Sb	Te	I	Xe
Palladium	Silver	Cadmium	Indium	Tin	Antimony	Tellurium	Iodine	Xenon
106.42	107.87	112.41	114.82	118.71	121.76	127.60	126.90	131.29
78	79	80	81	82	83	84	85	86
Pt	Au	Hg	Tl	Pb	Bi	Po	At	Rn
Platinum	Gold	Mercury	Thallium	Lead	Bismuth	Polonium	Astatine	Radon
195.08	196.97	200.59	204.38	207.2	208.98	(209)	(210)	(222)
110	111	112	113	114	115	116	117	118
Ds	Rg	Cn	Uut	Fl	Uup	Lv	Uus	Uuo
Darmstadtium	Roentgenium	Copernicium	Ununtrium	Flerovium	Ununpentium	Livermorium	Ununseptium	Ununoctium
(271)	(272)	(285)	(284)	(289)	(288)	(293)	(294)	(294)

63	64	65	66	67	68	69	70	71
Eu	Gd	Tb	Dy	Ho	Er	Tm	Yb	Lu
Europium	Gadolinium	Terbium	Dysprosium	Holmium	Erbium	Thulium	Ytterbium	Lutetium
151.96	157.25	158.93	162.50	164.93	167.26	168.93	173.05	174.97
95	96	97	98	99	100	101	102	103
Am	Cm	Bk	Cf	Es	Fm	Md	No	Lr
Americium	Curium	Berkelium	Californium	Einsteinium	Fermium	Mendelevium	Nobelium	Lawrencium
(243)	(247)	(247)	(251)	(252)	(257)	(258)	(259)	(262)

References

Physical Science Refresher

Atoms and Elements

Every object in the universe is made of matter. **Matter** is anything that takes up space and has mass. All matter is made of atoms. An **atom** is the smallest particle into which an element can be divided and still be the same element. An **element**, in turn, is a substance that cannot be broken down into simpler substances by chemical means. Each element consists of only one kind of atom. An element may be made of many atoms, but they are all the same kind of atom.

Atomic Structure

Atoms are made of smaller particles called **electrons, protons**, and **neutrons**. Electrons have a negative electric charge, protons have a positive charge, and neutrons have no electric charge. Together, protons and neutrons form the **nucleus,** or small dense center, of an atom. Because protons are positively charged and neutrons are neutral, the nucleus has a positive charge. Electrons move within an area around the nucleus called the **electron cloud**. Electrons move so quickly that scientists cannot determine their exact speeds and positions at the same time.

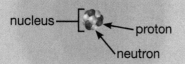

electron cloud

nucleus —— proton

neutron

Atomic Number

To help distinguish one element from another, scientists use the atomic numbers of atoms. The **atomic number** is the number of protons in the nucleus of an atom. The atoms of a certain element always have the same number of protons.

When atoms have an equal number of protons and electrons, they are uncharged, or electrically neutral. The atomic number equals the number of electrons in an uncharged atom. The number of neutrons, however, can vary for a given element. Atoms of the same element that have different numbers of neutrons are called **isotopes**.

Periodic Table of the Elements

In the periodic table, each element in the table is in a separate box. And the elements are arranged from left to right in order of increasing atomic number. That is, an uncharged atom of each element has one more electron and one more proton than an uncharged atom of the element to its left. Each horizontal row of the table is called a **period**. Changes in chemical properties of elements across a period correspond to changes in the electron arrangements of their atoms.

Each vertical column of the table is known as a **group.** A group lists elements with similar physical and chemical properties. For this reason, a group is also sometimes called a family. The elements in a group have similar properties because their atoms have the same number of electrons in their outer energy level. For example, the elements helium, neon, argon, krypton, xenon, and radon all have similar properties and are known as the noble gases.

Molecules and Compounds

When two or more elements join chemically, they form a **compound**. A compound is a new substance with properties different from those of the elements that compose it. For example, water, H_2O, is a compound formed when hydrogen (H) and oxygen (O) combine. The smallest complete unit of a compound that has the properties of that compound is called a **molecule**. A chemical formula indicates the elements in a compound. It also indicates the relative number of atoms of each element in the compound. The chemical formula for water is H_2O. So, each water molecule consists of two atoms of hydrogen and one atom of oxygen. The subscript number after the symbol for an element shows how many atoms of that element are in a single molecule of the compound.

Chemical Equations

A chemical reaction occurs when a chemical change takes place. A chemical equation describes a chemical reaction using chemical formulas. The equation indicates the substances that react and the substances that are produced. For example, when carbon and oxygen combine, they can form carbon dioxide, shown in the equation below: $C + O_2 \longrightarrow CO_2$

Acids, Bases, and pH

An **ion** is an atom or group of chemically bonded atoms that has an electric charge because it has lost or gained one or more electrons. When an acid, such as hydrochloric acid, HCl, is mixed with water, it separates into ions. An **acid** is a compound that produces hydrogen ions, H^+, in water. The hydrogen ions then combine with a water molecule to form a hydronium ion, H_3O^+. A **base**, on the other hand, is a substance that produces hydroxide ions, OH^-, in water.

To determine whether a solution is acidic or basic, scientists use pH. The **pH** of a solution is a measure of the hydronium ion concentration in a solution. The pH scale ranges from 0 to 14. Acids have a pH that is less than 7. The lower the number, the more acidic the solution. The middle point, pH = 7, is neutral, neither acidic nor basic. Bases have a pH that is greater than 7. The higher the number is, the more basic the solution.

The pH of Some Common Materials

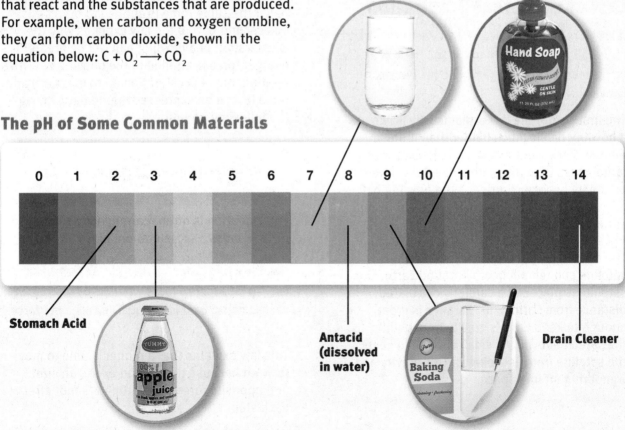

Stomach Acid

Antacid (dissolved in water)

Drain Cleaner

References

Physical Laws and Useful Equations

Law of Conservation of Mass

Mass cannot be created or destroyed during ordinary chemical or physical changes.

The total mass in a closed system is always the same no matter how many physical changes or chemical reactions occur.

Law of Conservation of Energy

Energy can be neither created nor destroyed.

The total amount of energy in a closed system is always the same. Energy can be changed from one form to another, but all of the different forms of energy in a system always add up to the same total amount of energy, no matter how many energy conversions occur.

Law of Universal Gravitation

All objects in the universe attract each other by a force called gravity. The size of the force depends on the masses of the objects and the distance between the objects.

The first part of the law explains why lifting a bowling ball is much harder than lifting a marble. Because the bowling ball has a much larger mass than the marble does, the amount of gravity between Earth and the bowling ball is greater than the amount of gravity between Earth and the marble.

The second part of the law explains why a satellite can remain in orbit around Earth. The satellite is placed at a carefully calculated distance from Earth. This distance is great enough to keep Earth's gravity from pulling the satellite down, yet small enough to keep the satellite from escaping Earth's gravity and wandering off into space.

Newton's Laws of Motion

Newton's first law of motion states that an object at rest remains at rest, and an object in motion remains in motion at constant speed and in a straight line unless acted on by an unbalanced force.

The first part of the law explains why a football will remain on a tee until it is kicked off or until a gust of wind blows it off. The second part of the law explains why a bike rider will continue moving forward after the bike comes to an abrupt stop. Gravity and the friction of the sidewalk will eventually stop the rider.

Newton's second law of motion states that the acceleration of an object depends on the mass of the object and the amount of force applied.

The first part of the law explains why the acceleration of a 4 kg bowling ball will be greater than the acceleration of a 6 kg bowling ball if the same force is applied to both balls. The second part of the law explains why the acceleration of a bowling ball will be greater if a larger force is applied to the bowling ball. The relationship of acceleration (a) to mass (m) and force (F) can be expressed mathematically by the following equation:

$$acceleration = \frac{force}{mass}, \text{ or } a = \frac{F}{m}$$

This equation is often rearranged to read force = mass × acceleration, or $F = m \times a$

Newton's third law of motion states that whenever one object exerts a force on a second object, the second object exerts an equal and opposite force on the first.

This law explains that a runner is able to move forward because the ground exerts an equal and opposite force on the runner's foot after each step.

Average speed

$$\text{average speed} = \frac{\text{total distance}}{\text{total time}}$$

Example:
A bicycle messenger traveled a distance of 136 km in 8 h. What was the messenger's average speed?

$$\frac{136 \text{ km}}{8 \text{ h}} = 17 \text{ km/h}$$

The messenger's average speed was **17 km/h**.

Average acceleration

$$\text{average acceleration} = \frac{\text{final velocity} - \text{starting velocity}}{\text{time it takes to change velocity}}$$

Example:
Calculate the average acceleration of an Olympic 100 m dash sprinter who reached a velocity of 20 m/s south at the finish line. The race was in a straight line and lasted 10 s.

$$\frac{20 \text{ m/s} - 0 \text{ m/s}}{10 \text{ s}} = 2 \text{ m/s/s}$$

The sprinter's average acceleration was **2 m/s/s south.**

Net force
Forces in the Same Direction

When forces are in the same direction, add the forces together to determine the net force.

Example:
Calculate the net force on a stalled car that is being pushed by two people. One person is pushing with a force of 13 N northwest, and the other person is pushing with a force of 8 N in the same direction.

$$13 \text{ N} + 8 \text{ N} = 21 \text{ N}$$

The net force is **21 N northwest**.

Forces in Opposite Directions

When forces are in opposite directions, subtract the smaller force from the larger force to determine the net force. The net force will be in the direction of the larger force.

Example:
Calculate the net force on a rope that is being pulled on each end. One person is pulling on one end of the rope with a force of 12 N south. Another person is pulling on the opposite end of the rope with a force of 7 N north.

$$12 \text{ N} - 7 \text{ N} = 5 \text{ N}$$

The net force is **5 N south.**

Pressure

Pressure is the force exerted over a given area. The SI unit for pressure is the pascal. Its symbol is Pa.

$$\text{pressure} = \frac{\text{force}}{\text{area}}$$

Example:
Calculate the pressure of the air in a soccer ball if the air exerts a force of 10 N over an area of 0.5 m^2.

$$\text{pressure} = \frac{10 \text{N}}{0.5 \text{ m}^2} = \frac{20 \text{N}}{\text{m}^2} = 20 \text{ Pa}$$

The pressure of the air inside the soccer ball is **20 Pa.**

Reading and Study Skills

A How-To Manual for Active Reading

This book belongs to you, and you are invited to write in it. In fact, the book won't be complete until you do. Sometimes you'll answer a question or follow directions to mark up the text. Other times you'll write down your own thoughts. And when you're done reading and writing in the book, the book will be ready to help you review what you learned and prepare for tests.

Active Reading Annotations

Before you read, you'll often come upon an Active Reading prompt that asks you to underline certain words or number the steps in a process. Here's an example.

Active Reading

12 **Identify** In this paragraph, number the sequence of sentences that describe replication.

Marking the text this way is called **annotating,** and your marks are called **annotations.** Annotating the text can help you identify important concepts while you read.

There are other ways that you can annotate the text. You can draw an asterisk (*) by vocabulary terms, mark unfamiliar or confusing terms and information with a question mark (?), and mark main ideas with a double underline. And you can even invent your own marks to annotate the text!

Other Annotating Opportunities

Keep your pencil, pen, or highlighter nearby as you read, so you can make a note or highlight an important point at any time. Here are a few ideas to get you started.

- Notice the headings in red and blue. The blue headings are questions that point to the main idea of what you're reading. The red headings are answers to the questions in the blue ones. Together these headings outline the content of the lesson. After reading a lesson, you could write your own answers to the questions.

- Notice the bold-faced words that are highlighted in yellow. They are highlighted so that you can easily find them again on the page where they are defined. As you read or as you review, challenge yourself to write your own sentence using the bold-faced term.

- Make a note in the margin at any time. You might
  - Ask a "What if" question
  - Comment on what you read
  - Make a connection to something you read elsewhere
  - Make a logical conclusion from the text

Use your own language and abbreviations. Invent a code, such as using circles and boxes around words to remind you of their importance or relation to each other. Your annotations will help you remember your questions for class discussions, and when you go back to the lesson later, you may be able to fill in what you didn't understand the first time you read it. Like a scientist in the field or in a lab, you will be recording your questions and observations for analysis later.

Active Reading Questions

After you read, you'll often come upon Active Reading questions that ask you to think about what you've just read. You'll write your answer underneath the question. Here's an example.

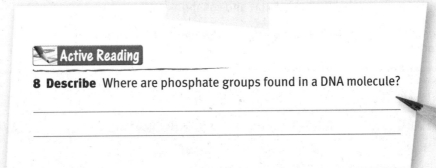

Active Reading

8 Describe Where are phosphate groups found in a DNA molecule?

_____

_____

This type of question helps you sum up what you've just read and pull out the most important ideas from the passage. In this case the question asks you to **describe** the structure of a DNA molecule that you have just read about. Other times you may be asked to do such things as **apply** a concept, **compare** two concepts, **summarize** a process, or **identify a cause-and-effect** relationship. You'll be strengthening those critical thinking skills that you'll use often in learning about science.

Reading and Study Skills

Using Graphic Organizers to Take Notes

Graphic organizers help you remember information as you read it for the first time and as you study it later. There are dozens of graphic organizers to choose from, so the first trick is to choose the one that's best suited to your purpose. Following are some graphic organizers to use for different purposes.

To remember lots of information	To relate a central idea to subordinate details	To describe a process	To make a comparison
• Arrange data in a Content Frame • Use Combination Notes to describe a concept in words and pictures	• Show relationships with a Mind Map or a Main Idea Web • Sum up relationships among many things with a Concept Map	• Use a Process Diagram to explain a procedure • Show a chain of events and results in a Cause-and-Effect Chart	• Compare two or more closely related things in a Venn Diagram

Content Frame

1 Make a four-column chart.

2 Fill the first column with categories (e.g., snail, ant, earthworm) and the first row with descriptive information (e.g., group, characteristic, appearance).

3 Fill the chart with details that belong in each row and column.

4 When you finish, you'll have a study aid that helps you compare one category to another.

Invertebrates

NAME	GROUP	CHARACTERISTICS	DRAWING
snail	mollusks	mangle	
ant	arthropods	six legs, exoskeleton	
earthworm	segmented worms	segmented body, circulatory and digestive systems	
heartworm	roundworms	digestive system	
sea star	echinoderms	spiny skin, tube feet	
jellyfish	cnidarians	stinging cells	

Combination Notes

1 Make a two-column chart.

2 Write descriptive words and definitions in the first column.

3 Draw a simple sketch that helps you remember the meaning of the term in the second column.

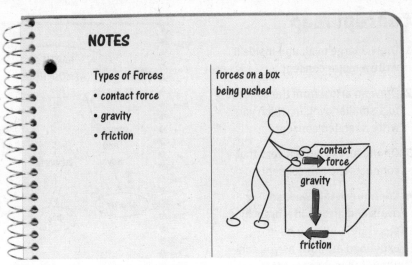

Mind Map

1 Draw an oval, and inside it write a topic to analyze.

2 Draw two or more arms extending from the oval. Each arm represents a main idea about the topic.

3 Draw lines from the arms on which to write details about each of the main ideas.

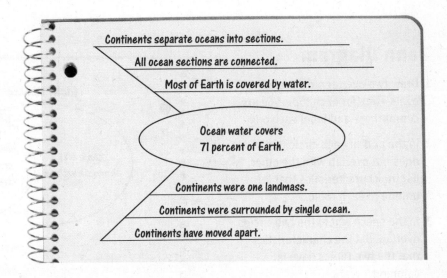

Main Idea Web

1 Make a box and write a concept you want to remember inside it.

2 Draw boxes around the central box, and label each one with a category of information about the concept (e.g., definition, formula, descriptive details).

3 Fill in the boxes with relevant details as you read.

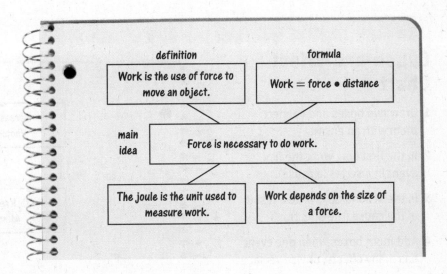

Reading and Study Skills

Concept Map

1 Draw a large oval, and inside it write a major concept.

2 Draw an arrow from the concept to a smaller oval, in which you write a related concept.

3 On the arrow, write a verb that connects the two concepts.

4 Continue in this way, adding ovals and arrows in a branching structure, until you have explained as much as you can about the main concept.

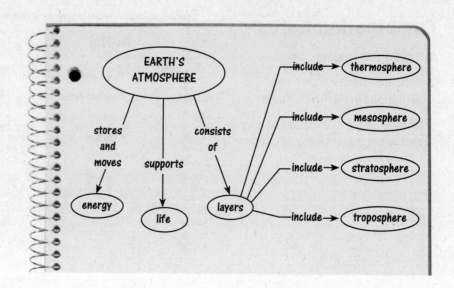

Venn Diagram

1 Draw two overlapping circles or ovals—one for each topic you are comparing—and label each one.

2 In the part of each circle that does not overlap with the other, list the characteristics that are unique to each topic.

3 In the space where the two circles overlap, list the characteristics that the two topics have in common.

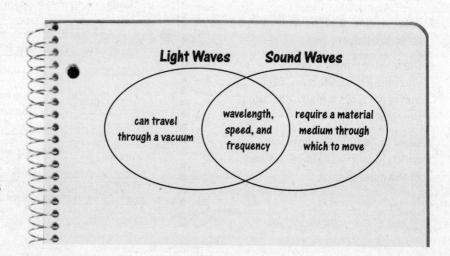

Cause-and-Effect Chart

1 Draw two boxes and connect them with an arrow.

2 In the first box, write the first event in a series (a cause).

3 In the second box, write a result of the cause (the effect).

4 Add more boxes when one event has many effects, or vice versa.

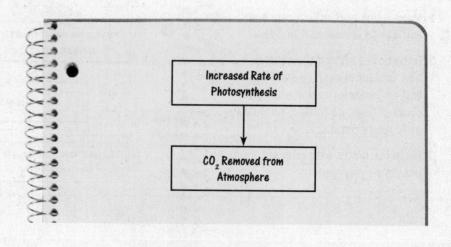

Process Diagram

A process can be a never-ending cycle. As you can see in this technology design process, engineers may backtrack and repeat steps, they may skip steps entirely, or they may repeat the entire process before a useable design is achieved.

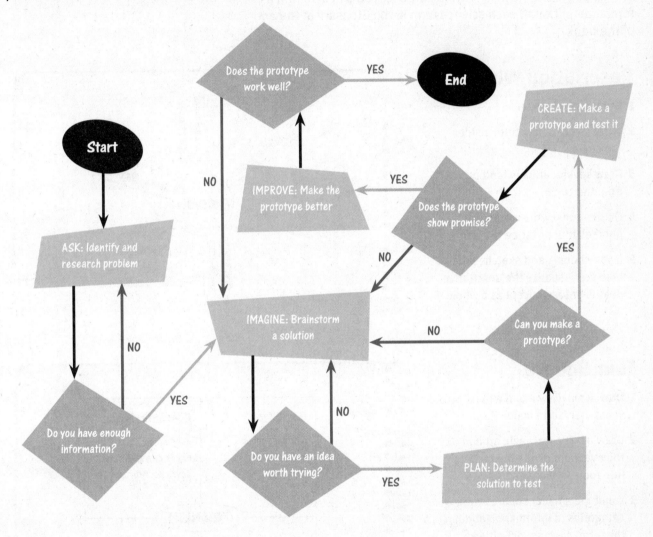

Reading and Study Skills

Using Vocabulary Strategies

Important science terms are highlighted where they are first defined in this book. One way to remember these terms is to take notes and make sketches when you come to them. Use the strategies on this page and the next for this purpose. You will also find a formal definition of each science term in the Glossary at the end of the book.

Description Wheel

1 Draw a small circle.

2 Write a vocabulary term inside the circle.

3 Draw several arms extending from the circle.

4 On the arms, write words and phrases that describe the term.

5 If you choose, add sketches that help you visualize the descriptive details or the concept as a whole.

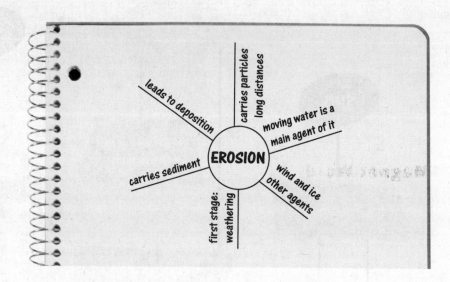

Four Square

1 Draw a small oval and write a vocabulary term inside it.

2 Draw a large rectangle around the oval, and divide the rectangle into four smaller squares.

3 Label the smaller squares with categories of information about the term, such as: definition, characteristics, examples, non-examples, appearance, and root words.

4 Fill the squares with descriptive words and drawings that will help you remember the overall meaning of the term and its essential details.

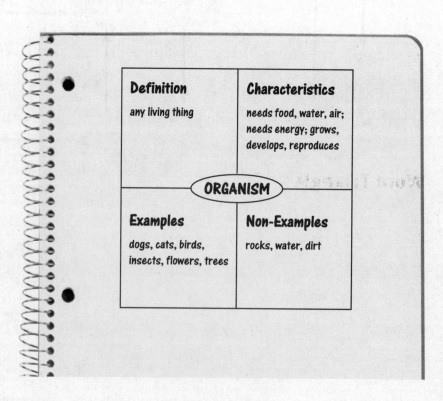

Frame Game

1 Draw a small rectangle, and write a vocabulary term inside it.

2 Draw a larger rectangle around the smaller one. Connect the corners of the larger rectangle to the corners of the smaller one, creating four spaces that frame the word.

3 In each of the four parts of the frame, draw or write details that help define the term. Consider including a definition, essential characteristics, an equation, examples, and a sentence using the term.

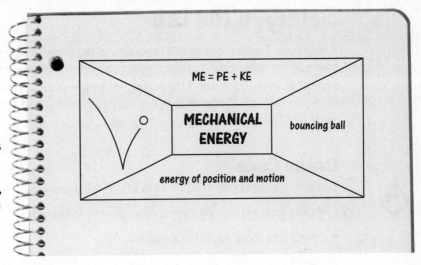

Magnet Word

1 Draw horseshoe magnet, and write a vocabulary term inside it.

2 Add lines that extend from the sides of the magnet.

3 Brainstorm words and phrases that come to mind when you think about the term.

4 On the lines, write the words and phrases that describe something essential about the term.

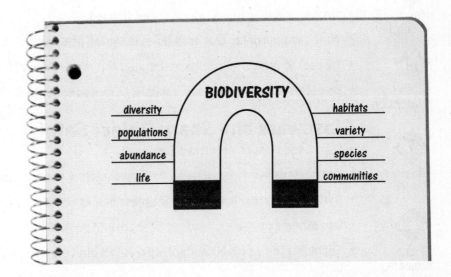

Word Triangle

1 Draw a triangle, and add lines to divide it into three parts.

2 Write a term and its definition in the bottom section of the triangle.

3 In the middle section, write a sentence in which the term is used correctly.

4 In the top section, draw a small picture to illustrate the term.

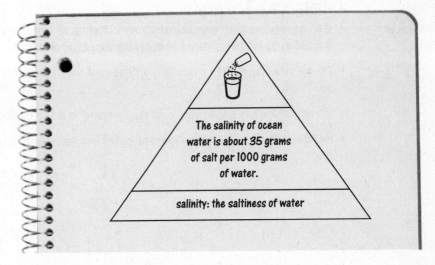

Science Skills

Safety in the Lab

Before you begin work in the laboratory, read these safety rules twice. Before starting a lab activity, read all directions and make sure that you understand them. Do not begin until your teacher has told you to start. If you or another student are injured in any way, tell your teacher immediately.

Dress Code

Eye Protection

- Wear safety goggles at all times in the lab as directed.
- If chemicals get into your eyes, flush your eyes immediately.
- Do not wear contact lenses in the lab.
- Do not look directly at the sun or any intense light source or laser.

Hand Protection

- Do not cut an object while holding the object in your hand.
- Wear appropriate protective gloves as directed.

Clothing Protection

- Wear an apron or lab coat at all times in the lab as directed.
- Tie back long hair, secure loose clothing, and remove loose jewelry.
- Do not wear open-toed shoes, sandals, or canvas shoes in the lab.

Glassware and Sharp Object Safety

Glassware Safety

- Do not use chipped or cracked glassware.
- Use heat-resistant glassware for heating or storing hot materials.
- Notify your teacher immediately if a piece of glass breaks.

Sharp Objects Safety

- Use extreme care when handling all sharp and pointed instruments.
- Cut objects on a suitable surface, always in a direction away from your body.

Chemical Safety

Chemical Safety

- If a chemical gets on your skin, on your clothing, or in your eyes, rinse it immediately (shower, faucet or eyewash fountain) and alert your teacher.
- Do not clean up spilled chemicals unless your teacher directs you to do so.
- Do not inhale any gas or vapor unless directed to do so by your teacher.
- Handle materials that emit vapors or gases in a well-ventilated area.

Electrical
Safety

Electrical Safety

- Do not use equipment with frayed electrical cords or loose plugs.
- Do not use electrical equipment near water or when clothing or hands are wet.
- Hold the plug housing when you plug in or unplug equipment.

Heating
Safety

Heating and Fire Safety

- Be aware of any source of flames, sparks, or heat (such as flames, heating coils, or hot plates) before working with any flammable substances.
- Know the location of lab fire extinguishers and fire-safety blankets.
- Know your school's fire-evacuation routes.
- If your clothing catches on fire, walk to the lab shower to put out the fire.
- Never leave a hot plate unattended while it is turned on or while it is cooling.
- Use tongs or appropriate insulated holders when handling heated objects.
- Allow all equipment to cool before storing it.

Wafting

Plant
Safety

Animal
Safety

Plant and Animal Safety

- Do not eat any part of a plant.
- Do not pick any wild plants unless your teacher instructs you to do so.
- Handle animals only as your teacher directs.
- Treat animals carefully and respectfully.
- Wash your hands thoroughly after handling any plant or animal.

Proper
Waste
Disposal

Hygienic
Care

Cleanup

- Clean all work surfaces and protective equipment as directed by your teacher.
- Dispose of hazardous materials or sharp objects only as directed by your teacher.
- Keep your hands away from your face while you are working on any activity.
- Wash your hands thoroughly before you leave the lab or after any activity.

Science Skills

Designing, Conducting, and Reporting an Experiment

An experiment is an organized procedure to study something under specific conditions. Use the following steps of the scientific method when designing or conducting a controlled experiment.

1 Identify a Research Problem

Every day, you make observations by using your senses to gather information. Careful observations lead to good questions, and good questions can lead you to an experiment. Imagine, for example, that you pass a pond every day on your way to school, and you notice green scum beginning to form on top of it. You wonder what it is and why it seems to be growing. You list your questions, and then you do a little research to find out what is already known. A good place to start a research project is at the library. A library catalog lists all of the resources available to you at that library and often those found elsewhere. Begin your search by using:

- keywords or main topics.

- similar words, or synonyms, of your keyword.

The types of resources that will be helpful to you will depend on the kind of information you are interested in. And, some resources are more reliable for a given topic than others. Some different kinds of useful resources are:

- magazines and journals (or periodicals)—articles on a topic.

- encyclopedias—a good overview of a topic.

- books on specific subjects—details about a topic.

- newspapers—useful for current events.

The Internet can also be a great place to find information. Some of your library's reference materials may even be online. When using the Internet, however, it is especially important to make sure you are using appropriate and reliable sources. Websites of universities and government agencies are usually more accurate and reliable than websites created by individuals or businesses. Decide which sources are relevant and reliable for your topic. If in doubt, check with your teacher.

Take notes as you read through the information in these resources. You will probably come up with many questions and ideas for which you can do more research as needed. Once you feel you have enough information, think about the questions you have on the topic. Then, write down the problem that you want to investigate. Your notes might look like these.

Research Questions	Research Problem	Library and Internet Resources
• How do algae grow? • How do people measure algae? • What kind of fertilizer would affect the growth of algae? • Can fertilizer and algae be used safely in a lab? How?	How does fertilizer affect the algae in a pond?	Pond fertilization: initiating an algal bloom – from University of California Davis website. Blue-Green algae in Wisconsin waters-from the Department of Natural Resources of Wisconsin website.

As you gather information from reliable sources, record details about each source, including author name(s), title, date of publication, and/or web address. Make sure to also note the specific information that you use from each source. Staying organized in this way will be important when you write your report and create a bibliography or works cited list. Recording this information and staying organized will help you credit the appropriate author(s) for the information that you have gathered.

Representing someone else's ideas or work as your own, (without giving the original author credit), is known as plagiarism. Plagiarism can be intentional or unintentional. The best way to make sure that you do not commit plagiarism is to always do your own work and to always give credit to others when you use their words or ideas.

Current scientific research is built on scientific research and discoveries that have happened in the past. This means that scientists are constantly learning from each other and combining ideas to learn more about the natural world through investigation. But, a good scientist always credits the ideas and research that they have gathered from other people to those people. There are more details about crediting sources and creating a bibliography under step 9.

2 Make a Prediction

A prediction is a statement of what you expect will happen in your experiment. Before making a prediction, you need to decide in a general way what you will do in your procedure. You may state your prediction in an if-then format.

Prediction

If the amount of fertilizer in the pond water is increased, then the amount of algae will also increase.

Science Skills

3 Form a Hypothesis

Many experiments are designed to test a hypothesis. A hypothesis is a tentative explanation for an expected result. You have predicted that additional fertilizer will cause additional algae growth in pond water; your hypothesis should state the connection between fertilizer and algal growth.

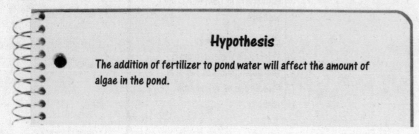

Hypothesis

The addition of fertilizer to pond water will affect the amount of algae in the pond.

4 Identify Variables to Test the Hypothesis

The next step is to design an experiment to test the hypothesis. The experimental results may or may not support the hypothesis. Either way, the information that results from the experiment may be useful for future investigations.

Experimental Group and Control Group

An experiment to determine how two factors are related has a control group and an experimental group. The two groups are the same, except that the investigator changes a single factor in the experimental group and does not change it in the control group.

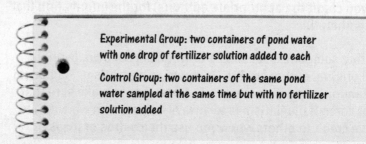

Experimental Group: two containers of pond water with one drop of fertilizer solution added to each

Control Group: two containers of the same pond water sampled at the same time but with no fertilizer solution added

Variables and Constants

In a controlled experiment, a variable is any factor that can change. Constants are all of the variables that are kept the same in both the experimental group and the control group.

The independent variable is the factor that is manipulated or changed in order to test the effect of the change on another variable. The dependent variable is the factor the investigator measures to gather data about the effect.

Independent Variable	Dependent Variable	Constants
Amount of fertilizer in pond water	Growth of algae in the pond water	• Where and when the pond water is obtained • The type of container used • Light and temperature conditions where the water is stored

5 Write a Procedure

Write each step of your procedure. Start each step with a verb, or action word, and keep the steps short. Your procedure should be clear enough for someone else to use as instructions for repeating your experiment.

Procedure

1. Use the masking tape and the marker to label the containers with your initials, the date, and the identifiers "Jar 1 with Fertilizer," "Jar 2 with Fertilizer," "Jar 1 without Fertilizer," and "Jar 2 without Fertilizer."

2. Put on your gloves. Use the large container to obtain a sample of pond water.

3. Divide the water sample equally among the four smaller containers.

4. Use the eyedropper to add one drop of fertilizer solution to the two containers labeled, "Jar 1 with Fertilizer," and "Jar 2 with Fertilizer".

5. Cover the containers with clear plastic wrap. Use the scissors to punch ten holes in each of the covers.

6. Place all four containers on a window ledge. Make sure that they all receive the same amount of light.

7. Observe the containers every day for one week.

8. Use the ruler to measure the diameter of the largest clump of algae in each container, and record your measurements daily.

Science Skills

6 Experiment and Collect Data

Once you have all of your materials and your procedure has been approved, you can begin to experiment and collect data. Record both quantitative data (measurements) and qualitative data (observations), as shown below.

Algal Growth and Fertilizer

Date and Time	Experimental Group		Control Group		Observations
	Jar 1 with Fertilizer (diameter of algal clump in mm)	Jar 2 with Fertilizer (diameter of algal clump in mm)	Jar 1 without Fertilizer (diameter of algal clump in mm)	Jar 2 without Fertilizer (diameter of algal clump in mm)	
5/3 4:00 p.m.	0	0	0	0	condensation in all containers
5/4 4:00 p.m.	0	3	0	0	tiny green blobs in Jar 2 with fertilizer
5/5 4:15 p.m.	4	5	0	3	green blobs in Jars 1 and 2 with fertilizer and Jar 2 without fertilizer
5/6 4:00 p.m.	5	6	0	4	water light green in Jar 2 with fertilizer
5/7 4:00 p.m.	8	10	0	6	water light green in Jars 1 and 2 with fertilizer and Jar 2 without fertilizer
5/8 3:30 p.m.	10	18	0	6	cover off of Jar 2 with fertilizer
5/9 3:30 p.m.	14	23	0	8	drew sketches of each container

Drawings of Samples Viewed Under Microscope on 5/9 at 100x

Jar 1 with Fertilizer

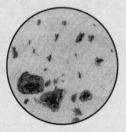
Jar 2 with Fertilizer

Jar 1 without Fertilizer

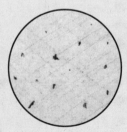
Jar 2 without Fertilizer

7 Analyze Data

After you complete your experiment, you must analyze all of the data you have gathered. Tables, statistics, and graphs are often used in this step to organize and analyze both the qualitative and quantitative data. Sometimes, your qualitative data are best used to help explain the relationships you see in your quantitative data.

Computer graphing software is useful for creating a graph from data that you have collected. Most graphing software can make line graphs, pie charts, or bar graphs from data that has been organized in a spreadsheet. Graphs are useful for understanding relationships in the data and for communicating the results of your experiment.

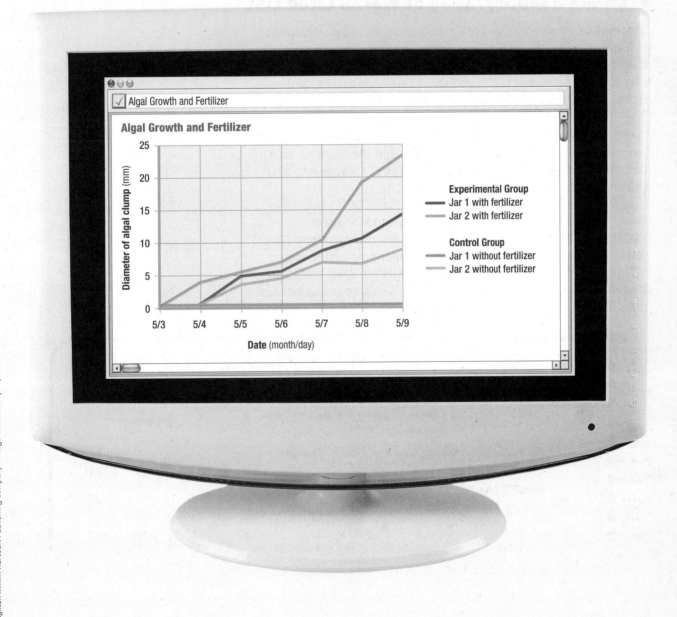

Science Skills

8 Make Conclusions

To draw conclusions from your experiment, first, write your results. Then, compare your results with your hypothesis. Do your results support your hypothesis? What have you learned?

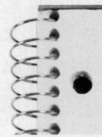

Conclusion

More algae grew in the pond water to which fertilizer had been added than in the pond water to which fertilizer had not been added. My hypothesis was supported. I conclude that it is possible that the growth of algae in ponds can be influenced by the input of fertilizer.

9 Create a Bibliography or Works Cited List

To complete your report, you must also show all of the newspapers, magazines, journals, books, and online sources that you used at every stage of your investigation. Whenever you find useful information about your topic, you should write down the source of that information. Writing down as much information as you can about the subject can help you or someone else find the source again. You should at least record the author's name, the title, the date and where the source was published, and the pages in which the information was found. Then, organize your sources into a list, which you can title Bibliography or Works Cited.

Usually, at least three sources are included in these lists. Sources are listed alphabetically, by the authors' last names. The exact format of a bibliography can vary, depending on the style preferences of your teacher, school, or publisher. Also, books are cited differently than journals or websites. Below is an example of how different kinds of sources may be formatted in a bibliography.

BOOK: Hauschultz, Sara. Freshwater Algae. Brainard, Minnesota: Northwoods Publishing, 2011.

ENCYCLOPEDIA: Lasure, Sedona. "Algae is not all just pond scum." Encyclopedia of Algae. 2009.

JOURNAL: Johnson, Keagan. "Algae as we know it." Sci Journal, vol 64. (September 2010): 201-211.

WEBSITE: Dout, Bill. "Keeping algae scum out of birdbaths." Help Keep Earth Clean. News. January 26, 2011. <www.SaveEarth.org>.

Using a Microscope

Scientists use microscopes to see very small objects that cannot easily be seen with the eye alone. A microscope magnifies the image of an object so that small details may be observed. A microscope that you may use can magnify an object 400 times—the object will appear 400 times larger than its actual size.

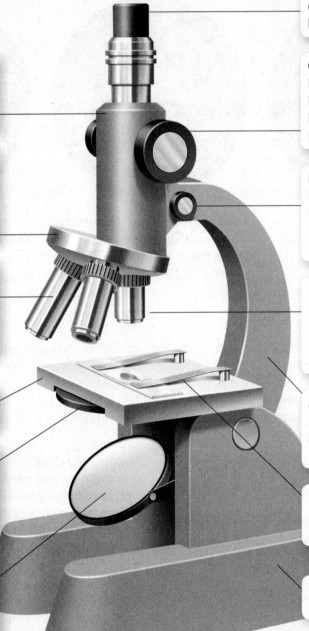

Eyepiece Objects are viewed through the eyepiece. The eyepiece contains a lens that commonly magnifies an image ten times.

Coarse Adjustment This knob is used to focus the image of an object when it is viewed through the low-power lens.

Fine Adjustment This knob is used to focus the image of an object when it is viewed through the high-power lens.

Low-Power Objective Lens This is the smallest lens on the nosepiece. It magnifies images about 10 times.

Arm The arm supports the body above the stage. Always carry a microscope by the arm and base.

Stage Clip The stage clip holds a slide in place on the stage.

Base The base supports the microscope.

Body The body separates the lens in the eyepiece from the objective lenses below.

Nosepiece The nosepiece holds the objective lenses above the stage and rotates so that all lenses may be used.

High-Power Objective Lens This is the largest lens on the nosepiece. It magnifies an image approximately 40 times.

Stage The stage supports the object being viewed.

Diaphragm The diaphragm is used to adjust the amount of light passing through the slide and into an objective lens.

Mirror or Light Source Some microscopes use light that is reflected through the stage by a mirror. Other microscopes have their own light sources.

Science Skills

Measuring Accurately

Precision and Accuracy

When you do a scientific investigation, it is important that your methods, observations, and data be both precise and accurate.

Low precision: The darts did not land in a consistent place on the dartboard.

Precision, but not accuracy: The darts landed in a consistent place, but did not hit the bull's eye.

Prescision and accuracy: The darts landed consistently on the bull's eye.

Precision

In science, *precision* is the exactness and consistency of measurements. For example, measurements made with a ruler that has both centimeter and millimeter markings would be more precise than measurements made with a ruler that has only centimeter markings. Another indicator of precision is the care taken to make sure that methods and observations are as exact and consistent as possible. Every time a particular experiment is done, the same procedure should be used. Precision is necessary because experiments are repeated several times and if the procedure changes, the results might change.

Example

Suppose you are measuring temperatures over a two-week period. Your precision will be greater if you measure each temperature at the same place, at the same time of day, and with the same thermometer than if you change any of these factors from one day to the next.

Accuracy

In science, it is possible to be precise but not accurate. *Accuracy* depends on the difference between a measurement and an actual value. The smaller the difference, the more accurate the measurement.

Example

Suppose you look at a stream and estimate that it is about 1 meter wide at a particular place. You decide to check your estimate by measuring the stream with a meter stick, and you determine that the stream is 1.32 meters wide. However, because it is difficult to measure the width of a stream with a meter stick, it turns out that your measurement was not very accurate. The stream is actually 1.14 meters wide. Therefore, even though your estimate of about 1 meter was less precise than your measurement, your estimate was actually more accurate.

Graduated Cylinders

How to Measure the Volume of a Liquid with a Graduated Cylinder

- Be sure that the graduated cylinder is on a flat surface so that your measurement will be accurate.

- When reading the scale on a graduated cylinder, be sure to have your eyes at the level of the surface of the liquid.

- The surface of the liquid will be curved in the graduated cylinder. Read the volume of the liquid at the bottom of the curve, or meniscus (muh-NIHS-kuhs).

- You can use a graduated cylinder to find the volume of a solid object by measuring the increase in a liquid's level after you add the object to the cylinder.

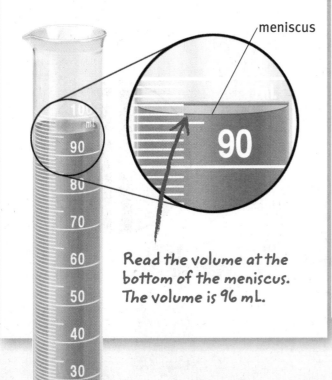

meniscus

Read the volume at the bottom of the meniscus. The volume is 96 mL.

Metric Rulers

How to Measure the Length of a Leaf with a Metric Ruler

1. Lay a ruler flat on top of the leaf so that the 1-centimeter mark lines up with one end. Make sure the ruler and the leaf do not move between the time you line them up and the time you take the measurement.

2. Look straight down on the ruler so that you can see exactly how the marks line up with the other end of the leaf.

3. Estimate the length by which the leaf extends beyond a marking. For example, the leaf below extends about halfway between the 4.2-centimeter and 4.3-centimeter marks, so the apparent measurement is about 4.25 centimeters.

4. Remember to subtract 1 centimeter from your apparent measurement, since you started at the 1-centimeter mark on the ruler and not at the end. The leaf is about 3.25 centimeters long (4.25 cm − 1 cm = 3.25 cm).

Science Skills

Triple Beam Balance

This balance has a pan and three beams with sliding masses, called riders. At one end of the beams is a pointer that indicates whether the mass on the pan is equal to the masses shown on the beams.

How to Measure the Mass of an Object

1 Make sure the balance is zeroed before measuring the mass of an object. The balance is zeroed if the pointer is at zero when nothing is on the pan and the riders are at their zero points. Use the adjustment knob at the base of the balance to zero it.

2 Place the object to be measured on the pan.

3 Move the riders one notch at a time away from the pan. Begin with the largest rider. If moving the largest rider one notch brings the pointer below zero, begin measuring the mass of the object with the next smaller rider.

4 Change the positions of the riders until they balance the mass on the pan and the pointer is at zero. Then add the readings from the three beams to determine the mass of the object.

300 g	position of largest rider
90 g	position of middle rider
+ 3 g	position of smallest rider
393 g	mass of beaker and water

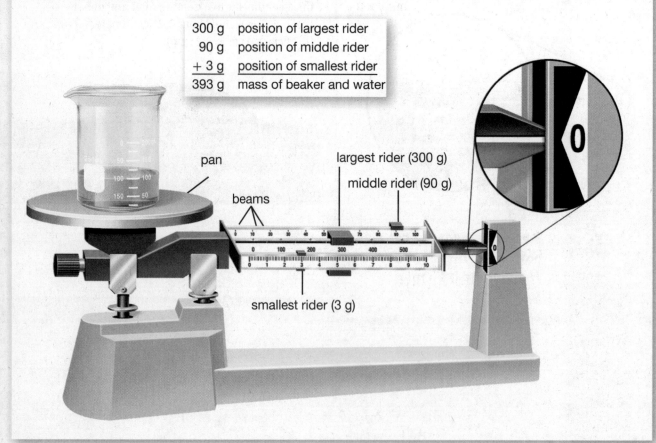

© Houghton Mifflin Harcourt Publishing Company

Using the Metric System and SI Units

Scientists use International System (SI) units for measurements of distance, volume, mass, and temperature. The International System is based on powers of ten and the metric system of measurement.

Basic SI Units		
Quantity	Name	Symbol
length	meter	m
volume	liter	L
mass	gram	g
temperature	kelvin	K

SI Prefixes		
Prefix	Symbol	Power of 10
kilo-	k	1000
hecto-	h	100
deca-	da	10
deci-	d	0.1 or $\frac{1}{10}$
centi-	c	0.01 or $\frac{1}{100}$
milli-	m	0.001 or $\frac{1}{1000}$

Changing Metric Units

You can change from one unit to another in the metric system by multiplying or dividing by a power of 10.

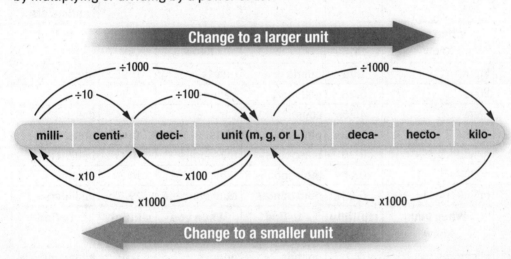

Example

Change 0.64 liters to milliliters.
1 Decide whether to multiply or divide.
2 Select the power of 10.

Change to a smaller unit by multiplying

mL ◀──── x 1000 ──── L

0.64 x 1000 = 640.

ANSWER 0.64 L = 640 mL

Example

Change 23.6 grams to kilograms.
1 Decide whether to multiply or divide.
2 Select the power of 10.

Change to a larger unit by dividing

g ──── ÷ 1000 ────▶ kg

26.3 ÷ 1000 = 0.0263

ANSWER 23.6 g = 0.0236 kg

Science Skills

Converting Between SI and U.S. Customary Units

Use the chart below when you need to convert between SI units and U.S. customary units.

SI Unit	From SI to U.S. Customary			From U.S. Customary to SI		
Length	**When you know**	**multiply by**	**to find**	**When you know**	**multiply by**	**to find**
kilometer (km) = 1000 m	kilometers	0.62	miles	miles	1.61	kilometers
meter (m) = 100 cm	meters	3.28	feet	feet	0.3048	meters
centimeter (cm) = 10 mm	centimeters	0.39	inches	inches	2.54	centimeters
millimeter (mm) = 0.1 cm	millimeters	0.04	inches	inches	25.4	millimeters
Area	**When you know**	**multiply by**	**to find**	**When you know**	**multiply by**	**to find**
square kilometer (km²)	square kilometers	0.39	square miles	square miles	2.59	square kilometers
square meter (m²)	square meters	1.2	square yards	square yards	0.84	square meters
square centimeter (cm²)	square centimeters	0.155	square inches	square inches	6.45	square centimeters
Volume	**When you know**	**multiply by**	**to find**	**When you know**	**multiply by**	**to find**
liter (L) = 1000 mL	liters	1.06	quarts	quarts	0.95	liters
	liters	0.26	gallons	gallons	3.79	liters
	liters	4.23	cups	cups	0.24	liters
	liters	2.12	pints	pints	0.47	liters
milliliter (mL) = 0.001 L	milliliters	0.20	teaspoons	teaspoons	4.93	milliliters
	milliliters	0.07	tablespoons	tablespoons	14.79	milliliters
	milliliters	0.03	fluid ounces	fluid ounces	29.57	milliliters
Mass	**When you know**	**multiply by**	**to find**	**When you know**	**multiply by**	**to find**
kilogram (kg) = 1000 g	kilograms	2.2	pounds	pounds	0.45	kilograms
gram (g) = 1000 mg	grams	0.035	ounces	ounces	28.35	grams

Temperature Conversions

Even though the kelvin is the SI base unit of temperature, the degree Celsius will be the unit you use most often in your science studies. The formulas below show the relationships between temperatures in degrees Fahrenheit (°F), degrees Celsius (°C), and kelvins (K).

$$°C = \frac{5}{9}\ (°F - 32) \qquad °F = \frac{9}{5}\ °C + 32 \qquad K = °C + 273$$

Examples of Temperature Conversions		
Condition	**Degrees Celsius**	**Degrees Fahrenheit**
Freezing point of water	0	32
Cool day	10	50
Mild day	20	68
Warm day	30	86
Normal body temperature	37	98.6
Very hot day	40	104
Boiling point of water	100	212

Math Refresher

Performing Calculations

Science requires an understanding of many math concepts. The following pages will help you review some important math skills.

Mean

The mean is the sum of all values in a data set divided by the total number of values in the data set. The mean is also called the *average*.

Example

Find the mean of the following set of numbers: 5, 4, 7, and 8.

Step 1   Find the sum.

$$5 + 4 + 7 + 8 = 24$$

Step 2   Divide the sum by the number of numbers in your set. Because there are four numbers in this example, divide the sum by 4.

$$24 \div 4 = 6$$

Answer The average, or mean, is 6.

Median

The median of a data set is the middle value when the values are written in numerical order. If a data set has an even number of values, the median is the mean of the two middle values.

Example

To find the median of a set of measurements, arrange the values in order from least to greatest. The median is the middle value.

13 mm   14 mm   16 mm   21 mm   23 mm

Answer The median is 16 mm.

Mode

The mode of a data set is the value that occurs most often.

Example

To find the mode of a set of measurements, arrange the values in order from least to greatest and determine the value that occurs most often.

13 mm, 14 mm, 14 mm, 16 mm, 21 mm, 23 mm, 25 mm

Answer The mode is 14 mm.

A data set can have more than one mode or no mode. For example, the following data set has modes of 2 mm and 4 mm:

2 mm   2 mm   3 mm   4 mm   4 mm

The data set below has no mode, because no value occurs more often than any other.

2 mm   3 mm   4 mm   5 mm

Math Refresher

Ratios

A **ratio** is a comparison between numbers, and it is usually written as a fraction.

Example

Find the ratio of thermometers to students if you have 36 thermometers and 48 students in your class.

Step 1   Write the ratio.

$$\frac{36 \text{ thermometers}}{48 \text{ students}}$$

Step 2   Simplify the fraction to its simplest form.

$$\frac{36}{48} = \frac{36 \div 12}{48 \div 12} = \frac{3}{4}$$

The ratio of thermometers to students is 3 to 4 or 3:4.

Proportions

A **proportion** is an equation that states that two ratios are equal.

$$\frac{3}{1} = \frac{12}{4}$$

To solve a proportion, you can use cross-multiplication. If you know three of the quantities in a proportion, you can use cross-multiplication to find the fourth.

Example

Imagine that you are making a scale model of the solar system for your science project. The diameter of Jupiter is 11.2 times the diameter of the Earth. If you are using a plastic-foam ball that has a diameter of 2 cm to represent the Earth, what must the diameter of the ball representing Jupiter be?

$$\frac{11.2}{1} = \frac{x}{2 \text{ cm}}$$

Step 1   Cross-multiply.

$$\frac{11.2}{1} = \frac{x}{2}$$

$$11.2 \times 2 = x \times 1$$

Step 2   Multiply.

$$22.4 = x \times 1$$

$$x = 22.4 \text{ cm}$$

You will need to use a ball that has a diameter of 22.4 cm to represent Jupiter.

Rates

A **rate** is a ratio of two values expressed in different units. A unit rate is a rate with a denominator of 1 unit.

Example

A plant grew 6 centimeters in 2 days. The plant's rate of growth was $\frac{6 \text{ cm}}{2 \text{ days}}$.

To describe the plant's growth in centimeters per day, write a unit rate.

Divide numerator and denominator by 2:

$$\frac{6 \text{ cm}}{2 \text{ days}} = \frac{6 \text{ cm} \div 2}{2 \text{ days} \div 2}$$

Simplify: $= \frac{3 \text{ cm}}{1 \text{ day}}$

Answer   The plant's rate of growth is 3 centimeters per day.

Percent

A **percent** is a ratio of a given number to 100. For example, 85% = 85/100. You can use percent to find part of a whole.

Example
What is 85% of 40?

Step 1 Rewrite the percent as a decimal by moving the decimal point two places to the left.

$$0.85$$

Step 2 Multiply the decimal by the number that you are calculating the percentage of.

$$0.85 \times 40 = 34$$

85% of 40 is 34.

Decimals

To **add** or **subtract decimals,** line up the digits vertically so that the decimal points line up. Then, add or subtract the columns from right to left. Carry or borrow numbers as necessary.

Example
Add the following numbers: 3.1415 and 2.96.

Step 1 Line up the digits vertically so that the decimal points line up.

$$\begin{array}{r} 3.1415 \\ + 2.96 \\ \hline \end{array}$$

Step 2 Add the columns from right to left, and carry when necessary.

$$\begin{array}{r} 3.1415 \\ + 2.96 \\ \hline 6.1015 \end{array}$$

The sum is 6.1015.

Fractions

A **fraction** is a ratio of two nonzero whole numbers.

Example
Your class has 24 plants. Your teacher instructs you to put 5 plants in a shady spot. What fraction of the plants in your class will you put in a shady spot?

Step 1 In the denominator, write the total number of parts in the whole.

$$\frac{?}{24}$$

Step 2 In the numerator, write the number of parts of the whole that are being considered.

$$\frac{5}{24}$$

So, $\frac{5}{24}$ of the plants will be in the shade.

Math Refresher

Simplifying Fractions

It is usually best to express a fraction in its simplest form. Expressing a fraction in its simplest form is called **simplifying a fraction**.

Example

Simplify the fraction $\frac{30}{45}$ to its simplest form.

Step 1   Find the largest whole number that will divide evenly into both the numerator and denominator. This number is called the greatest common factor (GCF).

Factors of the numerator 30:
1, 2, 3, 5, 6, 10, 15, 30

Factors of the denominator 45:
1, 3, 5, 9, 15, 45

Step 2   Divide both the numerator and the denominator by the GCF, which in this case is 15.

$$\frac{30}{45} = \frac{30 \div 15}{45 \div 15} = \frac{2}{3}$$

Thus, $\frac{30}{45}$ written in its simplest form is $\frac{2}{3}$.

Adding and Subtracting Fractions

To **add** or **subtract fractions** that have the same denominator, simply add or subtract the numerators.

Examples

$\frac{3}{5} + \frac{1}{5} = ?$ and $\frac{3}{4} - \frac{1}{4} = ?$

Step 1   Add or subtract the numerators.

$$\frac{3}{5} + \frac{1}{5} = \frac{4}{} \text{ and } \frac{3}{4} - \frac{1}{4} = \frac{2}{}$$

Step 2   Write in the common denominator, which remains the same.

$$\frac{3}{5} + \frac{1}{5} = \frac{4}{5} \text{ and } \frac{3}{4} - \frac{1}{4} = \frac{2}{4}$$

Step 3   If necessary, write the fraction in its simplest form.

$\frac{4}{5}$ cannot be simplified, and $\frac{2}{4} = \frac{1}{2}$.

To **add** or **subtract** fractions that have **different denominators,** first find the least common denominator (LCD).

Examples

$\frac{1}{2} + \frac{1}{6} = ?$ and $\frac{3}{4} - \frac{2}{3} = ?$

Step 1   Write the equivalent fractions that have a common denominator.

$$\frac{3}{6} + \frac{1}{6} = ? \text{ and } \frac{9}{12} - \frac{8}{12} = ?$$

Step 2   Add or subtract the fractions.

$$\frac{3}{6} + \frac{1}{6} = \frac{4}{6} \text{ and } \frac{9}{12} - \frac{8}{12} = \frac{1}{12}$$

Step 3   If necessary, write the fraction in its simplest form.

$\frac{4}{6} = \frac{2}{3}$, and $\frac{1}{12}$ cannot be simplifed.

Multiplying Fractions

To **multiply fractions,** multiply the numerators and the denominators together, and then simplify the fraction to its simplest form.

Example

$\frac{5}{9} \times \frac{7}{10} = ?$

Step 1   Multiply the numerators and denominators.

$$\frac{5}{9} \times \frac{7}{10} = \frac{5 \times 7}{9 \times 10} = \frac{35}{90}$$

Step 2   Simplify the fraction.

$$\frac{35}{90} = \frac{35 \div 5}{90 \div 5} = \frac{7}{18}$$

Dividing Fractions

To **divide fractions**, first rewrite the divisor (the number you divide by) upside down. This number is called the reciprocal of the divisor. Then multiply and simplify if necessary.

Example

$\frac{5}{8} \div \frac{3}{2} = ?$

Step 1   Rewrite the divisor as its reciprocal.

$\frac{3}{2} \rightarrow \frac{2}{3}$

Step 2   Multiply the fractions.

$\frac{5}{8} \times \frac{2}{3} = \frac{5 \times 2}{8 \times 3} = \frac{10}{24}$

Step 3   Simplify the fraction.

$\frac{10}{24} = \frac{10 \div 2}{24 \div 2} = \frac{5}{12}$

Using Significant Figures

The **significant figures** in a decimal are the digits that are warranted by the accuracy of a measuring device.

When you perform a calculation with measurements, the number of significant figures to include in the result depends in part on the number of significant figures in the measurements. When you multiply or divide measurements, your answer should have only as many significant figures as the measurement with the fewest significant figures.

Examples

Using a balance and a graduated cylinder filled with water, you determined that a marble has a mass of 8.0 grams and a volume of 3.5 cubic centimeters. To calculate the density of the marble, divide the mass by the volume.

Write the formula for density: $\text{Density} = \frac{mass}{volume}$

Substitute measurements: $= \frac{8.0 \, g}{3.5 \, cm^3}$

Use a calculator to divide: $\approx 2.285714286 \, g/cm^3$

Answer Because the mass and the volume have two significant figures each, give the density to two significant figures. The marble has a density of 2.3 grams per cubic centimeter.

Using Scientific Notation

Scientific notation is a shorthand way to write very large or very small numbers. For example, 73,500,000,000,000,000,000,000 kg is the mass of the moon. In scientific notation, it is 7.35×10^{22} kg. A value written as a number between 1 and 10, times a power of 10, is in scientific notation.

Examples

You can convert from standard form to scientific notation.

Standard Form	Scientific Notation
720,000	7.2×10^5
5 decimal places left	Exponent is 5.
0.000291	2.91×10^{-4}
4 decimal places right	Exponent is −4.

You can convert from scientific notation to standard form.

Scientific Notation	Standard Form
4.63×10^7	46,300,000
Exponent is 7.	7 decimal places right
1.08×10^{-6}	0.00000108
Exponent is −6.	6 decimal places left

Math Refresher

Making and Interpreting Graphs

Circle Graph

A circle graph, or pie chart, shows how each group of data relates to all of the data. Each part of the circle represents a category of the data. The entire circle represents all of the data. For example, a biologist studying a hardwood forest in Wisconsin found that there were five different types of trees. The data table at right summarizes the biologist's findings.

Wisconsin Hardwood Trees	
Type of tree	**Number found**
Oak	600
Maple	750
Beech	300
Birch	1,200
Hickory	150
Total	3,000

How to Make a Circle Graph

1 To make a circle graph of these data, first find the percentage of each type of tree. Divide the number of trees of each type by the total number of trees, and multiply by 100%.

$$\frac{600 \text{ oak}}{3,000 \text{ trees}} \times 100\% = 20\%$$

$$\frac{750 \text{ maple}}{3,000 \text{ trees}} \times 100\% = 25\%$$

$$\frac{300 \text{ beech}}{3,000 \text{ trees}} \times 100\% = 10\%$$

$$\frac{1,200 \text{ birch}}{3,000 \text{ trees}} \times 100\% = 40\%$$

$$\frac{150 \text{ hickory}}{3,000 \text{ trees}} \times 100\% = 5\%$$

2 Now, determine the size of the wedges that make up the graph. Multiply each percentage by 360°. Remember that a circle contains 360°.

$$20\% \times 360° = 72° \qquad 25\% \times 360° = 90°$$

$$10\% \times 360° = 36° \qquad 40\% \times 360° = 144°$$

$$5\% \times 360° = 18°$$

3 Check that the sum of the percentages is 100 and the sum of the degrees is 360.

$$20\% + 25\% + 10\% + 40\% + 5\% = 100\%$$

$$72° + 90° + 36° + 144° + 18° = 360°$$

4 Use a compass to draw a circle and mark the center of the circle.

5 Then, use a protractor to draw angles of 72°, 90°, 36°, 144°, and 18° in the circle.

6 Finally, label each part of the graph, and choose an appropriate title.

A Community of Wisconsin Hardwood Trees

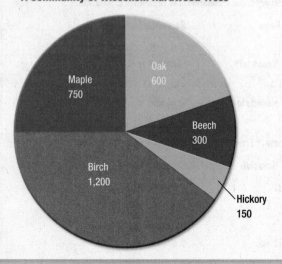

Line Graphs

Line graphs are most often used to demonstrate continuous change. For example, Mr. Smith's students analyzed the population records for their hometown, Appleton, between 1910 and 2010. Examine the data at right.

Because the year and the population change, they are the variables. The population is determined by, or dependent on, the year. Therefore, the population is called the **dependent variable,** and the year is called the **independent variable**. Each year and its population make a **data pair**. To prepare a line graph, you must first organize data pairs into a table like the one at right.

Population of Appleton, 1910–2010	
Year	Population
1910	1,800
1930	2,500
1950	3,200
1970	3,900
1990	4,600
2010	5,300

How to Make a Line Graph

1 Place the independent variable along the horizontal (*x*) axis. Place the dependent variable along the vertical (*y*) axis.

2 Label the *x*-axis "Year" and the *y*-axis "Population." Look at your greatest and least values for the population. For the *y*-axis, determine a scale that will provide enough space to show these values. You must use the same scale for the entire length of the axis. Next, find an appropriate scale for the *x*-axis.

3 Choose reasonable starting points for each axis.

4 Plot the data pairs as accurately as possible.

5 Choose a title that accurately represents the data.

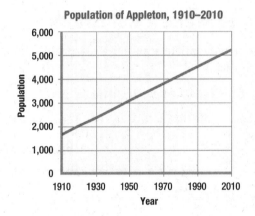

Population of Appleton, 1910–2010

How to Determine Slope

Slope is the ratio of the change in the *y*-value to the change in the x-value, or "rise over run."

1 Choose two points on the line graph. For example, the population of Appleton in 2010 was 5,300 people. Therefore, you can define point A as (2010, 5,300). In 1910, the population was 1,800 people. You can define point B as (1910, 1,800).

2 Find the change in the *y*-value.
(*y* at point A) − (*y* at point B) =
5,300 people − 1,800 people =
3,500 people

3 Find the change in the *x*-value.
(*x* at point A) − (*x* at point B) =
2010 − 1910 = 100 years

4 Calculate the slope of the graph by dividing the change in *y* by the change in *x*.

$$slope = \frac{change\ in\ y}{change\ in\ x}$$

$$slope = \frac{3,500\ people}{100\ years}$$

$$slope = 35\ people\ per\ year$$

In this example, the population in Appleton increased by a fixed amount each year. The graph of these data is a straight line. Therefore, the relationship is **linear**. When the graph of a set of data is not a straight line, the relationship is **nonlinear**.

Math Refresher

Bar Graphs

Bar graphs can be used to demonstrate change that is not continuous. These graphs can be used to indicate trends when the data cover a long period of time. A meteorologist gathered the precipitation data shown here for Summerville for April 1–15 and used a bar graph to represent the data.

Precipitation in Summerville, April 1–15			
Date	Precipitation (cm)	Date	Precipitation (cm)
April 1	0.5	April 9	0.25
April 2	1.25	April 10	0.0
April 3	0.0	April 11	1.0
April 4	0.0	April 12	0.0
April 5	0.0	April 13	0.25
April 6	0.0	April 14	0.0
April 7	0.0	April 15	6.50
April 8	1.75		

How to Make a Bar Graph

1 Use an appropriate scale and a reasonable starting point for each axis.

2 Label the axes, and plot the data.

3 Choose a title that accurately represents the data.

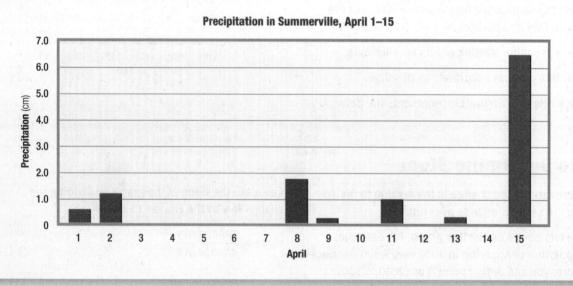

Precipitation in Summerville, April 1–15

Glossary

Pronunciation Key							
Sound	**Symbol**	**Example**	**Respelling**	**Sound**	**Symbol**	**Example**	**Respelling**
ă	a	pat	PAT	ŏ	ah	bottle	BAHT'l
ā	ay	pay	PAY	ō	oh	toe	TOH
âr	air	care	KAIR	ô	aw	caught	KAWT
ä	ah	father	FAH•ther	ôr	ohr	roar	ROHR
är	ar	argue	AR•gyoo	oi	oy	noisy	NOYZ•ee
ch	ch	chase	CHAYS	o͝o	u	book	BUK
ĕ	e	pet	PET	o͞o	oo	boot	BOOT
ĕ (at end of a syllable)	eh	settee lessee	seh•TEE leh•SEE	ou	ow	pound	POWND
ĕr	ehr	merry	MEHR•ee	s	s	center	SEN•ter
ē	ee	beach	BEECH	sh	sh	cache	CASH
g	g	gas	GAS	ŭ	uh	flood	FLUHD
ĭ	i	pit	PIT	ûr	er	bird	BERD
ĭ (at end of a syllable)	ih	guitar	gih•TAR	z	z	xylophone	ZY•luh•fohn
ī	y eye (only for a complete syllable)	pie island	PY EYE•luhnd	z	z	bags	BAGZ
				zh	zh	decision	dih•SIZH•uhn
îr	ir	hear	HIR	ə	uh	around broken focus	uh•ROWND BROH•kuhn FOH•kuhs
j	j	germ	JERM	ər	er	winner	WIN•er
k	k	kick	KIK	th	th	thin they	THIN THAY
ng	ng	thing	THING	w	w	one	WUHN
ngk	ngk	bank	BANGK	wh	hw	whether	HWETH•er

A

abrasion (uh·BRAY·zhuhn) the process by which rock is reduced in size by the scraping action of other rocks driven by water, wind, and gravity (23)
abrasión proceso por el cual se reduce el tamaño de las rocas debido al efecto de desgaste de otras rocas arrastradas por el agua, el viento o la gravedad

absolute dating (AB·suh·loot DAYT·ing) any method of measuring the age of an event or object in years (108)
datación absoluta cualquier método que sirve para determinar la edad de un suceso u objeto en años

acid precipitation (AS·id prih·sip·ih·TAY·shuhn) rain, sleet, or snow that contains a high concentration of acids (24)
precipitación ácida lluvia, aguanieve o nieve que contiene una alta concentración de ácidos

alluvial fan (uh·LOO·vee·uhl FAN) a fan-shaped mass of material deposited by a stream when the slope of the land decreases sharply (33)
abanico aluvial masa en forma de abanico de materiales depositados por un arroyo cuando la pendiente del terreno disminuye bruscamente

asthenosphere (as·THEN·uh·sfir) the soft layer of the mantle on which the tectonic plates move (196)
astenosfera la capa blanda del manto sobre la que se mueven las placas tectónicas

atmosphere (AT·muh·sfir) a mixture of gases that surrounds a planet, moon, or other celestial body (10)
atmósfera una mezcla de gases que rodea un planeta, una luna, u otras cuerpos celestes

atom (AT·uhm) the smallest unit of an element that maintains the properties of that element (142)
átomo la unidad más pequeña de un elemento que conserva las propiedades de ese elemento

B

barrier island (BAIR·ee·er EYE·luhnd) a long ridge of sand or narrow island that lies parallel to the shore (38)
isla barrera un largo arrecife de arena o una isla angosta ubicada paralela a la costa

beach (BEECH) an area of the shoreline that is made up of deposited sediment (38)
playa un área de la costa que está formada por sedimento depositado

biosphere (BY·uh·sfir) the part of Earth where life exists; includes all of the living organisms on Earth (11)
biosfera la parte de la Tierra donde existe la vida; comprende todos los seres vivos de la Tierra

C

chemical weathering (KEM·ih·kuhl WETH·er·ing) the chemical breakdown and decomposition of rocks by natural processes in the environment (24)
desgaste químico la descomposición química que sufren las rocas por procesos naturales del entorno

cleavage (KLEE·vij) in geology, the tendency of a mineral to split along specific planes of weakness to form smooth, flat surfaces (149)
exfoliación en geología, la tendencia de un mineral a agrietarse a lo largo de planos débiles específicos y formar superficies lisas y planas

climate (KLY·mit) the weather conditions in an area over a long period of time (88)
clima las condiciones del tiempo en un área durante un largo período de tiempo

composition (kahm·puh·ZISH·uhn) the chemical makeup of a rock; describes either the minerals or other materials in the rock (172)
composición la constitución química de una roca; describe los minerales u otros materiales presentes en ella

compound (KAHM·pownd) a substance made up of atoms of two or more different elements joined by chemical bonds (142)
compuesto una sustancia formada por átomos de dos o más elementos diferentes unidos por enlaces químicos

compression (kuhm·PRESH·uhn) stress that occurs when forces act to squeeze an object (221)
compresión estrés que se produce cuando distintas fuerzas actúan para estrechar un objeto

convection (kuhn·VEK·shuhn) the movement of matter due to differences in density; the transfer of energy due to the movement of matter (195, 210)
convección el movimiento de la materia debido a diferencias en la densidad; la transferencia de energía debido al movimiento de la materia

convergent boundary (kuhn·VER·juhnt BOWN·duh·ree) the boundary between tectonic plates that are colliding (208)
límite convergente el límite entre placas tectónicas que chocan

core (KOHR) the central part of Earth below the mantle (195)
núcleo la parte central de la Tierra, debajo del manto

creep (KREEP) the slow downhill movement of weathered rock material (52)

arrastre el movimiento lento y descendente de materiales rocosos desgastados

crust (KRUHST) the thin and solid outermost layer of Earth above the mantle (195)

corteza la capa externa, delgada y sólida de la Tierra, que se encuentra sobre el manto

cryosphere (KRY·oh·sfir) those portions of Earth's surface where water occurs in a solid form (9)

criosfera partes de la superficie de la Tierra donde el agua se encuentra en estado sólido

crystal (KRIS·tuhl) a solid whose atoms, ions, or molecules are arranged in a regular, repeating pattern (143)

cristal un sólido cuyos átomos, iones o moléculas están ordenados en un patrón regular y repetitivo

deformation (dee·fohr·MAY·shuhn) the bending, tilting, and breaking of Earth's crust; the change in the shape of rock in response to stress (218, 241)

deformación el proceso de doblar, inclinar y romper la corteza de la Tierra; el cambio en la forma de una roca en respuesta a la tensión

delta (DEL·tuh) a mass of material deposited in a triangular or fan shape at the mouth of a river or stream (33)

delta un depósito de materiales en forma de triángulo o abanico ubicado en la desembocadura de un río

deposition (dep·uh·ZISH·uhn) the process in which material is laid down (30, 157)

sublimación inversa el proceso por medio del cual un material se deposita

divergent boundary (dy·VER·juhnt BOWN·duh·ree) the boundary between two tectonic plates that are moving away from each other (209)

límite divergente el límite entre dos placas tectónicas que se están separando una de la otra

dune (DOON) a mound of wind-deposited sand that moves as a result of the action of wind (47)

duna un montículo de arena depositada por el viento que se mueve como resultado de la acción de éste

Earth system (ERTH SIS·tuhm) all of the nonliving things, living things, and processes that make up the planet Earth, including the solid Earth, the hydrosphere, the atmosphere, and the biosphere (6)

sistema terrestre todos los seres vivos y no vivos y los procesos que componen el planeta Tierra, incluidas la Tierra sólida, la hidrosfera, la atmósfera y la biosfera

earthquake (ERTH·kwayk) a movement or trembling of the ground that is caused by a sudden release of energy when rocks along a fault move (240)

terremoto un movimiento o temblor del suelo causado por una liberación súbita de energía que se produce cuando las rocas ubicadas a lo largo de una falla se mueven

elastic rebound (ee·LAS·tik REE·bownd) the sudden return of elastically deformed rock to its undeformed shape (241)

rebote elástico ocurre cuando una roca deformada elásticamente vuelve súbitamente a su forma no deformada

element (EL·uh·muhnt) a substance that cannot be separated or broken down into simpler substances by chemical means (142)

elemento una sustancia que no se puede separar o descomponer en sustancias más simples por medio de métodos químicos

energy budget (EN·er·jee BUHJ·it) the net flow of energy into and out of a system (14)

balance energético el flujo neto de energía que entra y sale de un sistema

epicenter (EP·ih·sen·ter) the point on Earth's surface directly above an earthquake's starting point, or focus (240, 255)

epicentro el punto de la superficie de la Tierra que queda justo arriba del punto de inicio, o foco, de un terremoto

erosion (ee·ROH·zhuhn) the process by which wind, water, ice, or gravity transports soil and sediment from one location to another (30, 157)

erosión el proceso por medio del cual el viento, el agua, el hielo o la gravedad transporta tierra y sedimentos de un lugar a otro

fault (FAWLT) a break in a body of rock along which one block moves relative to another (220, 241)
falla una grieta en un cuerpo rocoso a lo largo de la cual un bloque se mueve respecto de otro

floodplain (FLUHD·playn) an area along a river that forms from sediments deposited when the river overflows its banks (33)
llanura de inundación un área a lo largo de un río formada por sedimentos que se depositan cuando el río se desborda

focus (FOH·kuhs) the location within Earth along a fault at which the first motion of an earthquake occurs (240, 255)
foco el lugar dentro de la Tierra a lo largo de una falla donde ocurre el primer movimiento de un terremoto

folding (FOHLD·ing) the bending of rock layers due to stress (219)
plegamiento fenómeno que ocurre cuando las capas de roca se doblan debido a la compresión

fossil (FAHS·uhl) the trace or remains of an organism that lived long ago, most commonly preserved in sedimentary rock (81, 100)
fósil los indicios o los restos de un organismo que vivió hace mucho tiempo, comúnmente preservados en las rocas sedimentarias

geologic column (jee·ah·LAHJ·ik KAHL·uhm) an ordered arrangement of rock layers that is based on the relative ages of the rocks and in which the oldest rocks are at the bottom (101)
columna geológica un arreglo ordenado de capas de rocas que se basa en la edad relativa de las rocas y en el cual las rocas más antiguas están al fondo

geologic time scale (jee·uh·LAHJ·ik TYM SKAYL) the standard method used to divide Earth's long natural history into manageable parts (122)
escala de tiempo geológico el método estándar que se usa para dividir la larga historia natural de la Tierra en partes razonables

geology (jee·AHL·uh·jee) the scientific study of the origin, history, and structure of Earth and the processes that shape Earth (120)
geología el estudio científico del origen, la historia y la estructura del planeta Tierra y los procesos que le dan forma

geosphere (JEE·oh·sfir) the mostly solid, rocky part of Earth; extends from the center of the core to the surface of the crust (7)
geosfera la capa de la Tierra que es principalmente sólida y rocosa; se extiende desde el centro del núcleo hasta la superficie de la corteza terrestre

glacial drift (GLAY·shuhl DRIFT) the rock material carried and deposited by glaciers (48)
deriva glacial el material rocoso que es transportado y depositado por los glaciares

glacier (GLAY·sher) a large mass of ice that exists year-round and moves over land (48)
glaciar una masa grande de hielo que existe durante todo el año y se mueve sobre la tierra

groundwater (GROWND·waw·ter) the water that is beneath Earth's surface (34)
agua subterránea el agua que está debajo de la superficie de la Tierra

half-life (HAF·lyf) the time required for half of a sample of a radioactive isotope to break down by radioactive decay to form a daughter isotope (108)
vida media el tiempo que se requiere para que la mitad de una muestra de un isótopo radiactivo se descomponga por desintegración radiactiva y forme un isótopo hijo

hot spot (HAHT SPAHT) a volcanically active area of Earth's surface, commonly far from a tectonic plate boundary (234)
mancha caliente un área volcánicamente activa de la superficie de la Tierra que comúnmente se encuentra lejos de un límite entre placas tectónicas

humus (HYOO·muhs) dark, organic material formed in soil from the decayed remains of plants and animals (59)
humus material orgánico obscuro que se forma en la tierra a partir de restos de plantas y animales en descomposición

hydrosphere (HY·druh·sfir) the portion of Earth that is water (8)
hidrosfera la porción de la Tierra que es agua

ice core (EYES KOHR) a long cylinder of ice obtained from drilling through ice caps or ice sheets; used to study past climates (89)
testigo de hielo un cilindro largo de hielo que se obtiene al perforar campos de hielo o capas de hielo continentales; se usa para estudiar los climas del pasado

igneous rock (IG·nee·uhs RAHK) rock that forms when magma cools and solidifies (158)
roca ígnea una roca que se forma cuando el magma se enfría y se solidifica

intensity (in·TEN·sih·tee) in Earth science, the amount of damage caused by an earthquake (261)
intensidad en las ciencias de la Tierra, la cantidad de daño causado por un terremoto

L

landslide (LAND·slyd) the sudden movement of rock and soil down a slope (53)
derrumbamiento el movimiento súbito hacia abajo de rocas y suelo por una pendiente

lava (LAH·vuh) magma that flows onto Earth's surface; the rock that forms when lava cools and solidifies (228)
lava magma que fluye a la superficie terrestre; la roca que se forma cuando la lava se enfría y se solidifica

lithosphere (LITH·uh·sfir) the solid, outer layer of Earth that consists of the crust and the rigid upper part of the mantle (196)
litosfera la capa externa y sólida de la Tierra que está formada por la corteza y la parte superior y rígida del manto

loess (LUHS) fine-grained sediments of quartz, feldspar, hornblende, mica, and clay deposited by the wind (47)
loess sedimentos de grano fino de cuarzo, feldespato, horneblenda, mica y arcilla depositados por el viento

luster (LUHS·ter) the way in which a mineral reflects light (149)
brillo la forma en que un mineral refleja la luz

M-N

magma (MAG·muh) the molten or partially molten rock material containing trapped gases produced under Earth's surface (228)
magma el material rocoso total o parcialmente fundido que contiene gases atrapados que se producen debajo de la superficie terrestre

magnitude (MAG·nih·tood) a measure of the strength of an earthquake (260)
magnitud una medida de la intensidad de un terremoto

mantle (MAN·tl) the layer of rock between Earth's crust and core (195)
manto la capa de roca que se encuentra entre la corteza terrestre y el núcleo

matter (MAT·er) anything that has mass and takes up space (142)
materia cualquier cosa que tiene masa y ocupa un lugar en el espacio

mesosphere (MEZ·uh·sfir) the strong, lower part of the mantle between the asthenosphere and the outer core (196)
mesosfera la parte fuerte e inferior del manto que se encuentra entre la astenosfera y el núcleo externo

metamorphic rock (met·uh·MOHR·fik RAHK) a rock that forms from other rocks as a result of intense heat, pressure, or chemical processes (158)
roca metamórfica una roca que se forma a partir de otras rocas como resultado de calor intenso, presión o procesos químicos

mineral (MIN·er·uhl) a natural, usually inorganic solid that has a characteristic chemical composition and an orderly internal structure (142)
mineral un sólido natural, normalmente inorgánico, que tiene una composición química característica y una estructura interna ordenada

mudflow (MUHD·floh) the flow of a mass of mud or rock and soil mixed with a large amount of water (53)
flujo de lodo el flujo de una masa de lodo o roca y suelo mezclados con una gran cantidad de agua

O

oxidation (ahk·sih·DAY·shuhn) a chemical reaction in which a material combines with oxygen to form new material; in geology, oxidation is a form of chemical weathering (24)
oxidación una reacción química en la que un material se combina con oxígeno para formar un material nuevo; en geología, la oxidación es una forma de desgaste químico

P-Q

Pangaea (pan·JEE·uh) the supercontinent that formed 300 million years ago and that began to break up 200 million years ago (203)
Pangea el supercontinente que se formó hace 300 millones de años y que comenzó a separarse hace 200 millones de años

physical weathering (FIZ·ih·kuhl WETH·er·ing) the mechanical breakdown of rocks into smaller pieces that is caused by natural processes and that does not change the chemical composition of the rock material (20)
desgaste físico el rompimiento mecánico de una roca en pedazos más pequeños que ocurre por procesos naturales y que no modifica la composición química del material rocoso

plate tectonics (PLAYT tek·TAHN·iks) the theory that explains how large pieces of Earth's outermost layer, called tectonic plates, move and change shape (206)
tectónica de placas la teoría que explica cómo se mueven y cambian de forma las placas tectónicas, que son grandes porciones de la capa más externa de la Tierra

radioactive decay (ray·dee·oh·AK·tiv dee·KAY) the process in which a radioactive isotope tends to break down into a stable isotope of the same element or another element (108)

desintegración radiactiva el proceso por medio del cual un isótopo radiactivo tiende a desintegrarse y formar un isótopo estable del mismo elemento o de otro elemento

radiometric dating (ray·dee·oh·MET·rik DAYT·ing) a method of determining the absolute age of an object by comparing the relative percentages of a radioactive (parent) isotope and a stable (daughter) isotope (109)

datación radiométrica un método para determinar la edad absoluta de un objeto comparando los porcentajes relativos de un isótopo radiactivo (precursor) y un isótopo estable (hijo)

relative dating (REL·uh·tiv DAYT·ing) any method of determining whether an event or object is older or younger than other events or objects (94)

datación relativa cualquier método que se utiliza para determinar si un acontecimiento u objeto es más viejo o más joven que otros acontecimientos u objetos

rift zone (RIFT ZOHN) an area of deep cracks that forms between two tectonic plates that are pulling away from each other (162)

zona de rift un área de grietas profundas que se forma entre dos placas tectónicas que se están alejando una de la otra

rock (RAHK) a naturally occurring solid mixture of one or more minerals or organic matter (172)

roca una mezcla sólida de uno o más minerales o de materia orgánica que se produce de forma natural

rock cycle (RAHK SY·kuhl) the series of processes in which rock forms, changes from one type to another, is broken down or melted, and forms again by geologic processes (160)

ciclo de las rocas la serie de procesos por medio de los cuales una roca se forma, cambia de un tipo a otro, se destruye o funde y se forma nuevamente por procesos geológicos

rockfall (RAHK·fawl) the rapid mass movement of rock down a steep slope or cliff (53)

desprendimiento de rocas el movimiento rápido y masivo de rocas por una pendiente empinada o un precipicio

sandbar (SAND·bar) a low ridge of sand deposited along the shore of a lake or sea (38)

barra de arena un arrecife bajo de arena depositado a lo largo de la orilla de un lago o del mar

sea-floor spreading (SEE·flohr SPRED·ing) the process by which new oceanic lithosphere (sea floor) forms when magma rises to Earth's surface at mid-ocean ridges and solidifies, as older, existing sea floor moves away from the ridge (204)

expansión del suelo marino el proceso por medio del cual se forma nueva litósfera oceánica (suelo marino) cuando el magma sube a la superficie de la Tierra en las dorsales oceánicas y se solidifica, a medida que el antiguo suelo marino existente se aleja de la dorsal oceánica

sedimentary rock (sed·uh·MEN·tuh·ree RAHK) a rock that forms from compressed or cemented layers of sediment (158)

roca sedimentaria una roca que se forma a partir de capas comprimidas o cementadas de sedimento

seismic wave (SYZ·mik WAYV) a wave of energy that travels through Earth and away from an earthquake in all directions (255)

onda sísmica una onda de energía que viaja a través de la Tierra y se aleja de un terremoto en todas direcciones

seismogram (SYZ·muh·gram) a tracing of earthquake motion that is recorded by a seismograph (258)

sismograma una traza del movimiento de un terremoto registrada por un sismógrafo

shear stress (SHIR STRES) stress that occurs when forces act in parallel but opposite directions, pushing parts of a solid in opposite directions (220)

tensión de corte el estrés que se produce cuando dos fuerzas actúan en direcciones paralelas pero opuestas, lo que empuja las partes de un sólido en direcciones opuestas

shoreline (SHOHR·lyn) the boundary between land and a body of water (35)

orilla el límite entre la tierra y una masa de agua

soil (SOYL) a loose mixture of rock fragments, organic material, water, and air that can support the growth of vegetation (58)

suelo una mezcla suelta de fragmentos de roca, material orgánico, agua y aire en la que puede crecer vegetación

soil horizon (SOYL huh·RY·zuhn) each layer of soil within a soil profile (61)

horizonte del suelo una de las capas en que se divide el perfil del suelo; tiene características bien definidas, es relativamente uniforme y se encuentra casi paralela a la superficie terrestre

soil profile (SOYL PROH·fyl) a vertical section of soil that shows the layers, or horizons (61)

perfil del suelo una sección vertical de suelo que muestra las capas u horizontes

streak (STREEK) the color of a mineral in powdered form (148)

veta el color de un mineral en forma de polvo

subsidence (suhb·SYD·ns) the sinking of regions of Earth's crust to lower elevations (162)

hundimiento del terreno el hundimiento de regiones de la corteza terrestre a elevaciones más bajas

superposition (soo·per·puh·ZISH·uhn) a principle that states that younger rocks lie above older rocks if the layers have not been disturbed (95)

superposición un principio que establece que las rocas más jóvenes se encontrarán sobre las rocas más viejas si las capas no han sido alteradas

tectonic plate (tek·TAHN·ik PLAYT) a block of lithosphere that consists of the crust and the rigid, outermost part of the mantle (206, 231)

placa tectónica un bloque de litosfera formado por la corteza y la parte rígida y más externa del manto

tectonic plate boundary (tek·TAHN·ik PLAYT BOWN·duh·ree) the edge between two or more plates, classified as divergent, convergent, or transform by the movement taking place between the plates (241)

límite de placa tectónica el borde entre dos o más placas clasificado como divergente, convergente o transformante por el movimiento que se produce entre las placas

tension (TEN·shuhn) stress that occurs when forces act to stretch an object (221)

tensión estrés que se produce cuando distintas fuerzas actúan para estirar un objeto

texture (TEKS·cher) the quality of a rock that is based on the sizes, shapes, and positions of the rock's grains (173)

textura la cualidad de una roca que se basa en el tamaño, la forma y la posición de los granos que la forman

trace fossil (TRAYS FAHS·uhl) a fossilized structure, such as a footprint or a coprolite, that formed in sedimentary rock by animal activity on or within soft sediment (83)

fósil traza una estructura fosilizada, como una huella o un coprolito, que se formó en una roca sedimentaria por la actividad de un animal sobre sedimento blando o dentro de éste

transform boundary (TRANS·fohrm BOWN·duh·ree) the boundary between tectonic plates that are sliding past each other horizontally (209)

límite de transformación el límite entre placas tectónicas que se están deslizando horizontalmente una sobre otra

unconformity (uhn·kuhn·FOHR·mih·tee) a break in the geologic record created when rock layers are eroded or when sediment is not deposited for a long period of time (97)

disconformidad una ruptura en el registro geológico, creada cuando las capas de roca se erosionan o cuando el sedimento no se deposita durante un largo período de tiempo

uniformitarianism (yoo·nuh·fohr·mih·TAIR·ee·uh·niz·uhm) a principle that geologic processes that occurred in the past can be explained by current geologic processes (80)

uniformitarianismo un principio que establece que es posible explicar los procesos geológicos que ocurrieron en el pasado en función de los procesos geológicos actuales

uplift (UHP·lift) the rising of regions of Earth's crust to higher elevations (162)

levantamiento la elevación de regiones de la corteza terrestre a elevaciones más altas

vent (VENT) an opening at the surface of Earth through which volcanic material passes (228)

chimenea una abertura en la superficie de la Tierra a través de la cual pasa material volcánico

volcano (vahl·KAY·noh) a vent or fissure in Earth's surface through which magma and gases are expelled (228)

volcán una chimenea o fisura en la superficie de la Tierra a través de la cual se expulsan magma y gases

weathering (WETH·er·ing) the natural process by which atmospheric and environmental agents, such as wind, rain, and temperature changes, disintegrate and decompose rocks (20, 157)

meteorización el proceso natural por medio del cual los agentes atmosféricos o ambientales, como el viento, la lluvia y los cambios de temperatura, desintegran y descomponen las rocas

Index

Page numbers for definitions are printed in **boldface** type.
Page numbers for illustrations, maps, and charts are printed in *italics*.

21st Century Skills, 275
21st Century Skills: Technology and Coding, 275

A

abrasion, **23**
  by glaciers, 48
  by wind, 46
absolute dating, **108**
  Earth, 112, 113
  by radiocarbon dating, 111
  by radiometric dating, **109**–113
  using index fossils, 114–115
  using radioactive isotopes, 108
acid precipitation, **24**
Active Reading, lesson opener pages, 5, 19, 29, 45, 57, 79, 93, 107, 119, 141, 155, 171, 193, 201, 217, 227, 239, 253
active tendon system, 263, *263*
A horizon, 61
A How-To Manual for Active Reading, R18–R19
alluvial fan, **33**, *33*
alpine glacier, **49**
  landforms created by, 49, *49*
aluminum, life cycle of, 166–167
ammonite, 115
animal dung (trace fossil), 83, *83. See also* coprolite.
animal
  soil formation by, 59, *58–59*
  weathering caused by, 22
anticline, 219, *219*
Appalachian Mountains, *87*, 222
Archean Eon, 122, *122–123*
  defining events, 124
arctic soil, 63, *63*
arête, 49
asthenosphere, **196**
  tectonic plates and, 206, 208–209, 211
Atekwana, Estella, 214, *214*
atmosphere, **10**
atom, 142, *142*

B

bacteria, decomposition by, 59
Badlands National Park, South Dakota, *176*
Banda Aceh, Indonesia, 245
barite, *147*
barrier island, **38–39**, *38–39*

basalt, *175*
base isolator, 263, *263*
Basin and Range area, 221
bauxite, 166–167
beach, **38**
  deposition, 38
  erosion, 2–3, 35
B horizon, 61
Big Idea, 1, 75, 137, 189
biogeophysics, 214
biosphere, **11**
body wave, 256
Bonneville Salt Flats, Utah, *176*
boundary, tectonic plate, **241**
  convergent, **208**, *208*, 231, 233, *233*
  divergent, **209**, *209*, 231, 232, *232*
  earthquakes and, 241–243
  transform, **209**, 243, *243*
  volcano formation and, *231*, 231–233
breccia, *173*, 176
building construction,
  earthquakes and, 190–191, 244, 263, *263*
burrow (trace fossil), 83

C

calcite, *147, 150,* 158
caldera, 230, *230,* 233
Cambrian Explosion, 125
Cambrian Period, 125
canyon, created by erosion, 32
carbon
  in mineral formation, 144
  in radiocarbon dating, 111
carbonate, 147, *147*
Cascade Range, 233, *233*
catastrophism, 120–121
cave, 34
  sea cave, *36,* 37
Cenozoic Era, 122
  defining events, 127
channel, 32
chemical sedimentary rock, 176
chemical weathering, **24**
  by reactions with acid, 24–25
  by reactions with oxygen, 24
C horizon, 61
cinder cone, 229, *229,* 231, 232
cirque, 49
Citizen Science
  Mineral Resources, 138–139
  Preserving the Past, 76–77
  Save a Beach, 2–3

Stable Structures, 190–191
Classification of Living Things, R10–R11
clastic sedimentary rock, 176
clay particle, 62
cleavage (mineral), **149**
cliff dwelling, *163*
Cliff Palace, Colorado, *163*
climate, **88**
  geologic change and, 88
  soil formation and, 60
  soil type and, 63
coal, formation of, 85, 177
code, computer, 275, 280, *280,* 284
coding, 275
color
  of minerals, 148
  of soil, 63
Columbia Plateau, *230,* 234
composite volcano, 229, *229,* 233
composition (mineral), **172**
compositional layer (Earth), 194–195, *194–195*
compound, **142**, *142*
compression, **221**
  earthquakes and, 243
computer, 275, 276, 277
computer science, 276, 278, 279
computer scientist, 276–279
computer technology, 275–278
conchoidal fracture, 149
conglomerate (rock), 176
continental crust, 7, 195, *207*
continental drift, **202**. *See also* plate tectonics.
  continental change and, 203
  evidence from ocean trenches, 205
  evidence from sea floor, 204
continental glacier, 50
convection, 195, **210**
convergent boundary, **208**, *208,* 231, 233, *233*
  earthquake and, 243, *243*
  folded mountain and, 222
  reverse fault and, 221
  volcano formation and, 223, 233, *233*
coprolite, 83, *83*
coquina, 177
core, 7, **195**
  composition, 195
  inner, 196
  outer, 196
corundum, *147*
crater, volcanic, 230
Crater Lake, Oregon, 230
creep (mass movement), *52*

Cretaceous extinction, 127
crosscutting (relative dating), 98, 99
crust, 7, **195**
cryosphere, **9**
crystal, 109, **143**
    formation of mineral and, *174*
    radiometric dating and, 109
crystal structure, 143, *143*

D

daughter isotope, 108, *109*
deflation, 46
deformation, **218**, **241**
    elastic, 241
delta, **33**
density (mineral), 150
deposition, 30, **157**
    alluvial fan, 33
    barrier island, 38
    beach, 38
    delta, 33
    floodplain, 33
    by glacier, 48–50
    by mass movement, 52–53
    rock formation and, 95, 157,
        160–161
    sandbar, 38
    by water, *30*, 33, 35, 38
    by wind, 47, *47*
desert pavement, 46, *46*
desert soil, 63, *63*
Designing, Conducting, and Reporting
    an Experiment, R28–R34
diamond, *150*
dinosaur, mass extinction of, 121, 123,
    126
diorite, *174*
discharge (stream), 31
divergent boundary, **209**, *209*
    earthquake and, 243, *243*
    normal fault and, 221
    volcano formation and, 231, 232,
        232
dolomite, 145, *145*
dormant volcano, 228
Do the Math!, 10, 31, 110, 146, 172,
    197, 258
dune, **47**, *47*

E

Earth
    age of, 112, 113, 122
    asthenosphere, **196**
    compositional layers, 194–195,
        194–195
    core, 7, **195**, 196
    crust, 7, **195**
    lithosphere, **196**
    mantle, 7, **195**
    mesosphere, **196**
    physical layers, 196, *196*

earthquake, **240**, 245, 255–258
    body wave and, 256
    building construction and, 263, *263*
    cause of, 241, 254
    deformation and, **241**
    effects of, 244–245, 262–263
    elastic rebound and, **241**
    epicenter, **240**, 259, 263
    fault and, 241, 254
    focus, **240**
    intensity, **261**
    lag time, 259
    liquefaction, **262**
    location, 242, *242*
    magnitude, **260**, 262
    measuring, 258
    primary wave, 256
    secondary wave, 256
    seismic wave, **255–259**
    strength of, 255, 260
    surface wave, **257**
    tectonic plate boundary and,
        241–243
Earth system, **6**
    atmosphere, **10**
    biosphere, **11**
    cryosphere, **9**
    energy budget, **14**–15, *15*
    energy source, 14
    geosphere, **7**
    hydrosphere, **8**
earthy luster, *149*
East Pacific Rise, 232
elastic deformation, 241
elastic rebound, **241**
element, **142**
Enchanted Rock, Texas, *22*, *159*
energy
    in earthquakes, 255, 263
    in Earth system, 10, 14–15
    exchanged between Earth's
        spheres, 12–15
    solar, 10, 11, 13, 14
energy budget, **14**–15, *15*
Engage Your Brain, 5, 19, 29, 45, 57,
    79, 93, 107, 119, 141, 155, 171,
    193, 201, 217, 227, 239, 253
Engineering and Technology. *See
    also* STEM (Science, Technology,
    Engineering, and Mathematics).
    Analyzing the Life Cycles of
        Aluminum and Glass, 166–169
    Building a Seismometer, 248–251
environmental issue
    beach erosion, 2–3
    earthquake-safe buildings, 190–
        191, 244, 263
    global climate change, 15
    life cycle of natural resource,
        166–167
    melting polar ice, 15
    mining, 138–139
eon, **122**
epicenter, **240**
    distance from, 263
    location of, 259

epoch, **122**
era, **122**
erosion, 30, **157**. *See also* weathering.
    of barrier island, 39, *39*
    canyons and valleys formed by, 32
    by glacier, 48–50
    by groundwater, 34
    by mass movement, 52–53
    rock formation and, 157, 160,
        160–161
    of shoreline, 35–37
    by stream, 31–33
    by water, 30, *30–37*, *32–33*, 35,
        36–37, 39
    by wind, 46
erratic (boulder), *50*
Essential Question, 4, 18, 28, 44, 56,
    78, 92, 106, 118, 140, 154, 170,
    192, 200, 216, 226, 238, 252
exfoliation, 22
extinction event, 123, 126, 127
    catastrophes and, 121
extrusive igneous rock, 159, 175, *175*

F

fairy chimney, *157*
fault, 96, **220**, **241**
    compression and, 221
    earthquakes and, 241, 254
    normal, 221, *221*
    plane, 220
    reverse, 221, *221*
    shear stress and, 220, 243
    strike-slip, 220, *220*, 243
    tension and, 221
fault block, 220
fault-block mountain, 223
feldspar, *150*
    in composition of rocks, 172, *172*
fertility, 65
fissure, 175
fissure eruption, 230, 231
floodplain, **33**
fluorite, *147*
focus, **240**, **255**
folded mountain, 222
folding (rock), 96, **219**
foliated metamorphic rock, 178
foliation, **178**
footwall, 220–221
fossil, 81, **100**, *100*
    in amber and asphalt, 81
    frozen, 82
    index, 114–115
    limestone from, 177
    petrified, 82
    in sedimentary rock, 82, 84, 100
    trace, **83**
fossiliferous limestone, 177, *177*
fossil record, 84
fracture zone, 209
frost wedging, 21
fungus, soil formation by, 59

G

garnet, *144*
gas, 10. *See also* atmosphere.
geologic change, 80–89
  continental drift evidence, 86
  fossil evidence, 81–84
  ice core evidence, 89
  landform evidence, 87
  relative dating, 92–101
  sea-floor evidence, 88
  sedimentary rock evidence, 85
  tree evidence, 88
  uniformitarianism, **80**, 121
  volcanism, *80*
geologic column, **101**
geologic time scale, **122**–127, R4–R5
geologist, 215
geology, **120**
  earthquakes and, 262
geophysicist, 214
geosphere, **7**, *7*
Gila Cliff Dwellings, New Mexico, *163*
glacial dam, 51
glacial drift, **48**
glacier, 9, **48**
  alpine, 49
  continental, 50
  erosion and deposition by, 48–50
global warming, 15
gneiss, 159, *159*, 178, *178*
gold, 142, *145*
Gondwana, 203, *203*
gradient (streams), 31, *31*
grain, 173. *See also* texture.
Grand Canyon, 32, *121*
granite, *144*, 159, *172*
gravity
  erosion and deposition caused by,
    52–53
  weathering caused by, 23
Great Rift Valley, 232, *232*
greenhouse gases, 15
groundwater, **34**
  erosion caused by, 34
Guggenheim Museum, 151, *151*
gypsum, 145, *147*

H

Hadean Eon, 122, *122–123*
half-life, **108**
halide, 147, *147*
halite, 143, 145, *145*, 176, *176*
hanging wall, 220–221
hardness (mineral), 150
hardware, 276, 277
headland, 35, *36–37*
Hellas Crater, 99
hinge (rock), 219, *219*
horn (mountain), 49
hot spot, 231, **234**

humus, 59
Hutton, James, 121
hydrosphere, **8**

I–J

ice
  cryosphere, **9**
  as mineral, 142
  polar ice melting, 15
  weathering and, 21, *21*
ice cap, 9
ice core, **89**, *89*
Iceland, 232
ice wedging, 21, *21*
igneous rock, **158**
  dating, 114
  extrusive, 159, 175, *175*
  formation, 158
  intrusive, 159, 174, *174*
  in rock cycle, 160, *160–161*
  texture, 173
index fossil, *114*, 114–115
inner core, 196
inorganic substance, 143
intensity (earthquake), **261**
intrusion (rock), 96
intrusive igneous rock, 159, 174, *174*
irregular fracture (mineral), 149

K

kettle lake, *50*
Kilauea volcano, Hawaii, 234, *234*
kyanite, *147*

L

La Brea Tar Pits, California, 81
lag time, 259
lahar, 53
Lake Missoula, 51
landform
  continental movement and, 86–87
  created by alpine glacier, 49
  created by erosion, 32–34, *36–37*
  created by volcano, 229–230,
    229–230
  deposition and, 38
  geologic change and, 86–87
landslide, 53, *53*
Laurasia, 203, *203*
lava, **228**
  formation, 157
  minerals formed from, 143, 144,
    144
  in rock cycle, 160, *160–161*, 162
  rock formed from, 174–175
  viscosity, 229
lava plateau, 230, *230*

leaching, 61
Lesson Review, 17, 27, 41, 55, 67, 91,
  103, 117, 129, 153, 165, 181,
  199, 213, 225, 237, 247, 265
life cycle of natural resources,
  166–167
limestone, 85, 156, 158
  in cave formation, 34
  in composition of rocks, *172*
  formation, 177
  fossiliferous, 177, *177*
liquefaction, 262, *262*
lithosphere, **196**
  tectonic plates and, 206, 208–209,
    211
living things, 11. *See also* biosphere.
load (stream), 31, 33
loess, 47
longshore current, 35
Look It Up!, reference section, R1
  A How-To Manual for Active
    Reading, R18–R19
  Classification of Living Things,
    R10–R11
  Designing, Conducting, and
    Reporting an Experiment,
    R28–R34
  Geologic Time Scale, R4–R5
  Making and Interpreting Graphs,
    R46–R48
  Measuring Accurately, R36–R38
  Mineral Properties, R2–R3
  Performing Calculations, R41–R45
  Periodic Table of the Elements,
    R12–R13
  Physical Laws and Useful Equations,
    R16–R17
  Physical Science Refresher,
    R14–R15
  Safety in the Lab, R26–R27
  Star Charts for the Northern
    Hemisphere, R6–R7
  Using a Microscope, R35
  Using Graphic Organizers to Take
    Notes, R20–R23
  Using the Metric System and SI
    Units, R39–R40
  Using Vocabulary Strategies,
    R24–R25
  World Map, R8–R9
luster (mineral), **149**

M

magma, **228**
  formation, 157
  minerals formed by, 144, *144*, 145,
    145
  in rock cycle, 160, *160–161*, 162,
    162
  rock formed from, 157, 158, 159,
    174
  volcanoes formed by, 233

magma chamber, *174*, 230
magnitude, **260**, 262
Making and Interpreting Graphs, R46–R48
mantle, 7, **195**
mantle convection, 210
mantle plume, 234, *234*
mapping technician, 215
marble, 179, *179*
mass, 142
mass damper, 263, *263*
mass extinction, 123
mass movement, 52–53
Math Refresher, R41–R48
    Making and Interpreting Graphs, R46–R48
    Performing Calculations, R41–R45
matter, **142**
    exchanged between Earth's spheres, 13
meander, *32, 33*
Measuring Accurately, R36–R38
melting polar ice, 15
Merapi volcano, 120
mesosphere, **196**
Mesozoic Era
    defining events, 126
    extinction event, 123, 126
metallic luster, 149, *149*
metamorphic rock, **158**
    foliated, 178
    formation, 157, 158, 159
    nonfoliated, 179
    in rock cycle, 160, *160–161*
    texture, 173
metamorphism, 144, *144*
meteorite, radiometric dating and, 113, *113*
mica, 149
microorganism, soil formation and, 59
mid-ocean ridge
    continental drift and, 204, *204*
    volcanic formation and, 232
mineral, **142**–151
    chemical composition, 142
    classification, 146–147, *147*
    cleavage, **149**
    color, 148
    compounds in, 142
    density, 150
    elements in, 142
    formed by cooling magma and lava, 144, *144*
    formed by metamorphism, 144, *144*
    formed from solutions, 145, *145*
    fracture, 149
    in geosphere, 7
    hardness, 150
    luster, 149, *149*
    Mohs scale, 150, *150*
    nonsilicate, 146–147, *147*
    properties, 148–149, *148–149*, R2–R3

silicate, 146
    streak, **148**
Mineral Properties, R2–R3
Missoula, Lake, 51
Modified Mercalli scale, 261, *261*
Mohs hardness scale, 150, *150*
molecule, 142
Moment Magnitude scale, 260
mountain
    alpine glacial formation, 49
    continental drift and, 203
    fault-block, 223
    folded, 222
    tectonic plate movement and, *86,* 86–87
    volcanic, 223
Mt. Griggs, *223*
Mt. Mazama, Oregon, 230
Mt. St. Helens, 233
mud crack (sedimentary rock), 85
mudflow, **53**
mudstone, *173*
Munsell System of Color Notation, 63

N

native element, 142, 147, *147*
natural resources, life cycle of, 166–167
nitrogen
    in atmosphere, 10
    exchanged between Earth's spheres, 13
nonfoliated metamorphic rock, 179
nonmetallic luster, 149
nonsilicate minerals, 146–147, *147*
normal fault, 221, *221*

O

obsidian, 175
ocean
    continental drift and formation of, 203, *203*
oceanic crust, 7, 195, *207*
ocean current, 35
    deposition and, 35
ocean trench, 205, *205*
    continental drift and, 205
ocean wave
    deposition and, 35, 38
    erosion and, 35–37, 39
organic sedimentary rock, 177
organism, soil formation and, 59–60
outer core, 196
oxbow lake, 33, *33*
oxidation, **24**
oxide, 147, *147*
oxygen
    in atmosphere, 10
    weathering caused by, 24

P

Paleozoic Era, 122
    defining events, 125
    extinction event, 123
Palouse Falls, Washington, *230*
Pangaea, 86, *86,* **203**, *203*
    formation and breakup of, 125–127, 203, *203*
Panthalassa, 203, *203*
parent isotope, 108, *109*
parent rock, 58, 61
pearly luster, *149*
pegmatite, 144, *144*
People in Science
    Atekwana, Estella, 214, *214*
period, 122
Periodic Table of the Elements, R12–R13
Performing Calculations, R41–R45
permafrost, 9
Permian extinction, 126
petrification, 82
petrified wood, *82*
petroleum technician, 215
pH, soil, 64
Phacops rana fossil, *114,* 115
Phanerozoic Eon, 122, *122–123*
phyllite, 178, *178*
Physical Laws and Useful Equations, R16–R17
physical layers (Earth), 196, *196*
Physical Science Refresher, R14–R15
physical weathering, **20**–23
    caused by animal action, 22
    caused by plant growth, 23
    caused by pressure changes, 22
    caused by temperature change, 21
    caused by wind, water, and gravity, 23
plant
    soil formation and, 59–60
    weathering caused by, 23, 58
plate boundary, **241**
    convergent, **208**, *208*, 231, 233, *233*
    divergent, **209**, *209*, 231, 232, *232*
    earthquakes and, 241–243
    transform, **209**, *209*, 243, *243*
    volcano formation and, *231,* 231–233
plate tectonics, 206, *207. **See also*** tectonic plate; tectonic plate boundary.
pluton, *144*
polar ice, energy budget and, 15
pore space, soil, 64
potassium-argon dating, 112
Precambrian time, 122, *122–123*
    defining events, 124
precipitate, 145, *145*

pressure change
  rock formation and, 157, 159, 160, *160–161*, 178–179
  weathering and, 22
primary wave, 256. *See also* P wave.
programmer, 281, 284
programming, 275, 280, 281, 284
programming language, 280
Proterozoic Eon, 122, *122–123*
  defining events, 124
P wave, 256
Pyrenees Mountains, 222, *222*
pyrite, *147*
pyroclastic material, 229, *229*

quartz, 142, 143, *143*
  in composition of rocks, 172
  formed from magma and lava, 144
  hardness, *150*
quartzite, 179, *179*
Quaternary Period, 127

radioactive decay, **108**
radioactive isotope, 108
radiocarbon dating, 111
radiometric dating, **108**–113
  age of the Earth and, 113
  potassium-argon dating, 112
  radiocarbon dating, 111
  uranium-lead dating, 112
Reading and Study Skills, R18–R25
  A How-To Manual for Active Reading, R18–R19
  Using Graphic Organizers to Take Notes, R20–R23
  Using Vocabulary Strategies, R24–R25
References, R2–R17
  Classification of Living Things, R10–R11
  Geologic Time Scale, R4–R5
  Mineral Properties, R2–R3
  Periodic Table of the Elements, R12–R13
  Physical Laws and Useful Equations, R16–R17
  Physical Science Refresher, R14–R15
  Star Charts for the Northern Hemisphere, R6–R7
  World Map, R8–R9
relative dating, 94–101
  on Mars, 99
  using fossils, 100
  using geologic columns, 101
  using sedimentary rock, 95–98
resinous luster, *149*
reverse fault, 221, *221*
Richter scale, 260

ridge mantle, *207*
ridge push, 211
rift valley, 209, 214, 232
rift zone, **162**
Ring of Fire, 223, 231
ripple mark (sedimentary rock), 85, *85*
river, 32. *See also* stream.
rock, 172. *See also* igneous rock; metamorphic rock; sedimentary rock.
  abrasion and, 46
  absolute dating, **108**–109, 113–115
  biogeophysics and, 214
  classifying, 158–159, 172–173
  composition, **172**
  cycle, 160–162
  deflation and, 46
  deformation, *218*
  erosion and, 36–37
  exfoliation, 22
  in geosphere, 7
  as natural resource, 156
  relative dating, 94–101
  soil formation and, 58, 60
  texture, **173**
  weathering and, 20–25, 58, 157
rock cycle, **160**–162
  factors in, 160, *160–161*
  tectonic plate motion and, 162, *162*
rockfall, **53**
Rocky Mountains, *87*
rust, 24, *25*
rutile, 151

Safety in the Lab, R26–R27
San Andreas Fault, 209, 220
sandbar, **38**
sand particle, 62
sandstone, 85, *85*, *158*, 176
San Gabriel Mountains, 221
Scablands, 51
schist, 178, *178*
Science Skills, R26–R40
  Designing, Conducting, and Reporting an Experiment, R28–R34
  Measuring Accurately, R36–R38
  Safety in the Lab, R26–R27
  Using a Microscope, R35
  Using the Metric System and SI Units, R39–R40
sea arch, 37, *37*
sea cave, 36, *37*
sea cliff, *36–37*, 37
sea floor
  continental drift and, 204
  sediment as evidence of geologic change, 88
sea-floor spreading, **204**
  continental drift and, 204, *205*
sea stacks, 37, *37*

secondary wave, 256. *See also* S wave.
sediment, 30, 157
sedimentary rock, **158**
  absolute dating of, 114–115
  chemical, 176
  clastic, 176
  composition, 85, 158
  disturbances in, *96–97*, *96–97*
  features, 85, 158
  formation, 158
  fossils in, 82, 84, 100
  order of layers, 98
  organic, 177
  relative dating of, 94–101
  in rock cycle, 160, *160–161*
  superposition and, 95
  texture, 85, 158, 173
  unconformity and, 97
seismic wave, 240–241, **255**–259
  body wave, 256
  measuring, 258
  surface wave, 257
seismogram, 249, *249*, **258**
seismometer, 248–249, *249*, 258, *258*
shear stress, **220**, 243
shear wave, 256
shield volcano, 229, *229*, 231, 232, 234
shoreline, **35**. *See also* beach.
Sierra Nevadas, 223
silica compound, 142–143, *142–143*
silicate mineral, 7, 146
silicate tetrahedron, 146
silicon, 142, 146
silky luster, *149*
silt particle, 62
silver, 142, *147*
sinkhole, *1*, 34
slab pull, 211
slate, 178, *178*
smelting, 166, *167*
software, 266–271
soil, **58**
  climate and, 63, *63*
  color, 63
  composition, 62
  developed and undeveloped, 60
  fertility, 65
  formation, *58–59*, 58–60
  horizon, **61**
  layers of, 61
  pH, 64
  pore space, 64
  texture, 62
  types of, 63, *63*
soil chemistry, 64
soil horizon, **61**
soil profile, 61, *61*
solar energy
  atmosphere and, 10
  for biosphere, 11
  exchanged between Earth's spheres, 13, 14
solid, 142
solution, 145

source code, 280, 281
South American tectonic plate, *207*
S-P time method, 259
stalactite, *25, 34*
stalagmite, *25*
Star Charts for the Northern
 Hemisphere, R6–R7
STEM (Science, Technology,
 Engineering, and Mathematics).
 See also Engineering and
 Technology.
  Analyzing Technology, Analyzing
  the Life Cycles of Aluminum and
  Glass, 166–169
  Engineering Design Process,
  Building a Seismometer, 248–251
streak (mineral), **148**
stream, 31–33. *See also* water.
strike-slip fault, 220, *220*, 243
subduction zone, 208, 211, 243
submetallic luster, *149*
subsidence, **162**
sulfate, 147, *147*
sulfide, 147, *147*
sun, 14. *See also* solar energy.
superposition (relative dating), **95**, *99*
surface wave, 257, 263
surveying technician, 215
S wave, 256
syncline, 219, *219*

Take It Home, 3, 77, 105, 139, 191
talc, 143, *150*
tectonic plate, 86, **206**, **231**
 anticline and, 219, *219*
 continental and oceanic plate, 206
 deformation and, 218
 mantle convection, 210
 mountain building and, 222–223
 ridge push, 211
 rock cycle and, 162, *162*
 slab pull, 211
 subduction, 211
 synclines, 219, *219*
 theory of plate tectonics, 206, *207*
 volcano formation and, 231–233
tectonic plate boundary, **241**
 convergent, **208**, *208*, 231, 233,
  233
 divergent, **209**, *209*, 231, 232, *232*
 earthquake and, 241–243
 transform, **209**, 243, *243*
 volcano formation and, *231*,
  231–233
temperate soil, 63, *63*
temperature
 convection and, **195**
 rock formation and, 157, 159, 160,
  160–161, 178–179
 weathering and, 21
tension (rock), **221**, 243
Tertiary Period, 127
Teton Mountains, *223*

texture, **173**
 of igneous rock, 174, 175
 of sedimentary rock, 85
 of soil, 62
Think Science
 Forming a Hypothesis, 104–105
 Searching the Internet, 42–43
tilting (sedimentary rock), 96
titanium, 151
topaz, *144, 150*
topography, soil formation and, 60
topsoil, 61. *See also* A horizon.
trace fossil, **83**
track (trace fossil), 83, *83*
transform boundary, **209**, *209*, 243,
 243
  strike-slip fault and, 220
tree, evidence of geologic change and,
 88
triangulation, 259, *259*
Triassic-Jurassic extinction, 123
tropical soil, 63, *63*
Tropites fossil, 115
tsunami, 244, 245
21st Century Skills, 275
21st Century Skills: Technology and
 Coding, 275

ultraviolet (UV) ray, 10
unconformity (sedimentary rock),
 96–**97**, *97*
uniformitarianism, **80**, 121
uplift, **162**, 222
uranium-lead dating, 112
Using a Microscope, R35
Using Graphic Organizers to Take
 Notes, R20–R23
Using the Metric System and SI Units,
 R39–R40
Using Vocabulary Strategies, R24–R25
UV (ultraviolet) ray, 10

valley
 created by water erosion, 32
 created by glaciers, 49
vent, volcano, **228**
viscosity, 229
Visual Summary, 16, 26, 40, 54, 66,
 90, 102, 116, 128, 152, 164, 180,
 198, 212, 224, 236, 246, 264
vitreous luster, *149*
volcanic crater, 230
volcanic mountain, 223, 229
volcano, **228**–235
 calderas, 230, *230*
 characteristics, 228
 craters, 230
 eruption as catastrophic event, 120
 fissures, 230
 formation, 231–234

 landforms created by, 229–230,
  229–230
 lava, **228**–229
 lava plateau, 230, *230*
 living near, 235
 magma, *228*
 magma chamber, 230
 pyroclastic material, 229, *229*
volume, 142

waste stream, 166–167
water
 for biosphere, 11
 cycle of, 12
 erosion and deposition caused by,
  30–39
 mineral precipitates from, 145, *145*
 hydrosphere and, 8
wave, ocean
 deposition and, 35, 38
 erosion and, 35–37, 39
wave, seismic, 240–241, **255**–259
 body waves, 256
 measuring, 258
 surface waves, 257
wave-cut platform, *36–37, 37*
waxy luster, *149*
weathering, **20**–25, **157**
 abrasion, *23*
 caused by animal action, 22
 caused by plant growth, 23
 caused by pressure changes, 22
 caused by reactions with acid,
  24–25
 caused by reactions with oxygen,
  24
 caused by temperature change, 21
 caused by wind, water, and gravity,
  23
 chemical, **24**–25
 physical, **20**–23
 rock formation and, 157, 160,
  160–161
 soil formation and, 58
Wegener, Alfred, 202
White Cliffs of Dover, *177*
Why It Matters, 39, 51, 99, 151, 163,
 235, 245
wind
 abrasion caused by, 23, 46
 deflation caused by, 46
 deposition of dunes and loess, 47
World Map, R8–R9

Yellowstone National Park, 234